De Gaulle
and the
Anglo-Saxons

DE GAULLE
and the
ANGLO-SAXONS

John Newhouse

THE VIKING PRESS

New York

First published in 1970 by The Viking Press, Inc.
625 Madison Avenue, New York, N.Y. 10022

Published simultaneously in Canada by
The Macmillan Company of Canada Limited

SBN 670–26618–3

Library of Congress catalog card number: 76–94849

Printed in U.S.A. by H. Wolff Book Mfg., Co.

Acknowledgments

Abelard-Schuman, Ltd.: For excerpts from *The Edge of
the Sword* by Charles de Gaulle. Copyright © 1960 by
Criterion Books. All rights reserved. Reprinted by permission of Abelard-Schuman, Ltd.

FOR I.N.H.

FOR I.M.H.

Foreword

This is a book about relations between France, the United States, and Great Britain in the period starting just before General de Gaulle's return to power and ending with his abrupt withdrawal eleven years later. I have tried to explain the attitudes and policies adopted during those years by the three governments, and to describe the issues, events, and phenomena which most influenced the remarkable relationship that linked de Gaulle and his American and British counterparts.

To assess at this time the high points and themes of the troubled diplomacy of the Western powers in the Gaullist era might be judged premature, or immoderately bold. Many of the important documents are not yet available. Yet some of them have appeared, the content of others is known, and the gist of still more can be found in this book.

The writer of this kind of contemporary history relies on the willingness of the people directly involved to speak frankly of what they know. Most of this book draws upon information obtained in private conversations, and the individuals concerned cannot, except in rare cases, be identified. (Where published material is used source notes are, of course, provided.) But in London, Paris, and Washington, many persons at all levels of the governments, many of them still in public service or politics, devoted a great deal of time to contribute to my knowledge and understanding of what happened during moments of history in which they themselves participated. I am indebted to them all. They do not, of course, bear any responsibility for the book's conclusions or its point of view. The responsibility is mine.

I should also acknowledge with thanks the support and encouragement I received, while preparing the book, from Ben T. Moore, Director of the Tocqueville Series; Richard E. Neustadt, Director of the Institute of Politics in the John F. Kennedy School of Government, Harvard University; and Philip E. Mosely, Director of the European Institute, Columbia University. I am grateful as well to Alastair Buchan, until recently the Director of the Institute for Strategic Studies, and his colleagues, who kindly allowed me to use I.S.S. as an operating base during my research on the essentially British aspects of the history. A final note of thanks to Christine de Rougemont, who took on the unenviable job of typing the manuscript.

J. N.

Contents

Contents

De Gaulle
and the
Anglo-Saxons

1

On the Eve of Power

"Leaders of men," writes Charles de Gaulle, "are remembered
less for the usefulness of what they have achieved than for the
sweep of their endeavors. . . . In the concourse of great men
Napoleon will always rank higher than Parmentier." [1]

Parmentier introduced the potato into French life.

De Gaulle's achievement was to end the war in Algeria. He
was maneuvered back to power for that and nothing more. By
1958 nobody else could have banished the colonial incubus,
and, out of power, de Gaulle refused to deploy his prestige behind the efforts of Fourth Republic leaders struggling with the
pernicious Algerian issue. Quite the contrary, in fact. To him,
these men were only pawns in a system whose feeble claims to
legitimacy were mocked by the glory and brilliance of France,
and by the shame and degradation into which the French had
fallen. For them, on the other hand, summoning de Gaulle was
a last throw of the dice. France was edging toward anarchy and
civil war. Perhaps de Gaulle could calm the passions, could
arbitrate and then choose, and finally the affair would be liquidated. The pressures in French political life released by a settlement of the Algerian war would then oblige the legendary

figure to withdraw again—this time permanently—to the bleak fastness of Colombey-les-Deux-Églises.

This is not at all how de Gaulle saw matters. The issue of Algeria would be, rather, a squalid prelude to the great work of his life. He, de Gaulle, would take France out from under Anglo-Saxon domination. The neighboring states of Western Europe would be molded into a French-led coalition. The Cold War would give way to *détente;* words like "bipolarity" would fall from fashion; the long American shadow over European affairs would fade. And then those old allies and former enemies, France and Russia, Continental Europe's two nuclear powers—each with its own magnetic field—would fulfill their vocations as leaders, the one West to Center, the other East to Center. Together, they would contain the German phoenix. Beyond Europe, old France, citadel of modern civilization, would become the arbiter between those greater powers but lesser societies, America and Russia.

Was it—is it—entirely visionary? Could it work? Probably not. At heart de Gaulle was a realist and sensitive to the limits of French power, the restraints on French ambition. But in 1958, little matter. For the figure to whom history confided French legitimacy in June 1940 and who has embodied it ever since, nothing less than a great enterprise could animate France. Nothing less could restore her soul. The French must again be put to the service of France.

Exhausted by war and obsessed by Algeria, the French were scarcely ready for "endeavors" of "sweep." But then de Gaulle had no illusions about them. From 1940 on he had made the best with whatever was at hand. Nor were the prospects entirely dim. Resistance in France to Gaullist attitudes, where it existed, lacked real power and could be scattered easily. Take, for example, the issue of de Gaulle's presumed anti-Americanism. It found resonance among the right wing, embittered first by the United States' unwillingness to retrieve France's position in

Indochina in early 1954, and later by the absence of forthright American support for the epic Algerian struggle; alas, the United States had even abstained on uncongenial resolutions offered at the UN General Assembly concerning France's North African troubles—an unforgivable dereliction. On the left, the United States was (and is) seen as a menace to peace—a clumsy giant, alarmingly strong militarily, alarmingly unripe politically. Nor did America, with its putative dollar culture, seem to be on the side of virtue in the class struggle.

Yet fashion holds that the friendship and mutual respect forged between the French and American peoples over two centuries remain untouched by periodic crises between their governments. There is some truth in that, but not nearly so much as has been claimed down through the years by after-dinner speakers and editorialists. The famous friendship relies heavily on such symbols as Lafayette and the Statue of Liberty, on Pierre L'Enfant's architectural and urban planning, on the Louisiana Purchase, and so on. But it is not truly anchored in a history of close association and identity of view between Washington and Paris. Never a shot exchanged between French and American soldiers, it is true; and the Americans did arrive in 1917 and 1944. Still, the mutual respect of the two peoples is overlaid by misunderstanding and suspicion, and these are nourished by dissimilarity.

Between the French and the British the misunderstanding is less, but the warmth is scarcely any greater. Britain remains *perfide Albion* for many of the French; for as many British, France is only the beginning of a great non-English-speaking continental land mass reaching into Central Asia. The French are the cleverest of the inhabitants but among the least reliable, certainly the least governable—in a popular English view. And it is the unresolved quality of the French Revolution that is most disquieting. Republican France is traditionally weak, a constant temptation to the power across the Rhine; yet when

ruled in the Bonapartist tradition France becomes uncomfort-
ably strong and unsympathetic to British interests.

The French—and de Gaulle is no exception—find in Britain
the old culture and sense of civilization whose absence they reproach in the Americans. British style finds a certain acceptance, if not emulation, with *le tout Paris.* Still, since World
War II, respect for imperial Britain and her works has declined
in France, perhaps in rough proportion to the decline in British
fortunes. At a practical level, advanced sectors of French industry, such as aviation, have often been disillusioned when asso-
ciating on joint projects with British firms, which they find
slow, old-fashioned, and inefficient. But it is just as true that
less advanced sectors of French industry are, in the West European context, laggards in adapting to competitive modern-day
pressures, remaining protectionist in attitude, inward-looking,
and inefficient.

Since the war the French have observed a steady decline in
the world-wide influence of their habits, language, and culture.
They were humiliated by World War II, and since then they
have suffered military defeat and the loss of a colonial empire.
For a people which claims to represent a civilization, even to
seem to be dominated by another inspires notions that there is
a conspiracy against it, the more so since the conspiratorial
view of history tugs hard at the French instinct. Protestations
about the polycentric character of Anglo-Saxon civilization
have little or no effect on this tendency. De Gaulle has sometimes spoken of America as the daughter of Europe, but France
has influenced America's development less than any other major European country and, unlike the others, feels little kinship
with this European offspring. Listen to François Mauriac, dean
of French letters and de Gaulle's tireless Boswell, writing on the
eve of Dwight D. Eisenhower's visit to Paris in September
1959. The lofty language limns a deep-running current of
French opinion:

God willing, on September 2 as many Parisians will be found on the sidewalks acclaiming the President of the United States as there were on London's. . . . The jolts to *amour propre*, the bitterness of a nation which was once the greatest, which was even in Europe the only great, nation (since for a long time the term "great nation" really meant France)—all that must bow on September 2 to the President of the United States, above all to the admiration and gratitude aroused in the French people . . . by General Eisenhower.

But I, who preach to others, what are my real sentiments? What do I really feel? If I put the question to myself publicly on such a day, it is because I am sure of the answer. I am sure that I will be in the crowd on the Champs Élysées, and I will not be the least enthusiastic of those acclaiming our illustrious guest. Therein lies a contradiction I would like to clarify.

Ultimately my sympathy lies with the leader of a great people whom I certainly admire, but this people, by many aspects of their genius, is stranger to me than any other. I have never visited them. To what purpose? They have done a lot more than visit us. The rhythm of our daily life is adjusted to theirs. Their music orchestrates our days with millions of records. Thousands of films, on all the screens of Paris and in the provinces, impose their style on us in every way. . . . But beyond the cult, the adoration of technique, beyond all the techniques invented by man and to which man enslaves himself, is the folly of speed, this disease of staggers which affects all the sheep of the West, a trepidation that none of us escapes: an immoderation in all things, the one thing in the world that conforms least to our genius. . . .

I admire and I like the President of the United States, although nothing in me responds to the civilization he represents, against which I struggle, although it invades my own life and although each day I depend a little more on its techniques.[2]

The Suez episode of 1956 did more damage to France's relations with the Anglo-Saxons, especially the Americans, than any other episode in postwar history. It forced France's latent hostility to and mistrust of the Anglo-Saxons to the surface. Washington was seen to have betrayed its chief allies, and Britain abjectly to have deserted France and Israel at the first sign of disapproval in Washington.

Suez deeply divided British politics and forced Prime Minister Anthony Eden from public life. Among the lessons drawn by the Conservative party's hierarchy, not least by Harold Macmillan, was that never again could Britain permit herself the luxury of a basic policy conflict with the United States. But the effect of Suez in France was even more profound and pervasive. Whereas the affair divided Britain, it tended to unite France. And, far from reaching the same conclusion as the Tory hierarchy, the French had as their prevailing attitude the belief that Europe must find a way to manage its affairs without reference to the superpowers. The Suez crisis had much to do with encouraging the creation of the Common Market and animating France's nuclear program.

Paris considered the Suez Canal a primarily French enterprise. Gamal Abdal Nasser was the Levantine Beelzebub, back to whom could be traced many of France's troubles in Algeria. The commander of the French forces, General André Beaufre, notes in his memoir of Suez that the Algérie Française movement on the right and pro-Israel policies on the left were mutually reinforcing in the push for armed intervention.[3]

France's negotiations with Israel in preparation for the expedition against Egypt went forward secretly for some time before the British were brought in. Indeed, so secret was the planning that right to the end the Foreign Affairs Ministry, except for the Minister himself, was kept in the dark.[4] Colombey-les-Deux-Églises was, in fact, better informed than the Quai d'Orsay, since de Gaulle was briefed at every stage. His passion for action was aroused by Suez, but he was doubtful about the arrangements. A project of French inspiration had been, for all practical purposes, taken over by the British. Before the expedition was launched, he told a participating French officer involved in briefing him to "watch out. Having the British command at all echelons seems to me of no value." [5] Shortly after the crisis he unburdened himself to the French historian and journalist Jean-Raymond Tournoux (whom he saw frequently both during the "desert" years of his withdrawal at Colombey and later): Suez, he said,

> was well intended. For once we were doing something. But the operation was very difficult. It required perfect preparation at the political and military levels. We entrusted this to the British in every area. Why did we give them the command everywhere? They commanded on sea, they commanded on land, they commanded in the air.
>
> When I speak of political preparation, I think it was necessary to warn the Americans and say to them: "Now this is what we wish to do. If you don't approve . . . !" [6]

The failure of the Anglo-French-Israeli raid against Nasser confirmed de Gaulle in his bitter and despairing view of the Fourth Republic system and in his belief that France must be able to act alone in defending her interests. In concluding his post-mortem with Tournoux he mentioned his plan to visit the Sahara and noted: "The possibilities of this territory [the Sahara] are immense. But the regime will lose the Sahara, you will see. It has lost Indochina, Tunisia, Morocco. It will lose Algeria. It will also lose Alsace, Lorraine, Corsica, and Brittany. Only the Auvergne will remain to us, because nobody will want it."

Suez, as Hugh Thomas has said, destroyed the Entente Cordiale, "which thus died, as it was born, over Egypt." [7] The enterprise against Nasser was itself dead the moment the Eisenhower Administration refused to rescue Eden from the ensuing sterling crisis unless he agreed to accept a cease-fire.

What further proof for de Gaulle that only the boldest and most independent spirits could avoid becoming hostages to American power?

Since World War II Britain and France have struggled with the problem of how to maneuver American power to support their national interests. Their approaches to the problem have differed fundamentally. Britain seeks to influence Washington in her role as a privileged partner of the United States. France, on the other hand, has always used conventional methods to induce the United States to accept her views. This is not only because the French feel that the intimate Anglo-American arrangements during the war, plus the English language, have created a special relationship probably beyond their reach. The French attitude is really rooted in an old aversion (probably unique in Europe) to the role of *demandeur*. A typical French leader can be relied on never to put himself in the position of seeking by other than scrupulously correct and traditional diplomacy to obtain satisfaction for French interests. It is not just that the French are a proud people; it is a conviction (and instinctual feeling) that the potential pitfalls in the role of *demandeur* or junior partner (as in the case of Britain)—betrayal, disappointment, and failure—outweigh the possible gains over the long run. Best to drink from one's own glass, as de Gaulle has observed, while touching glasses all around. Even if a nation has relatively little power or enters a negotiation holding the weaker hand, the game is somehow to alter the balance so that the other party is maneuvered into seeking one's acceptance of *his* position in return for meeting one's own terms. Thus French negotiators, military as well as political, are generally characterized by their flair and mastery of the *dossiers*.

This diplomatic tendency accounts in part for the traditional sensitivity in Franco-American relations. Actual French differences with America have not normally exceeded Britain's, but the British learned how to work with—how to maneuver—the Americans, instead of just coping with them. The distinction is important; it was important before de Gaulle and would remain so. His predecessors' efforts to maneuver American power behind French policies, whether in Europe or the colonies, were on the whole unsuccessful. De Gaulle, on the other hand, never chose to avoid the role of *demandeur* or tried to maneuver American power, because he never expected or intended to do serious business with the United States after his return to power in 1958. The one thing he wanted from the Anglo-Saxons was assistance in matters concerning nuclear technology. But he would not ask for it himself, and he was not prepared to concede anything in return.

The United States' ambiguous, often contradictory policy on aiding France's nuclear-weapons program marked both the Eisenhower and Kennedy years. Few issues in the period between 1958 and 1963 pre-empted more of the time and thought of high officials, including the two Presidents. And perhaps none stimulated so much division, even bitterness, within the American government as the question whether to put American relations with France on the same footing as those with Great Britain.

The nuclear-sharing saga originates in the late Fourth Republic period, when French leaders entertained a well-founded suspicion that many in Washington wanted to discourage, if not prevent, a French nuclear-weapons capability. It was always clear that France, even without the inspiration of her Suez failure and other irritants, was determined to have such a capability. De Gaulle fueled and accelerated the nuclear program, and he established its military vocation, but he did not start it. The detonation of the first French atomic bomb (on February 13, 1960) was authorized by Prime Minister Félix Gaillard on April 11, 1958.

In the early and mid-1950s American support for France's nuclear programs was excluded on security grounds; French facilities were judged to be too deeply penetrated by the French Communist party. In the late 1950s this concern had been dissipated; in the words of one American official, those who still opposed helping France on security grounds were suffering from a "cultural lag." French personnel and security procedures were, in effect, "cleared" by the Central Intelligence Agency and the Atomic Energy Commission.

In 1956 the United States cut the price of the enriched uranium (U-235) she sold for foreign industrial use, presumably to discourage France from building an isotope-separation plant for the manufacture of fissile materials, either alone or with other European countries. At about this time the United States appears to have objected to the transfer of data by the British Atomic Energy Authority to its French counterpart regarding isotope-separation facilities.[8] She was within her rights here, as Anglo-American agreements required approval of both parties to any such transfer.

Some of the reasoning behind the American position was valid, some of it less so. First, as the British concede, their nuclear operations were not "compartmentalized," which meant that a French scientist gaining exposure to one area of the operations would inevitably gain access to quite a lot more. But it is also true that the AEC strongly opposed the creation of new gaseous-diffusion plants. The issue was put in economic terms—nobody else could make enriched uranium as cheaply as the Americans, so why bother?—but a simple desire to monopolize the new industry was doubtless closer to the heart of the matter.

Within both Britain and France strong pressures from military, industrial, and political sources were exerted to expand their respective nuclear capabilities. But for many reasons, most of them going back to the war years, the two nations were operating at different levels. The gap between the British and French programs was even greater than that between the British and American. The British, benefiting from an early association with the American nuclear program, exploded a thermonuclear bomb in 1957; the French did not follow suit until 1968, and their mastery of this technology is still not clearly established. The British, in fact, were ahead of the Americans in some areas of nuclear technology and their warhead technology was at least as advanced. Nevertheless, the seemingly unlimited scope of American resources and the limitations on Britain's foreshadowed an expansion of the gap between the two nations. Briefly, Britain needed nothing less than a restoration of the nuclear collaboration that had been achieved with America during the war in order to assure the "modernity" of her nuclear weapons and techniques. America's Atomic Energy Act, imposing strict controls on the dissemination of nuclear information, had been liberalized in 1954, but not enough to give Britain what she needed. To persuade Washington to make a much broader liberalization of the law was for many years among the highest goals of British foreign policy.

The irony of Britain's slow fall away from nuclear preeminence only sharpened her sense of frustration—and her resolve to regain lost ground. In 1940 and 1941 British-based scientists working on a uranium bomb had a long lead on their American colleagues; the question of merging the two national programs arose even at this early date and was then rejected by British authorities worried about American security procedures. The United States was not yet in the war, and London was reluctant to diffuse data that might fall into the hands of German scientists. This attitude changed as more and more of Britain's scientific resources began to be absorbed by the urgent demands of the radar program; and, of course, bombs were falling.

Just after the war new efforts were begun to merge British

and American nuclear programs. A Pentagon colonel named Lauris Norstad directed preparation of a paper proposing the United States' nuclear marriage with Britain. But the Klaus Fuchs affair erupted at about this time, confirming *American* doubts about *British* security! The initiative came to nothing.

The process of nuclear estrangement set in. The wartime agreements were repudiated by President Harry S. Truman (under the influence of Secretary of State James Byrnes). In 1950 Britain began to work on her own isotope-separation plant at Capenhurst and received no help from Washington on the immensely difficult gaseous-diffusion technology (which had originated in Britain). The only Briton to gain access to the American plant at Oak Ridge in this period was Lord Portal, Marshal of the Royal Air Force. He was not shown much, and later could report little except that he had needed a bicycle to travel from one end of the plant to the other.

Curiously, the Suez crisis hastened a *rapprochement*. The Eisenhower Administration, although less overwhelmed by Suez than the Conservative party had been, was nonetheless disturbed by the squall that had shattered the even and productive rhythm of Anglo-American relations. A post-Suez reconciliation, in the form of an Eisenhower-Macmillan conference at Bermuda, was held in March 1957. On all sides it appeared to have been a success. The bitterness was effaced. Britain agreed to deploy four squadrons of Thor liquid-fueled missiles (sixty in all) under joint control in the United Kingdom (Washington had been most anxious to find a home for these weapons), and the Americans, with a minimum of fuss, agreed to restore a close nuclear collaboration. Eisenhower wanted to do this for sentimental reasons, taking into account Britain's pioneering efforts in nuclear matters, a consideration eloquently recalled to him by Macmillan. The bargain was swiftly struck. At this time Washington wanted British support in the nuclear-test-ban negotiations just beginning their tortuous course. John Foster Dulles recognized that Britain would require substantial American help in her nuclear-weapons program if she were to accept the limitations of a test-ban agreement. So the State Department fell into line, leaving the AEC as the deepest pocket of resistance. Lewis Strauss, then Chairman of the AEC, continued to oppose helping the English on security grounds; he had seen numerous British promises regarding security procedures go unfulfilled. (Some elements in the AEC felt differently. Britain had first-rate people and a well-advanced program, especially in the design area; the benefits, it was thought, would be reciprocal.) But Strauss was outmaneuvered by the even more powerful Dulles. Even Admiral Hyman Rickover, a legendary protectionist in this area, acquiesced quietly.

Thus, the Bermuda conference led to the Plowden-Strauss accord (Lord Plowden was Chairman of the British Atomic Energy Authority) on the exchange of technology and weapons design. And this in turn led to the 1958 amendment to the McMahon Act, permitting release of weapons-design information to any ally that has made "substantial progress" toward a nuclear capability. The legislative history of the law—the record of what the Joint Commission on Atomic Energy reported to the Congress as a whole, plus the utterances of its senior members—left little doubt that Britain was intended as the sole beneficiary of the amendment.

At Bermuda the two governments had privately agreed that no third country—i.e., France—would figure in the exchanges to come, and the bilateral agreement they later reached confirmed this understanding. The French were not slow in sensing the drift of events, and they reacted accordingly. In May 1957 Defense Minister Maurice Bourgès-Maunoury put forward a new French defense policy, based, he said, on "the new conditions of war [which] . . . require that on the list of studies to be undertaken, the strategic reprisal weapon* must have priority." [9] Two months later, in July, construction of an isotope-separation plant (for U-235) was authorized.† Even before Suez, Bourgès-Maunoury had said: "[The Ministry of] National Defense, more than any other department, is concerned that an enriched uranium plant rapidly see the light of day." [10]

One direct French response to the exclusivity of the Anglo-Saxon arrangement was a folly that became known in a small and restricted circle as the Strauss–Chaban-Delmas agreements —named for Franz-Josef Strauss, West German Defense Minister at the time, who had much to do with the affair, and Jacques Chaban-Delmas, French Defense Minister in early 1958, who had relatively little to do with it. These were trinational arrangements (Italy was included) which provided that France's two partners would contribute to the construction of a French isotope-separation plant at Pierrelatte in return for certain technical advantages, some of which could have military application. The Quai d'Orsay strongly opposed this initiative for many obvious reasons: the reaction of the United States and Russia, as well as Great Britain, to a scheme that might stimulate West Germany's appetite for nuclear weapons was predictable and worrisome. Nevertheless, negotiations began in April 1957—just one month after the Eisenhower-Macmillan conference in Bermuda—and a secret protocol was informally agreed to in February 1958. The affair took on a more distinctly Franco-German coloration when Strauss accompanied Chaban-Delmas on a trip to the French nuclear installation in the Sahara a while later. It was agreed that in return for financial

---

* Meaning, in this context, a nuclear weapon capable of reaching the territory of a potential enemy or aggressor.
† The French parliament, in ratifying the treaty creating Euratom, made its approval contingent upon the government's commitment to constructing an isotope-separation plant.

assistance, West Germany would eventually gain access to France's nuclear-weapons technology.

All this was closely linked to France's role in the Suez affair. Much of the push for both projects came from Bourgès-Maunoury, first Defense Minister and then Prime Minister for three and a half months in this period, a strong personality with a distinguished Resistance record with the Free French. He, in turn, was deeply influenced by his *directeur de cabinet,* a *polytechnicien* named Abel Thomas. In diplomatic circles Thomas was considered an *éminence grise;* he was deeply hostile to and suspicious of the United States.

Often in the Fourth Republic, cabinet directors were strongly identified with the accomplishments of the ministers for whom they worked. Moreover, it is the custom in France to entrust large responsibility to relatively junior officials, some of them quite young. But only rarely does the junior member become the stronger or dominant figure. The French political scientist Alfred Grosser has said of these relationships:

> Whether open or hidden, the action of cabinet directors is often decisive. . . . Jacques Duhamel [now the leader of a group of centrist deputies and Minister of Agriculture] . . . entered Edgar Faure's cabinet in 1949. Becoming Deputy Director, then Director of Prime Minister Faure's cabinet, he played an important role in the Tunisian affair in 1952 and in the Moroccan drama in 1955. Still, the influence of the collaborator on the "patron" does not extend in this example to domination, which one cannot say in the cases of General Lecomte . . . chief of General Koenig's general staff in the Defense Ministry in 1955, or of Abel Thomas, Bourgès-Maunoury's cabinet director in the same ministry at the time of Suez.[11]

Tournoux, writing about Suez, describes Thomas simply as Bourgès-Maunoury's "alter ego." [12]

Both the Suez expedition and the inappropriately labeled

Strauss–Chaban-Delmas affairs were characterized by extreme secrecy and subterranean maneuvers designed to keep anyone from being fully informed. Even now it is difficult to reach the bottom of the latter or to measure its intended scope. But at the time, the prospect of Franco-German-Italian nuclear arrangements aroused considerable activity at the working levels in London and Washington. It is far from certain that "FIG," as it became known in the State Department (meaning France-Italy-Germany), influenced any of Washington's hastily conceived and uncoordinated offers of nuclear assistance to France in the months just prior to de Gaulle's return to power. Probably it did not have much real influence. So little was known of the arrangements that they remained primarily only of working-level concern. But the importance of this misguided affair lies in what it reveals about the attitudes of some nationalistic Frenchmen with power in the face of exclusive Anglo-American nuclear arrangements. It represented perhaps the first uncertain effort of Continental Europeans to free themselves from dependence on America for their security. De Gaulle, returning to power in the spring of 1958, would find much of the terrain to his liking.

De Gaulle's parliamentary group drew only four per cent of the French popular vote in the last election preceding his return to power. But Gaullist attitudes were current in a large part of French society. To take NATO as an example, the writ of the Supreme Allied Commander, Europe, covered France but did not extend to the British Isles. If the Anglo-American relationship was not a frankly anti-France conspiracy, it was clearly a *directoire-à-deux* of NATO. Close wartime associations were carried forward in the NATO framework. Language, of course, was also a factor. Then, as now, NATO was dominated by the United States, although then, unlike now, American policies were likely to be seasoned by expert British staff work.

Throughout the late 1940s and 1950s the Americans and British did all or most of the work to be done in SHAPE and on NATO's Military Committee. Traditional British excellence in military staff work, together with the British officers' more expert use of the common language, meant that what began as an American policy would often emerge with a strong pinch of British flavoring.

At the level of high policy the so-called doctrine of massive retaliation offers an instructive example. Although rightly identified with the early years of Eisenhower's Administration, the concept was first put forward by Air Chief Marshal Sir John Slessor, and it reflected the thinking at the time of the British military planning staff. This, of course, was long before Robert McNamara and the methodology of the RAND Corporation social scientists he brought into the Pentagon. In the early and mid-1950s the Pentagon was still feeling its way; more than a few didn't know their jobs, and the methodology didn't exist.

It would not be easy to show that Britain's leverage with the Americans in NATO returned her any real benefits. Britain did help to turn aside various suggestions for NATO reform, many of which amounted to enlarging the West German (also possibly the Italian) role, largely at French expense. But the French never showed any gratitude, and the larger West German role has come about through events.

Sophisticated circles in the French government and press tended to favor the principle of collective security—treaty arrangements and so on—but to look upon NATO itself as a tiresome but rather harmless enterprise. It didn't matter much if the Americans did control it. It was, after all, normal, since Americans supplied most of NATO's plausible strength. Still others in France who took an interest didn't mind too much about the British privileges, provided that France's participation could be made to seem correspondingly important. For them it was chiefly a question of cosmetics, of an optical enlargement and sharpening of France's position in the largely American chain of command. One recalls the remark of Perken, in André Malraux's novel *The Royal Way:* "You French, you love these men who attach more importance . . . to playing a role than to achieving something."

De Gaulle was to touch responsive chords with both these points of view. He was to concede the utility of the North Atlantic Treaty, while downgrading the North Atlantic Treaty Organization structure. And he would lose no time in demanding formal and explicit *global* parity for France with the Anglo-Saxons in return for his cooperation in NATO.

But NATO was never really the issue between France and the Anglo-Saxons. NATO was seldom at the center of France's preoccupations or, for that matter, Britain's. As long as the American commitment to defend Europe remained valid, France and Britain were free to pursue other interests in the accepted and traditional manner.

The fact is that French and British postwar foreign-policy priorities have never been the same as the United States', which for more than twenty years sought first and foremost to prevent an expansion of Soviet influence in Europe and to anchor West Germany to the Western Alliance system. France and Britain, during most of this period, were absorbed in re-establishing themselves; in strengthening their positions vis-à-vis the reviving power of West Germany and vis-à-vis each other; and in ridding themselves, by one means or another, of their old dependencies.

The issue of NATO and the issue of nuclear weapons—the question of whether Europeans should have larger responsibilities in nuclear strategy and control of nuclear weapons (a "co-determinate" responsibility, as it became known)—were closely related and really overlapped. At least, for the Americans and West Germans they were closely related; much less so for France and Britain, both determined to deploy, as one of the badges of sovereignty (or, better, as virility symbols), for which West Germany was and is ineligible, independent nuclear forces.

By 1957 these interrelated issues were at the center of the tangled relations between France, Britain, and the United States. As if it were not already tense enough, the matter was sharpened by the Soviet Union's dazzling technological achievements and its power politics. Successful test flights of a Sputnik and then an intercontinental ballistic missile (ICBM) moved the Western nations to huddle together, to undergo self-examination of one sort or another (a *New Yorker* cartoon showed a woman remarking to her husband, "Well, it's been quite a week. They got the ICBM and we got the Edsel"), and to take "new looks" at NATO mechanisms. Even more disturbing, Russia was deploying medium-range ballistic missiles (MRBMs) in Eastern Europe, targeted on West European cities. Mixed into all this were the first stirrings of interest in a nuclear-test-ban treaty. And, in a speech delivered in August, Dulles had entered the word "proliferation" into the lexicon of the atomic age.

A mirror image of the tensions between allies was by now visible within the American government. Differences on such issues as nuclear aid to France aroused strong feelings (destined to run higher after de Gaulle's arrival on the scene). Each of the contesting points of view was rooted in some basic given of American policy, as is always true in bureaucratic struggles. Some elements in both the State Department and uniformed services argued that since France would eventually have nuclear weapons, why not provide enough help to spare her part of the enormous investment in resources and time she would have to make, in return for France's more vigorous participation in NATO and other political dividends that might come from having her dependent on American technology. Still others, centered in the Defense Department's International

Security Affairs bureau (ISA), favored aiding France for balance-of-payments reasons.

Resistance to helping France, found in other parts of the State Department and in Congress, was largely inspired by two concerns. The first was the "German argument." Jean Monnet's dictum, never do for France what you are not eventually willing to do for Germany, had taken hold, especially in the State Department. Then there was the proliferation argument, which held that it was America's duty to discourage *any* spread of nuclear weapons, *not* to contribute to their spread, whatever the rationale. If it was too late to undo the nuclear accord with Great Britain, the line should at least be drawn before the next pretender—in this case, France. Admittedly, France one day probably would have nuclear arms whatever the United States did, but American policy should make this as expensive and drawn-out as possible. With occasional exceptions, this was the policy followed by the Administrations of Eisenhower, Kennedy, and Johnson.

By the summer of 1957 Dulles and Eisenhower were preparing to offer their NATO Continental allies access to nuclear weapons stockpiled in Europe under a "double veto" system. (The United States would retain custody of the warheads, while the ally would operate the weapons.) Sputnik's autumn debut inspired a further decision to deploy American IRBMs (the liquid-fueled Thors and Jupiters) on allied soil. These first-generation missiles had been built in great haste and had only modest strategic value; still, they were America's only ballistic missiles, and Washington was determined to find European hosts for a large number of them. Eisenhower argued that the nuclear stockpiling arrangement would make it unnecessary for the Europeans to make their own nuclear weapons.[13] And something was needed to counter the Soviet missiles soon to be aimed at West European cities.

At a meeting of NATO heads of government in Paris in December Dulles presented the "stockpiling" plan, and attached a sweetener in the form of an offer to give interested allies the technical data needed for building the propulsion system of a nuclear submarine, *provided* Congress agreed. The United States would negotiate bilateral accords with each interested ally. As usual the British were in a special position, having already been assured of receiving the submarine technology and having agreed at Bermuda to accept Thors. The French, Dutch, and Italians showed interest in the submarine offer, but none of the Continental allies wanted the vulnerable, slow-reacting missiles on their territory, where they might invite a pre-emptive Soviet attack. In the end, only the Italians and Turks (along with the British) agreed to take the dubious weapons. Eisenhower later commented to some of his aides that it would have been better to dump them in the ocean instead of trying to dump them on our allies.

By the winter of 1957–1958 a broad debate was going on within the Pentagon, especially in the civilian-dominated ISA. The historic political instability of countries like France and Italy seemed to some to argue against giving them access to nuclear weapons. But the scales were tipped to the other side of the issue by balance-of-payments pressure, by the Pentagon's craving to find a home for the Thors and Jupiters, and by the tempting logic of the notion that America's allies should not be denied arms that the Soviet Union already had. Indeed, while the December Paris meeting was going on, the Secretary and the Deputy Secretary of Defense, Neil McElroy and Donald Quarles, tried to persuade the French to take some Thors and Jupiters and to permit the United States to store nuclear weapons on French territory.

For many on the French side it was a long-awaited moment. McElroy and Quarles were nominally dealing only with Prime Minister Gaillard and Minister of Defense Chaban-Delmas. But the entire French defense community had been pointing to this occasion for years. As early as 1953 Washington had sought to deploy nuclear weapons in France, but the French, although permitting deployment in North Africa, refused it in metropolitan France. Even then, they were looking ahead to bargaining with Washington on nuclear matters.

Now they were prepared to make a deal. In return for giving the right sort of technical assistance to France, Washington could probably have nuclear storage rights and might even get rid of some Thors and Jupiters. They were not very specific, but then neither were the Americans. McElroy and Quarles made broad but not very precise offers of assistance. The French were sufficiently impressed, however, to provide the American Embassy in Paris with information about their nuclear program which before they had scrupulously withheld. It was a gesture obviously designed to reassure those in Washington who might still harbor doubts about French security procedures.

Next, the French requested the United States government's approval to buy the guidance system for the Polaris missile and certain highly sensitive material and data. This squarely posed the issue of helping France to acquire a fully modern ballistic-missile technology. The American Embassy in Paris supported the requests, while the American Embassy to NATO, also in Paris, opposed them. A similar pattern was developing in the State Department itself, where numerous officers with traditional responsibility for country affairs favored helping France, while others dealing with NATO and regional affairs (in the section of the Department known as RA, or Regional Affairs, Europe) were strongly opposed. Most of the latter had also opposed, or were at best lukewarm about, the special nuclear link with Britain.

The United States was, in fact, groping for a position on the nuclear-proliferation issue. The lines were forming within the

State Department and between the State and Defense Departments. In London the same lines formed in Whitehall, where the Ministry of Defence was always more pro-French than the Foreign Office, just as the Pentagon was always first to plead the French case, with the State Department (backed by the Joint Atomic Energy Committee) putting up the stiffest resistance.

This conflict between defense officials and diplomats is hardly a new one, and it affects many policy issues. People who run defense ministries are usually eager to offset the heavy cost of their programs by selling hardware. And then there is the great game of military politics, which tends to have a wholly independent existence since it is played by soldiers and defense bureaucrats of friendly countries often without strict regard to the official policies of their respective governments. The players are united by a common interest in the techniques of weaponry, and this dynamic tends to put them into more intimate contact with each other than is true of the diplomats.

In Paris the weakness and impermanence of the Fourth Republic's civilian governments strengthened the relative position of French defense technicians in dealing with their opposite numbers in Washington and London. It added another dimension to the game of military politics. But this very absence of a reliable political authority, sharpened during the Algerian war, caused the State Department and Foreign Office to be even warier than usual about helping France's nuclear development.

Washington said no to Gaillard's request for the Polaris guidance system. Although this refusal was an important precedent in setting the tone of Franco-American nuclear diplomacy, few French leaders were surprised—or even had time to give the matter serious attention. They were by then too caught up in their futile efforts to subdue the furies let loose by the drama in Algeria. And the passions of many Frenchmen were fed by vagrant anxieties, among them the suspicion that the United States was conspiring to take France's place in North Africa.

Washington's real attitude was well reported on February 28, 1958, by *Le Monde*'s Washington correspondent:

> There is fundamental agreement [here] with Foreign Minister Christian Pineau [when he says] that the departure of France from North Africa would be a disaster for the West. The Americans, it is said, are convinced that the French presence is indispensable and necessary and are certainly not searching to substitute themselves. But people don't believe that Lacoste's pacification policy will assure this French presence. [Lacoste was France's Resident General in Algeria.]
>
> It must be repeated that Washington has always had a realistic and pragmatic attitude about the Algerian affair. If Lacoste's policy had worked, Washington would have rallied to it, although with some repugnance and some serious fears for the future. . . . Briefly, they are more and more convinced here that there is no military solution to the Algerian problem and that the possibilities of a political settlement are being sabotaged in Algiers and by an active minority of the French parliament, playing on the weakness and fear of the government.

A few days earlier, French Air Force elements had bombed and strafed the Tunisian border village of Sakhiet, killing sixty-nine persons. The incident was awkward for American officials who were pressing the French case for nuclear weapons: the bombing was a direct violation of French government orders forbidding this kind of reprisal against Tunisian villages harboring Algerian rebels, and it had been done without the knowledge of the Prime Minister, the Minister of Defense, or the Minister for Tunisian Affairs.[14] Habib Bourguiba, President of Tunisia, immediately demanded the withdrawal of all French forces from the country, including those at the naval base of Bizerte.

At this point Washington and London moved in, proposing a good-offices mission. Whatever the original merit of this initiative—and it doesn't seem to have had much—it had an important part in bringing down Gaillard, then the most promising young man in French politics and Prime Minister of the Fourth Republic's last real government. Moderate elements in French public life were offended by what seemed to them an intolerable intrusion in French affairs on the part of the Anglo-Saxons; the less moderate found their suspicions that the United States had designs on North Africa vindicated.* The Gaullists, by and large, needed little convincing. A month before de Gaulle returned to power, Michel Debré, who would be his first Prime Minister, wrote in the Gaullist newspaper *Carrefour:* "The official position of the United States can be summarized as follows: It does not want France to be an atomic power. It does not wish France to remain an African or Saharan power. It does not hope that France will recover her political independence." [15]

By then France needed de Gaulle. The French people were ready for Gaullism in more ways than they would admit, or perhaps even understand.

---

* The good-offices mission was more a British than an American inspiration. But the Americans at this time were inaugurating a small program of military assistance to Tunisia; this also irritated the French and confirmed the darkest suspicions of many of them.

2

The General

De Gaulle was acutely aware of his prestige in America and Britain. He exaggerated when he regarded himself as a factor in American Presidential politics, but his calculation that, whatever the political weather, he would hold a wide Anglo-American following was valid—at least until partially undermined by his excesses of 1967 and early 1968.

In an age of uncertain priorities de Gaulle was a leader who knew what he wanted for his country. This sureness, combined with the granitic character and brilliant style of the man, inspired trust. Many Americans and British, accustomed to de Gaulle's angry—often violent—verbal excesses, found him more sinned against than sinning. And in Britain and America, as in France, de Gaulle found support among ordinary people, politicians, civil servants, and in the academic community. Because Washington treated him with skepticism and hostility for much too long during the war, many Americans swung to the other extreme and gave him the benefit of every doubt in his innumerable disputes with their government. And the British, who followed Sir Winston Churchill in sticking with de Gaulle from start to finish—no matter how difficult this was—could not easily disabuse themselves about a man who seemed to them to measure up to his own self-portrait.

Quite a number of Americans and Englishmen who think seriously about relations with France suspect that de Gaulle was "lost" to the Anglo-Saxons during the war, thanks chiefly to President Franklin Delano Roosevelt. But this implies that de Gaulle might have been "available" as an ally in the conventional long-term sense. He never was available in those terms. De Gaulle's wartime conflicts with his overburdened colleagues at 10 Downing Street and the White House affected his attitude toward the Anglo-Saxons, but they did not define it. They fed the Gaullist bias, but the effects of his tenure in the Élysée Palace were anticipated by a set of attitudes that had been formed much earlier.

De Gaulle arrived in London in June 1940, a fully formed French nationalist of a familiar breed: a product of the upper-bourgeois, pious, intellectual milieu deeply marked by France's capitulation to Prussia in 1871 and her diplomatic retreat before Britain at Fashoda. The spirit which animated the Parisian household in which de Gaulle and his four siblings grew up was monarchist and *revanchist*.

World War I made the lesson of 1871 indelible: Germany must be confined, if not dominated, by a combination of diplomatic encirclement and military force. The application of these traditional methods, de Gaulle believed, would require a great and solitary chief, whose qualities he set forth in his book *The Edge of the Sword*, written in 1932. This book still offers the sharpest single glimpse of de Gaulle's thoughts, while the three volumes of his war memoirs—longer, but richer in precise clues—provide another path to understanding the man. Together, the early and later works establish the essential distinction between de Gaulle and his contemporaries—his mystical sense that France's exalted destiny was his own.

Churchill established a lasting pattern when he sought to mediate Free France's difficulties with the United States (though usually, but not always, yielding to Washington in the end). At a time when everyone would have liked to scuttle de Gaulle—the winter of 1942–1943—he and Eden perceived that there was nobody else to build up. Thanks largely to Britain's efforts, de Gaulle was an established figure in France and, perhaps more important, controlled most of the resistance "nets" established there. For Churchill he may have been the "monster of Hampstead," but he was also the "constable of France." On the American side, only the Office of Strategic Services and the Army appeared to accept this. The White House and State Department—that is to say, Roosevelt and Cordell Hull—went on resisting, somewhat willfully, to the end. In backing General Henri Giraud, a simple soldier and political innocent—a man who, unlike de Gaulle, could claim no support in France—the Americans lost de Gaulle's respect. He could understand their earlier support of Admiral Jean Darlan, who, after all, was the link to Vichy France. Never Giraud.

The wartime conflicts between de Gaulle and the Anglo-Saxons arose from the difference in their ultimate purposes. Washington and London were absorbed in winning the war, de Gaulle in restoring France, France's "rank," and France's influence in her dependent territories. In de Gaulle's view, the outcome of the war had been settled on December 7, 1941.

In mid-1941 de Gaulle and the British clashed over who would administer the French-mandated territories, Lebanon and Syria. De Gaulle threatened to use Free French troops to displace British forces if necessary, a gesture which provoked his colleagues in London to appeal to him formally for restraint. Upon winning this battle of wills de Gaulle dispatched to London the following reproach:

> I measured, better than anyone else, the grave national and international consequences that could have resulted from a rup-

ture between Free France and England. That is precisely why I
had to bring England face to face with the consequences, in case
she acted in an unacceptable manner toward us. . . . I understand that the British were irritated but that irritation is unim-
portant compared to our duty to France. . . . Mr. Churchill
will understand without doubt that he can only lean on something
that offers resistance. . . .

In conclusion, I invite you to close ranks and to permit no
suggestion that my conduct does not follow my policies exactly.
Our grandeur and our force consists uniquely in the intransigence we show in defending the rights of France.[1]

While it is true that the Churchill government did not always
resist the temptation to exploit France's enfeebled position, especially in Lebanon and Syria, Churchill and Eden performed
notable services of lasting value to de Gaulle and to France,
unfailingly backing de Gaulle's political claims and, later,
France's demand for a position in Germany as one of the victorious occupying powers and for permanent membership on the
United Nations Security Council. (Washington also backed
France's membership on the Council.) At the Teheran Conference Josef Stalin, on the other hand, surprised Roosevelt by
observing that it was Pétain, not de Gaulle, who represented
"the real physical France." Stalin also did not consider that
France could be trusted with any strategic positions outside her
own borders after the war, and doubted that de Gaulle was a
factor.[2] Then, at Yalta, Stalin at first refused to allow French
participation in the occupation of Germany, and Roosevelt
sided with him throughout most of the conference. But, as
Harry Hopkins noted, "Winston and Anthony fought like
tigers for France."[3] Yet de Gaulle, while formally acknowledging his debt to the English, seemed to remember, or chose to
remember, only the dark side of his association with them.
After returning to power in 1958 he was no less hostile to Britain than to America. The fact is, de Gaulle returned to power

determined to rid France, and if possible Europe, of the Anglo-Saxon domination which, to him, was clearer than the truth.

To the Western political leaders of the postwar period—Eisenhower, Macmillan, Konrad Adenauer, and John F. Kennedy—de Gaulle was one of them, a Christian Democratic moderate whose nationalism was tempered by a recognition that the societies of the West comprised a distinct politico-economic system whose maintenance required close co-operation. Moreover, de Gaulle was the last of those whose experience linked the Cold War not just with World War II but with the "Great War" and the dreary, puerile politics carried on between the wars and against which he struggled. For them de Gaulle was almost legendary, somewhat larger than life; difficult and demanding, yes; proud to a slightly comic point; claiming to incarnate French legitimacy; but a wise and far-seeing figure, another pillar of strength in the West, perhaps even the *deus ex machina* destined to make the French Republic work.

In greater or lesser degree, this is how he appeared to all of them. Each was wrong and each, in his turn, was victimized. De Gaulle was a creature from another part of the forest; he had no modern counterpart in the West or East. Obsessed by power (of which he had never had much), he sought relentlessly to diminish that of his nominal allies in order to supplant them. A French-led Western Europe, in his view, would settle the German question with Moscow; the role of arbiter between America and Russia would provide France's global vocation. All the rest was rhetoric.

Kennedy may have understood some of this, but he grasped it too late for the perception to benefit him very much. Adenauer had a long association with de Gaulle and, if often disappointed, was never disabused. For him, de Gaulle belonged to the postwar Christian Democratic political environment within which Adenauer had worked with de Gasperi, Robert Schuman, and others to rebuild Western Europe and give it the vocation of unity. De Gaulle was a forbidding figure, difficult and even worrisome at the beginning of their association, but the very strength of his character could help Adenauer toward the promised land of European unity, while stiffening the British and American attitude toward the menace from the East. What sort of European unity? Adenauer was ready to accept whatever formula or configuration best suited the General. He shared de Gaulle's doubts and suspicions of the German people; Adenauer would by choice and necessity remain the junior partner, charged with delivering the Germans (west of the Elbe) into the saner world of a West European political system guaranteed by American power. De Gaulle's France would lead; nobody else could.

Adenauer lived long enough to see de Gaulle withdraw from NATO, halt the European-unity movement in its tracks, and launch a diplomacy designed to isolate West Germany from Washington and confine its dynamic in a Franco-Russian security system. One wonders what Adenauer thought at the end. He had from the start been the victim of a double game. De Gaulle skillfully played on his predilections in persuading him that the Fifth Republic was his only reliable ally; at the same time he tried to persuade the Russians (never with any real success) that he, de Gaulle, was their only possible *interlocuteur valable* in the West. (From time to time de Gaulle indicated a willingness to trade German interests for some recognition from Moscow.)

Unlike Adenauer, who may not have wanted to face the truth, Macmillan ended with no illusions. Of all the Western leaders he knew de Gaulle best, but he was to fall farthest and hardest. As Prime Minister, Macmillan was well served by the Foreign Office's generally wary and skeptical attitude toward de Gaulle. But he himself was considerably less skeptical and in any case tended to believe that what could not be achieved in normal diplomatic channels might be arranged through his personal intervention with de Gaulle. (De Gaulle encouraged his tendency to rely on their association during the war, when Macmillan felt he had gained the confidence of the improbable figure in dealing with him as Churchill's special representative in North Africa.) Macmillan carried his illusions as far as his meeting with de Gaulle at Rambouillet in December 1962. But he left Rambouillet disabused, his foreign policy in ruins, his government, already grown old in office, further enfeebled, his party bearish.

Macmillan and de Gaulle met privately seven times, and the last three meetings, easily the most important, form a kind of triptych. The first took place at Macmillan's Sussex estate, Birch Grove, in November 1961, shortly after Great Britain's formal application to join the Common Market; the second was at the Château de Champs near Paris in the spring of 1962; and the last was at Rambouillet six months later. In reviewing what happened at these meetings one is struck by the brutality and artfulness of de Gaulle's style. Macmillan was seeking to gain British entry into Europe. De Gaulle, after realizing that Macmillan was serious, sparred with him. But not until he had settled the Algerian war and gotten past his parliamentary elections could he crush the enterprise. And he wasted no time once he found himself in open water. In the thirteen months between Birch Grove and Rambouillet an episodic, highly charged drama was enacted, offering a rare glimpse of statecraft as practiced by one of the ablest "Anglo-Saxons" and of the totally different method of de Gaulle, master of *Realpolitik*.

Eisenhower and Kennedy were both tempted by de Gaulle. For Eisenhower de Gaulle was the old comrade in arms, misunderstood and insulted by Roosevelt and Hull. He wanted to cooperate, and was always hopeful that avenues would open. But de Gaulle and Dulles between them kept the avenues blocked, each tacitly recognizing that their purposes were, by and large, mutually exclusive.

Kennedy constantly tried to find means of cooperating with de Gaulle, and this effort preoccupied him to an unfortunate degree. Almost from the first his admiration for de Gaulle's singular qualities warred with his instinct and judgment. Slowly Kennedy's suspicions hardened into a cold realism. He was to say just before his death that de Gaulle clearly required in his relations with Washington "a certain amount of tension." By then communications between Paris and Washington were all but nonexistent; there was little serious work to be done; Lyndon Johnson would be spared the Gaullist temptation that had so distracted his predecessors.

A large fund of good will was available to de Gaulle at the start of the Eisenhower Administration; the same was true of Kennedy's, more than willing to ignore the past and start afresh. If he had chosen, de Gaulle could have established a relationship with Washington that in time would have surpassed Britain's. The "special relationship" between the United States and Britain, which had seemed to be achieving a new level of intimacy in the period just following de Gaulle's return to power, was actually beginning a slow but steady decline, reflecting Britain's declining world position. De Gaulle could have become America's privileged partner—the European spokesman and *interlocuteur* that Washington had always wanted. But this was of no interest to him; his purpose was to detach Europe from America, not to strengthen her links with or, in his view, her dependence on America. One recalls the conversation he had with Churchill in the terrible summer of 1940: "Mr. Churchill and I agreed modestly in drawing from the events which had smashed the West this commonplace but final conclusion: when all is said and done, Great Britain is an island; France, the cape of a continent; America, another world." [4]

Whatever happened in the ensuing years, de Gaulle continued to assign political finality to this geographical "commonplace."

From time to time de Gaulle felt obliged to deny the charge that he was anti-American or anti-British. Strictly speaking, he was probably right. He was a French nationalist whose devotion was borne up to exalted heights by a total commitment to the "certain idea" of France he set forth in the opening passage of his memoirs. France's interest, as he defined it, might one day require close relations with America. Thus, anti-Americanism, although a useful chord to strike from time to time, was not to be formalized as policy.

On the other hand, de Gaulle's view of France, as he said himself, was "inspired as much by sentiment as by reason." This sentimental aspect harbored within it his hostility and grudges against the Anglo-Saxons. It accounts in part for the violent overtones of de Gaulle's cultivated and lofty style.

The unsentimental aspect of de Gaulle feared American power, because it seemed to block realization of a great role for France. And he claimed to see an imperial design in most American purposes. Britain was a threat only insofar as she was a stalking horse for Washington. Thus, she had to be denied a continental role until she had shed her heavy American baggage and given up any claims or pretensions to power that might jeopardize France's pre-eminence in Western Europe.

There may have been no room for anti-Americanism per se in the Gaullist vision of France, but it had an explicitly anti-German content. To be anti-German was normal for a French nationalist of de Gaulle's vintage and formation. America may threaten to stifle French civilization, to prevent its light from radiating throughout the world, but America is not a primordial threat to France or her real rival for the leadership of Western Europe. Germany is. One day America will go back to being a Western Hemisphere and Pacific power, leaving Europe to the Europeans. Then, as before, Germany might well be the most powerful state in Western and Central Europe. Therefore, Germany must remain subordinate to France.

De Gaulle's anti-Germanism can be seen in the sentimental and the positive sides of his thinking. As he said, again in the article of faith with which he opened his memoirs:

> The positive side of my mind . . . assures me that France is not really herself unless in the front rank; that only vast enterprises are capable of counterbalancing the ferments of dispersal which are inherent in her people; that our country, as it is, surrounded by the others, as they are, must aim high and hold itself straight, on pain of mortal danger. In short, to my mind, France cannot be France without greatness.

For "others, as they are," read "Germany," about whose people de Gaulle had deep and complex feelings. Indeed, no other people except possibly the French themselves moved him to such passion. His writings and speeches reveal respect mixed with profound distaste and, perhaps, fear.

In 1934, in *Vers l'Armée de Métier* (*The Army of the Future*), de Gaulle contrasted "Gaulois et Germains" in a lengthy plea for a mobile mechanized French army. Neither people was spared much, but the depth of his animus against the Germans shows clearly through the forbidding prose:

> . . . an assortment of powerful but troubled instincts; of born artists without taste; of technicians faithful to feudalism; of warlike heads of families; of restaurants built as temples; of factories in the forests; of gothic palaces serving as toilets; of noble warriors vomiting their beer . . . romantic toward noon, warlike in the evening; a sublime yet glaucous sea where the

fisherman's net hauls up monsters and treasures; a cathedral whose multicolored nave . . . becomes a symphony for the senses, for the mind, the soul, the emotions, the light and the religion of the world, but whose gloomy transept, echoing a barbaric din, offends the eyes, the spirit, and the heart.[5]

He might have been pronouncing an anathema. Noting first that the alternate victories of Gauls and Germans have neither settled the quarrel nor slaked their mutual taste for it, he argued that temperamental differences sharpen the bitterness and perpetuate a constant state of suspicion.

In the summer of 1966, on the eve of a voyage to East Africa and Cambodia, de Gaulle gathered round him a number of senior members of his government and staff and began ruminating about his life and the heavy responsibilities he bore; he contemplated his mortality with a solemnity inspired, apparently, by the abrupt change in climate he was about to experience and the onerous routine a trip of this sort would impose on one of his years. This led to a reminiscent appraisal of various peoples he knew well—his own, the Anglo-Saxons, and so on—a characteristically unflattering recital, with history invoked to sustain the main charges. He ended with the Germans, upon whom he pronounced a one-word judgment: *"maléfique"* (unnaturally pernicious). His audience, however familiar with his views, was impressed by the depth of feeling that inspired this solitary expletive. And they must have appreciated, if they had not fully done so before, that however far from Paris his foreign policy might take him, that policy in the end assumed that only Germany threatened France.

One of the earliest influences on de Gaulle and his "certain idea" of France was Henri Bergson, said to have been a friend of de Gaulle's father. His effect can be glimpsed in a passage from *The Edge of the Sword:*

It is Bergson . . . who has shown that the only way in which the human mind can make direct contact with reality is by intuition, by combining instinct with intelligence. Our intelligence can furnish us with the theoretic, general, abstract knowledge of what is, but only instinct can give the practical, particular and concrete *feel* of it. . . .

The problems of war are marked by an obscurity which the human mind cannot pierce unaided. . . . Great war leaders have always been aware of the importance of instinct. Was not what Alexander called his "hope," Caesar his "luck" and Napoleon his "star" simply the fact that they knew they had a particular gift of making contact with realities sufficiently closely to dominate them? [6]

Charles Péguy gave Bergson credit for having "broken our chains," and Péguy's lyrical nationalism in turn also left its mark on de Gaulle's attitudes (the distance he was careful to take from both capitalism and the Church, for example).

Other, less irreproachable spirits also shaped the Gaullist view of France. These were chiefly Charles Maurras and Maurice Barrès, extreme nationalists whose works, for those who read them now—and not many do—seem rather quaint, though discredited, period pieces. On the evidence, de Gaulle never accepted their racism and extreme rightism (de Gaulle's father opposed the Dreyfus proceedings, a courageous position in his circle), but he most surely drew upon their work in developing his mystical attachment to the land; his exaltation of national independence in pure (and unattainable) form; his contempt for political parties and other groups as prejudicial to the supreme national interest. The picture of the Champagne countryside around Colombey-les-Deux Églises drawn by de Gaulle at the end of his memoirs recalls Barrès.* "De Gaulle

---

* Barrès and de Gaulle had in common an attachment to the north of France and took little interest in the southern part of the country.

emerges from Barrès," a biographer has written, "as Churchill from Kipling." [7] The larger figure of Maurras taught de Gaulle's generation that the national interest—above all, national power and prestige—must dominate all other interests. Maurras dreamed of a monarchic, strongly led France maneuvering between the "giant empires," drawing in her wake a "cloud of small nations jealous of their independence." [8] "Maurras was so right as to become mad," de Gaulle is reported to have said.[9] Certain of Maurras's pre-World War I writings offer a blueprint of the Gaullist foreign policy that came a half-century later.

The imprint of these figures was an overlay on the French culture which enveloped de Gaulle from birth and for which he felt a passion that seems never to have dimmed. Out of his intimacy with French history and literature grew his epic view of France "endlessly oscillating between greatness and decline";[10] a France always betrayed by the weakness or divisiveness of her leadership until some great figure—a Joan of Arc, an Henri IV, a Bonaparte, Clemenceau, or Poincaré—aroused her "genius for renewal." De Gaulle made an early identification with this sacred handful: "I was convinced that France would have to go through gigantic trials, that the interest of life consisted in one day rendering her some signal service, and that I would have the occasion to do so." [11]

The decade before World War II was de Gaulle's most creative period; he was in his forties and at the height of his intellectual powers. It was during this period that his most important work aside from the memoirs, *The Edge of the Sword,* was published.

The edge of the sword, as seen by de Gaulle, was a military elite "conscious of the pre-eminent role it has to play" and in possession of the "philosophy proper to the soldier." The famous foreword to the book is a panegyric on force:

. . . prerequisite of movement and the midwife of progress . . . force has ruled empires, and dug the grave of decadence: force gives laws to the peoples and controls their destinies. . . .

How can we understand Greece without Salamis, Rome without the legions, Christianity without the sword, Islam without the scimitar, our own Revolution without Valmy, the League of Nations without the victory of France? The self-sacrifice of individuals for the sake of the community, suffering made glorious—these two things which are the basic elements of the profession of arms—respond to both our moral and aesthetic concepts. The noblest teachings of philosophy and religion have found no higher ideals.[12]

In the opening chapter and the following four essays on qualities of leadership de Gaulle offers a virtual self-portrait, for it is hard to doubt that he saw himself as the model leader already in possession of these yet unexploited attributes of leadership. Four years earlier, in 1928, he had written to his friend and confidant Lucien Nachin: "Ah, how bitter it is to be in harness these days. But it is necessary. One day, they will attach themselves to my coattails so as to save France." [13] *

The essays on character and leadership are the most memorable. Before the challenge of events, he says,

. . . the man of character has recourse to himself. His instinctive response is to leave his mark on action, to take responsibility for it, to make it *his own business* . . . he embraces action with the pride of a master; for if he takes a hand in it, it will become his, and he is ready to enjoy success on condition that is really *his own.* . . . Without him there is but the dreary task of the slave; thanks to him, it becomes the divine sport of the hero. . . .

Whatever the cost to himself, he looks for no higher reward

* One biographer, Jean Lacouture, dissents, saying that de Gaulle wrote "our" coattails, not "my." The text of the letter, as reproduced in his *De Gaulle* (Paris: Éditions du Seuil, 1965, pp. 31–32), leaves room for doubt.

than the harsh pleasure of knowing himself to be the man responsible. . . .

And so it comes that the authorities dread any officer who has the gift of making decisions and cares nothing for routine and soothing words. "Swollen-headed and undisciplined" is what the mediocrities say of him, treating the thoroughbred with a tender mouth as they would a donkey which refused to move, not realizing that asperity is, more often than not, the reverse side of a strong character, that you can only lean on something that offers resistance.[14] *

And the long essay on prestige is perhaps even more revealing:

What the masses once granted to birth or office, they now give to those who can assert themselves. . . . The mainspring of command is now to be found in the personal prestige of the leader. . . .

First and foremost, there can be no prestige without mystery, for familiarity breeds contempt. . . . In the designs, demeanor and the mental operations of a leader there must be always a "something" which others cannot altogether fathom, which puzzles them, stirs them and rivets their attention. . . . If one is to influence men's minds, one must observe them carefully and make it clear that each has been marked out from among his fellows, but only on condition that this goes with a determination to give nothing away, to hold in reserve some piece of secret knowledge which may at any moment intervene, and the more effectively from being in the nature of a surprise. The latent faith of the masses will do the rest. . . .

It is . . . from the contrast between inner power and outward control that ascendancy is gained. . . . Aloofness, character and the personification of greatness, these qualities it is that surround with prestige those who are prepared to carry a burden which is too heavy for lesser mortals. The price they

* This phrase cropped up nine years later (mid-1941) in the reproach de Gaulle dispatched to his colleagues in London which is quoted early in this chapter. (See pages 30–31.)

have to pay for leadership is unceasing self-discipline, the constant taking of risks, and a perpetual inner struggle . . . whence that vague sense of melancholy which hangs about the skirts of majesty, in things no less than in people. One day, somebody said to Napoleon, as they were looking at an old and noble monument: "How sad it is!" "Yes," came the reply, "as sad as greatness." [15]

Like his other writings of the prewar period, *The Edge of the Sword* reached a small elite; reissued after the war and translated into English, it found a wider audience. Yet some readers were alarmed by what seemed to them a preference for the discipline of a dictatorial society. And indeed, de Gaulle's contempt for the masses and for lesser figures is everywhere visible; the juxtaposition of Napoleon with the potato innovator merely hints at this characteristic. But despite the language and whatever the Maurras-Barrès influence de Gaulle was never a man of the far right. His political associations in the 1930s (especially with Paul Reynaud) belie this impression. In 1936 the great socialist Léon Blum, hearing of the stir de Gaulle was making in some Parisian intellectual circles, arranged to meet him. Blum found him a pessimistic and misanthropic character of the Clemenceau type, but the impression he left was a positive and indelible one.[16] The record sustains de Gaulle when he says he is neither Bonaparte nor Boulanger. (He is less plausible when denying his bourgeois background, which he does. De Gaulle's complete contempt for the *bourgeoisie française* is recorded in *The Edge of the Sword*. Yet the failure of his own class to rally to him in larger numbers during the war disappointed him.)

Two years after *The Edge of the Sword* de Gaulle published *Vers l'Armée de Métier*. These two brief works together support the Gaullists' claim for his prophetic gifts, a doubtful one when measured in the light of the attitudes and positions he was to take in the postwar years. But in the early 1930s he was a Cassandra, seeing inertia and decay everywhere. It wasn't only that he was one of a small handful of European strategists pressing for military reform, pleading for a modern and mechanized army. As always with de Gaulle, foreign policy was the dominant consideration. This was the period following Hitler's assumption of power, to which France reacted by negotiating a treaty with the Soviet Union, concluded after some delay in 1935 and intended to guarantee Soviet aid in discouraging Hitler from putting pressure on such East European states as Czechoslovakia and Poland. De Gaulle understood that the plausibility of such a policy—the credibility of France's guarantees to those threatened states—would require stress on mobile, mechanized forces, and that the static Maginot Line deployment to which the General Staff was so devoted was of little use in support of the general goal. Agreement with Russia on containing Germany, and having the most modern weapons in the service of a united France and of an authentically French policy—these were de Gaulle's objectives before and after World War II. They remained so throughout the postwar period, whatever the fashion or attitudes of the moment.

As de Gaulle saw it, Russia is a brake on Germany in Europe and on American imperialism in the world. For the Russians, as de Gaulle defined their interests, France is a brake on Germany in Western Europe and had nuisance value in the Atlantic Alliance.

De Gaulle masked his intentions, confiding them to nobody, seeking always to feint the other players out of position, and keeping in reserve "for the masses" that "piece of secret knowledge," that "surprise" he recommends in *The Edge of the Sword*. But this was all tactics. The objectives never changed, and he has defined them for the public record with prodigal clarity and frequency. The most famous and perhaps most useful reference can be found in *Salvation*, the last volume of his memoirs. It is essential for French security* to prevent the rise of another German Reich, he argues, and then goes on:

> To cooperate with East and West and, if need be, contract the necessary alliances on one side or the other without ever accepting any kind of dependency . . . to persuade the states along the Rhine, the Alps, and the Pyrenees to form a political, economic, and strategic bloc; to establish this organization as one of the three world powers and, should it be necessary, as the arbiter between the Soviet and Anglo-American camps. Since 1940, my every word and act had been dedicated to establishing these possibilities.[17]

It must be remembered that this third and final volume of the memoirs, not published until October 1959, was completed after de Gaulle returned to power in 1958. The goals he stated were for him as valid then as in 1946, and they would be as valid today as in 1958. They were the fixed, traditional goals of a romantic, unreconstructed nationalist, their iron firmness unaffected by de Gaulle's awareness that in the end it might all add up to little more than one man's dream. "This was the plan I had conceived knowing perfectly well that in such matters nothing turns out exactly as one had hoped." [18]

Turning toward Russia was instinctive to de Gaulle. "Perhaps, it would be possible," he continued, "to renew the old Franco-Russian solidarity which, though repeatedly betrayed and repudiated, remained no less a part of the natural order of things, as much in relation to the German menace as to the endeavors of Anglo-American hegemony." [19]

In December 1944 de Gaulle had gone to Moscow to negotiate another Franco-Russian treaty. He remarked to Stalin "how France envisaged the settlement of Germany's fate: no further sovereignty of the central German state on the left bank of the

* The word "security" is mistranslated as "primacy" in the American edition.

Rhine; the territories thus separated retaining their German character but receiving their autonomy . . . from the Western zone; the Ruhr placed under international control; the eastern frontier marked by the Oder and the Neisse." [20] Stalin, the realist, listened but offered little encouragement. A few weeks later the "Big Three" met at Yalta, with Stalin, as we have seen, opposing France as an occupying power in Germany. De Gaulle had no illusions about Stalin, but his deepest suspicions, as always, were of the Americans and British, who bore France "ill will" and, between the wars, "led us to renounce the guarantees and reparations which had been granted us in exchange for control of the Reich and the Ruhr." [21]

A month before de Gaulle's trip to Moscow Churchill had conferred with him in Paris, and he had also requested a meeting with Resistance groups. De Gaulle wrote: " 'I am going there,' he [Churchill] told me, 'to see the men of the insurrection!!' Perhaps, too, he cherished the hope of finding adversaries of de Gaulle among them." [22] Yet it was Churchill who had labored to undermine de Gaulle's rival, General Giraud, and it was Churchill, as much as anyone else, who pressed the idea that the Free French under General Jacques Leclerc should liberate Paris.

Because he saw America and Britain as competitive influences in Western Europe, de Gaulle's attitude toward them could modestly have been called defensive. With Russia, from whom he sought recognition and identity of purpose, the tone was different. He spoke of *"la vieille Russie de toujours"* (eternal Russia) as distinct from the impermanent Soviet system; "between France and Russia there is no political conflict of interests," he said after returning to power, and he stressed their long tradition of association.[23]

Much of de Gaulle's foreign policy was authentically French: a weak and divided Germany; suspicion of the British and Americans, especially the former; a certain affinity for

Russia west of the Ural Mountains and even alliance with her. But much was *not* typically French. While any French government would eventually have rebelled against the Anglo-American domination of NATO, no French leader other than de Gaulle would have sought methodically to withdraw France from the structure and to plot its destruction. Almost any French government would have attempted to build up a nuclear-weapons capability—at least, as long as Britain did. But only de Gaulle would have sought to replace the United States as the guarantor of Germany's non-nuclear status. Any French government would have maneuvered for special advantages within the Common Market (indeed, that was one of the achievements of de Gaulle's predecessors). But only de Gaulle would have insisted on dominating the structure, beginning with the domination of West Germany, France's only possible rival. (In June 1965 he boycotted and thus paralyzed the Common Market for six months to make that point, and he was always prepared to break it up on a given issue involving French interests.) Any French government could be counted on to wring all possible concessions from a British government applying to enter the Common Market. But perhaps only de Gaulle would have vetoed Britain no matter what the circumstances.

De Gaulle's virtuosity in exploiting latent and existing French sentiment served to mask the real nature of his foreign policy. He played skillfully on the anti-Americanism of the French mandarinate. He maneuvered intellectual support (and silenced opposition) on the left by attacking American power, on the right by asserting French power. French chauvinism was another card. On Day I of a de Gaulle-provoked crisis—take the Quebec affair—most French newspapers would record the shock waves and some deplore the gesture. On Day II, as a global reaction set in, many of the critics would begin to find reasonable explanations for de Gaulle's position, closing ranks behind him. Nearly everyone credited him with reasonable motives. Most often he was forgiven his exaggerations because he had at least expressed legitimate French tendencies. In fact, his policies mocked the French people by seeking ends far beyond their means and indeed their hopes: to replace the United States as protector of Western Europe; to dominate Germany, a larger, stronger, and more dynamic society; to build a nuclear force capable of reaching all points on the compass, even while Britain, already a thermonuclear power, was drawing back from the burdens of this technology; to arbitrate world conflicts by representing a neutral third force with political, if not military, power equal to that of the United States and the U.S.S.R.

These were the Gaullist purposes, pursued not strategically—de Gaulle was not much of a strategist—but by exploiting events and the mistakes of others. His model was Palmerston's England, which had "no allies, only interests." De Gaulle, it was said in Paris, was a ping-pong player, not a chess player. But he was more—a solitary figure in an endless drama, an Aeschylean character, condemned by his own will to eternal movement. And he ventured off to faraway places the better to strengthen his claim to speak for Europe. It was all performance, played for its own sake against a dazzling background of reflecting mirrors, and had little real content. The center of the public stage was held, but the real powers were not impressed. De Gaulle's most exuberantly defiant press conference, on November 27, 1967, was staged while Cyrus Vance, Washington's trouble shooter of the moment, was averting a dangerous Greco-Turkish war over Cyprus. The West Germans played the Gaullist game and waited for his disappearance to exploit their ability (constantly growing, thanks mainly to de Gaulle) to bargain with London, Paris, and Moscow.

While embodying the character and sense of drama prescribed in *The Edge of the Sword*, its author had also picked up some of the earthier qualities that go with political success. Call it cynicism or self-deception—it can be either, or a blend of both—almost any successful politician must be able to take a position for one reason while explaining it for another. De Gaulle's hostility toward the British was a good example. In *Salvation* he drew this gloomy conclusion from the Churchill-Eden visit to Paris in November 1944:

> It was apparent that England favored France's political reappearance, that she would continue to do so for reasons of equilibrium, tradition and security, that she desired a formal alliance with us, but would not consent to link her strategy with ours, believing herself in a position to function independently between Moscow and Washington, to limit their demands, but also to take advantage of them. The peace we French hoped to build in accord with what we regarded as logic and justice the British found it expedient to approach with formulas of empiricism and compromise.[24]

De Gaulle, who was to empiricism and the declining art of *Realpolitik* what Sutherland is to *bel canto,* was clearly aroused not by Churchill's "empiricism" but by his preferred position vis-à-vis Washington and Moscow. Or again, consider the catalogue of his objections to British membership in the Common Market: Britain was insular and maritime, tied to the old dominions of the Commonwealth; Britain must first reorient her agriculture and commerce; Britain's economic and financial liabilities would become Europe's and therefore must be corrected before she could become eligible. In fact, Britain's economic and financial weakness was the one factor that could have commended her to de Gaulle as an EEC member. A robust British economy would be yet another reason to veto; the last thing de Gaulle wanted was more competition. In truth, Britain would not be eligible in de Gaulle's eyes until her privileged position with Washington had ended and, still more important, until she had become measurably weaker than France, not just economically but politically and militarily. It wasn't that de Gaulle feared his Europe being dissolved in an Atlantic sea, but rather that he saw France's role diminished by Britain's presence in a closely knit European community.

De Gaulle seemed to believe that a softer Soviet policy would be hastened by a reduction of American influence in Europe; Moscow would be more disposed to make concessions to the West Europeans. The evidence, such as it was, did not support this thesis and few West or East Europeans agreed with him. But his attitude fit his purpose—to reduce American influence by supplanting it with French. His attitude recalled the Maurrasian dream: "This league of lesser peoples could entrust us with its military command, and the policy which the kings of France always followed, of blocking *the creation of any worldwide monarchy or the excessive growth of this or that coalition, would again triumphantly shine forth from Paris.*" [25]

What de Gaulle said about France's nuclear strike force was seldom related to its purpose. It deterred Moscow, he often noted, since it could "tear off an arm of the Soviet Union." In fact, the purpose of the *force de dissuasion* was political, not strategic. First and foremost, it pointed up the difference between France and Germany.

In short, everything the General did or said was for multiple reasons, some of which, like any effective politician, he actually believed. But his declaratory reasons often had little to do with his real purpose, although the possibility of some self-deception must be admitted.

De Gaulle was given to fits of gloom and despondency; these were often stimulated by large events, like the invasion of Czechoslovakia, which emphasized the flaws in his grand design. In such moods he envisaged another world war. He had been privately forecasting war between the Soviet Union and the United States, off and on, since 1946. And yet his nightmare was an understanding between the two great powers—a genuine dialogue that could lead to a settlement of the German problem without a key role for France. To discourage such an understanding was an enterprise never far from the center of Gaullist maneuver.

The Cuban missile crisis was one of those watershed episodes which leaves everything a bit clearer; for example, the identity of big-power interest in avoiding nuclear war. It also accented the inner conflict of the Gaullist argument, the duality of the design. Cuba proved, de Gaulle said later, that America cared more about the defense of its own geographic approaches than about Europe's defense.[26] But Cuba also aroused his fear of a Washington-Moscow dialogue. Thus, on one day de Gaulle was warning that Washington would abandon the defense of Europe, on another that America intended to settle Europe's future with the U.S.S.R. over the heads of the Europeans. In either case he was probing the American position for weakness.

Denunciation of the Soviet and American "blocs"—the "two hegemonies," as he liked to call them—was a basic theme of the Gaullist liturgy, reprised on every possible occasion—most recently in the French reaction to the Soviet invasion of Czechoslovakia, seen by de Gaulle as a consequence of the Yalta agreement. Yet this sworn enemy of blocs proposed in 1958 to Eisenhower and Macmillan that they create a three-nation bloc with "the responsibility of taking joint decisions on all political matters affecting world security. . . ."[27]

De Gaulle was untroubled by such inconsistencies; these were tactics. The so-called tridirectorate proposal was a tactical maneuver, *not* a serious proposal (as will be explained in the following chapter).

Briefly, de Gaulle was in motion, playing the age-old game. And there was the poignant—some would say tragic—aspect of the monumental figure. He alone was playing the game by traditional rules, the neoclassicist living in the nuclear age; a more romantic Richelieu in a less exalted epoch. De Gaulle was the leader with the intuitive knowledge of the uses of power but with no tolerance for the limits of power. An early prophet of European unity, he became the quixotic European separatist, driven to restore the concert of powers in an era dominated by the larger powers; an opponent of the balance of power, he lacked the means to alter it to purely French advantage.

And there, perhaps, was the ironic aspect of de Gaulle. The purity of his vision—the great "sweep of his endeavors"—set him apart and denied him fulfillment. With a less exalted design and somewhat more commitment to achievement than to endeavor, de Gaulle could have been more than the leader of a middle power, compelled in the end to accept the balance of power established by the "two hegemonies." He, and possibly only he, could have mobilized the countries of Western Europe into a community that could play something approaching the role he insisted belonged to France alone.

3

Seeding the Quarrel

Relief, heavily dosed with fresh anxiety, was the reaction in high places in most NATO countries to de Gaulle's return to power. Civil war and anarchy might now be averted, the Algerian war entrusted to the single personality with the prestige and strength to cope with it. But what would de Gaulle do about NATO, the Common Market, and disarmament? He was known to be implacably hostile to the European unity movement and all its works; his admiration for NATO was about what one might expect him to have for an Anglo-American fief centered on French territory. Toward the disarmament talks in Geneva he showed the predictable bias of someone moving in the opposite direction—trying to build a nuclear-weapons capability and determined to match, if not surpass, the British.

Just before de Gaulle's investiture various senior figures of the Fourth Republic made the trip to Colombey-les-Deux-Églises to sound him out on, among other things, these large issues. They heard nothing too alarming, but nothing very precise. On NATO de Gaulle spoke in general terms about reorganizing the structure so as to gain a larger role for France in European and world affairs. On the matter of uniting Europe he envisaged a *rassemblement des vieux pays autour de moi*—a grouping of the old countries around himself. On the Soviet Union he refused to commit himself to or even to comment on anything, and said merely that he would not allow Communist participation in his government. This was reassuring. At least he hadn't threatened to liquidate the Common Market, the Coal and Steel Community, and Euratom. (Indeed, he had no such intention, whatever his aversion to supranational enterprises. The Common Market might be just the means for obliging the laggard French economy to adapt to the pace of its more dynamic neighbors and for blowing fresh competitive winds through the archaic and fusty places of French commerce. And then if the EEC organization showed any political pretensions, one could speedily liquidate them and, if necessary, the Common Market, too.)

Algeria seemed to be all that mattered to the French in those early days of the Gaullist restoration. But insiders and high-level callers quickly discovered that the General was again "in play" on all fronts. One of his ministers recalls that when de Gaulle first summoned him in May 1958 he expected to be asked some searching questions about Algeria, but de Gaulle instead inquired whether he had given any thought to Communist China and the question of French recognition. Upon replying that this matter had not been much in his thoughts, he was advised to begin "reflecting" on it.[1]

Washington and London reached swift agreement that soundings had better be taken. Macmillan, an old colleague in the war, was the first to visit de Gaulle at the Hotel Matignon, official residence of French Prime Ministers, arriving on June 29, 1958, and departing two days later. Nothing of consequence was agreed upon, but Macmillan felt that this first encounter had gone well. De Gaulle complained about NATO; the present arrangements didn't suit him at all, the joint command being especially vexatious, and he talked of returning to some equivalent of a 1914 situation, with sector commands and each government receiving a veto over the actions of the other. He thought NATO's Standing Group in Washington should be strengthened. This was significant, as the Standing Group was the only instrument of the Alliance to which membership was confined to Britain, France, and the United States. With characteristic ambiguity de Gaulle outlined his soon-to-be-celebrated tridirectorate proposal, according to which those three countries would share equally in the decisions affecting their joint security in every part of the world. Macmillan either didn't grasp the point or, more likely, chose not to. But the Foreign Office *did* understand it. And it wasn't an entirely new thought. On July 4 Lord Montgomery called attention to the prospect of a strong and prosperous France, thanks to de Gaulle's return to power, and proposed a system in which NATO powers with global interests could evolve common policies to deal with these interests.[2]

The two men took a lengthy stroll in the deep Matignon garden after dinner one evening. De Gaulle did most of the talking. He expressed regret at having been so difficult to deal with during the war; the pitiful state of French affairs had left him then with no other course of action, he explained; his unwillingness to yield on even minor points had been Free France's only source of strength and self-confidence. Now that France was again on her feet—the situation more or less normalized—he looked forward to fruitful relations with Britain and Macmillan.

While he outlined his thoughts on France's place in the world, de Gaulle refused to be drawn out on precise points affecting Franco-British relations. Instead he returned constantly to Algeria, repeating each time that he would do his duty.

Macmillan felt that he had achieved a rapport with de Gaulle during this talk, and he reported him a man much improved from the difficult figure of the war years. Indeed, it turned out that Macmillan, a curiously sentimental man, was deeply moved by de Gaulle's constant references to "duty."

Four days later, on July 5, it was the turn of the grand panjandrum of American foreign policy, John Foster Dulles, who, while bearing little sympathy for de Gaulle's lofty estimate of France's place in the world, had great respect for de Gaulle himself. Even in the early days after the war and during de Gaulle's retreat from power, a time when most American "establishmentarians" had written him off, Dulles had sometimes seen de Gaulle in Paris, and he had never underrated his gifts or his prospects. De Gaulle, like Adenauer and Khrushchev, seemed to reciprocate this respect.

De Gaulle and Dulles were to meet three times tête-à-tête before the latter's death; there must have been something quite choice in these confrontations. The two had in common fifty-odd years of experience in world politics, but otherwise they stood in sharp contrast. De Gaulle was in style, attitude, and quality suited to any season of French history; Dulles, invincibly Calvinist, was to Europeans the very model of the modern American puritan.

By now the Gaullist idea of a trilateral sharing of the global burdens of defense was current in Washington as well as London. George Ball has written that prior to Dulles's first visit de Gaulle had told an American official that "France wished to play a central role in the development of Western strategy around the world and that she was unhappy that a German general had been selected for NATO's central European command." [3] (The American official was General Norstad, NATO's Supreme Commander.) Ball, whose account must be regarded as authentic, goes on to describe Dulles's and de Gaulle's disagreement on the tridirectorate concept. De Gaulle, he says, told Dulles "that unless France felt she were a 'world power' she would degenerate internally." He observed that

France had vital interests in the Sahara and the Middle East, but that West Germany "was not yet a major Western power and should be kept out of the directorate." Dulles replied that "a formalized 'world directorate' was unrealistic and would be resented by other Western and nonaligned countries." [4]

With agreement on this or that point excluded, the two men were inclined to let their differences take a philosophical turn. Thus, de Gaulle set forth his celebrated view of France as continental leader with a global vocation, while Dulles stressed joint activities and the NATO mechanism. Dulles saw the Communist countries as a menacing bloc forged by a common ideology; de Gaulle observed that the deeper reality was the existence of nations with different personalities and histories; their social systems were less important, he felt, and in any case not lasting. He conceded the threat of Soviet Russia, but felt that more and more it would become a matter of traditional Russian interests being asserted, as opposed to the insidious spread of the doctrine of a new Church Militant. De Gaulle saw the world as an ensemble of nations, Dulles as a system of two alliances, the one designed to check the malign purposes of the other.

Just one day before their meeting, on July 4, Britain and the United States had signed an agreement establishing closer nuclear cooperation; this followed passage of the amended United States atomic energy law—amended, it will be recalled, in Britain's favor. For Dulles's meeting with de Gaulle to occur on the following day could have been—and was—considered inopportune. But the coincidence probably served to sharpen the tone of the talks—to point up more clearly the gulf between the two leaders. One French paper captured well the attitude of much of its audience in suggesting that the amendments to the McMahon Act envisaged "the creation of an Anglo-U.S. atomic directorate, signaling and consolidating their preponderance in the Western camp. . . . All these arrangements can only make more apparent and more burdensome the hegemony of the English-speaking peoples at the heart of the Atlantic Alliance." [5]

Like Macmillan, Dulles knew that de Gaulle would never support a ban or limitation on nuclear testing until his own nuclear-weapons program was far enough along to do without tests. The message was plain. De Gaulle wasn't asking for assistance, and he never would. But he was telling the Anglo-Saxons that France's support of test-ban talks and the like would have to be paid for in the coin of technology. Dulles was also told that the United States would *not* be given the right to deploy nuclear weapons on French territory.

In return, Dulles, while making no effort to discourage de Gaulle's nuclear ambitions, left a clear impression that Washington would offer little help to the French nuclear program. He cited the restrictions of the atomic-energy laws and the pernicious effect that giving nuclear aid to France would have on the Federal Republic of Germany. He *did* offer the propulsion system for a nuclear submarine, provided Congress approved.

Little time was spent on the nuclear issue, even though both the Americans and the French knew it was central. De Gaulle and Dulles were, in fact, establishing a pattern that would endure: the nuclear issue would always be more a tacit than a current piece of business between Washington and Paris (or between London and Paris); yet, although seldom discussed, and even then never in depth, it was to be the dominant issue, in many ways the only issue, between de Gaulle and the Anglo-Saxons. For de Gaulle, nuclear weapons and his soaring hopes for France had a one-to-one relationship. To have access to Anglo-American expertise on inertial guidance systems, isotope separation, re-entry vehicles, warhead technology, and so on, would be incalculably beneficial to the French program. But the political price tag was always to be too high for the man of character. He would never water the noble wine of France's sovereign grandeur. Better to travel the nuclear path alone than to lose one's political direction in treacherous byways and short cuts.

De Gaulle never told his government *not* to seek aid from America or Britain, although his ambassador in Washington, Hervé Alphand, was at first forbidden to discuss the subject. He merely established that he would never pay a political price for nuclear technology; that being the case, he told his ministers and generals, the Anglo-Saxons would be unlikely to agree to give significant aid, but they were free to try to get it.

In the end de Gaulle was proved right, although it was a largely self-fulfilling prophecy. In return for very little—an occasional bow to NATO, a commitment to remain an active partner—de Gaulle at various moments could have had almost anything he wanted from the Americans and British. But even a gesture toward NATO was unthinkable. France "with free hands" was the eternal and supreme goal.

Dulles underrated neither de Gaulle's obdurate style nor France's place at the geographic heart of NATO. But like Dean Acheson before him, Dulles was even more sensitive to the problem of Germany. West Germany had to be anchored to the Western system and kept immune from nuclear temptation.

In the spring of 1958 the authentically German Defense Minister of the Federal Republic, Franz-Josef Strauss, in an interview with the prominent British socialist parliamentarian, Richard Crossman, had said, "I can guarantee there will be no German nuclear weapons for three, four or even five years. But after that, if other nations—particularly the French—make their own H-bomb, Germany may well be sucked in, too." [6] Strauss later remarked that when West Germany formally disavowed the right to fabricate atomic weapons, in signing the agreements creating the Western European Union in 1954, it was Dulles himself who had observed to Adenauer "that the Federal Republic's renunciation of these weapons followed from the *clausula rebus sic stantibus*" [7]—the standard legal phrase indicating that an agreement is in force only so long as the conditions under which it was made still apply. Dulles was acutely conscious that France's acquisition of nuclear weapons would represent a change in conditions. For Washington to advance the day when France would have this capability could well mean to advance the day of reckoning with Bonn.

De Gaulle and Dulles—architects of antagonistic policies each emerging from a set of alien fixed attitudes—were thus in solid agreement on one point: West Germany must on no account possess nuclear weapons or achieve independent access to them. Beyond that point they diverged sharply, de Gaulle wanting to check the German impulse with French power, Dulles fearful that French power would arouse the impulse and seeking constantly to reassure the West Germans about American guarantees, the reality of interdependence, the virtues of West European integration, and so on.

Neither man's comprehension of the other was complete. De Gaulle never really understood either the limits on American power or its purposes. He saw an isolationist America becoming an imperial America without even the grace of self-recognition. Words like interdependence and integration would better read United States' domination. Again, an element of self-deception—of believing what he found it convenient or satisfying to believe—doubtless helped to inspire this view. But Dulles was at least as dim on de Gaulle, however keen his appreciation of the latter's remarkable qualities and his ambitions for France. But then no other American official had perceived that de Gaulle's declared position had little, if anything, to do with what he really wanted. It was not parity with the United States and Britain in the Western system that he sought, but rather supremacy in Western Europe in order to have "free hands" everywhere else, including Moscow.

Since virtually nobody—certainly nobody at a high level—in London or Washington understood this, the general impression was that the *directoire à trois* for which de Gaulle seemed to be groping was the pinnacle of his vaulting ambition; it would, after all, give him a lasting political advantage over West Germany. Actually, de Gaulle was doing what he often did best—setting the scene for a *coup de théâtre* that would gain him the center of the stage, enhance his maneuverability, and present the other players with a kind of heads-I-win-tails-you-lose choice, which they might not even understand. Normally, de Gaulle built to such effects not with a strategic design but by clever manipulation of events. In the summer of 1958, however, he was atypically playing a strategic game.

His goal was *not* to harness France with America and Britain in a system for assuring the security and preservation of Western civilization. The real power of such a system, after all, would still be American. De Gaulle's purpose was to promote French political fortunes in the world and the spread of French language and culture. He was looking ahead to a quadripolar world system, the four power centers being Washington and Moscow, joined eventually—perhaps in the 1980s—by Peking and Paris. The Atlantic Alliance would be superseded; Great Britain, weakened by economic pressure and declining political fortune, might remain in the American orbit or might shift its allegiance to a French-led Europe.

Could this have been predicted? De Gaulle's dissent from Dulles's view of a world split into two ideological camps offered a clue of sorts, but not a very sharp one. His published works could not yet have illuminated the path of his thinking. *The Edge of the Sword* had not been translated into English and, while a new French edition had been issued, its Anglo-American readership was limited, to put it mildly; the third and most revealing volume of the memoirs was not yet completed (de Gaulle was still correcting galley proofs in the Élysée Palace in early 1959).

Still, de Gaulle had not left an entirely cold trail. His innumerable utterances during the "desert years" at Colombey-les-Deux-Églises are alive with clues:

> [The area bounded by the North Sea and the Mediterranean and drained by the Rhine is to become a grouping of which] the duty and dignity of becoming the center and the key falls to France.[8]

> Western Europe must be built. . . . But the physical and moral center of the formation is France.[9]

> As soon as France has a policy she will follow another path and take the Continent with her.[10]

> Europe requires a common defense system for which France has the responsibility of determining the guidelines and designating the leader.[11]

> Europe will not be organized if France does not assume its leadership. I mean a France on her feet and free of restraining ties.[12]

In the Gaullist calculation France was free to grow in strength and stature while her security was guaranteed by Washington. The absolute character of the American guarantee left him free to chop away at the American position in order to strengthen France's. One analyst saw this as de Gaulle's "elevator technique": conceding nothing, Gaullist France would climb in prestige and strength, the American commitments serving as elevator.[13] Equally, the French economy, once Europe's most worrisome invalid, would be borne up on the rising tide of the Common Market. Meanwhile, France was supposed gradually to assume control of a Western Europe whose security would become less and less an

American concern. This in turn would encourage Moscow to become more conciliatory—more "Russian" in her willingness to deal with Paris on the German issue. And so, at long last, the partition of Europe would become a matter to be settled by the two halves of Continental Europe:

> On our old continent, the organization of a western group, at the very least equivalent to that which exists in the east, may one day, without risk to the independence and the freedom of each nation and taking into account the probable evolution of political regimes, establish a European entente from the Atlantic to the Urals. Then Europe, no longer split in two by ambitions and ideologies that would become progressively out of date, would again be the heart of civilization.[14]

On the same distant horizon de Gaulle also saw inexorable and increasing Chinese pressure, pushing eternal Russia toward a European settlement:

> Doubtless, Soviet Russia, although having helped Communism become established in China, realizes that nothing can happen to prevent Russia—a white European nation which has conquered part of Asia, and, in short, is quite well endowed with land, mines, factories and wealth—nothing can happen to prevent it from having to reckon with the yellow multitude which is China—numberless and wretchedly poor, indestructible and ambitious, building by dint of violent efforts a power which cannot be kept within limits and looking around at the expanses over which it must one day spread.[15]

Thus, the eastern frontier of de Gaulle's Europe was the Ural Mountains, beyond which lay a vast area that might well be disputed one day by China. But the forces of a French-led Western Europe must never be committed to a struggle for what was clearly part of Asia.

De Gaulle's view as to how France would maintain the defensive power and strength required by this role was expressed in an address to students of France's three war colleges less than a year and a half after his return to power:

> What is obviously required is that we provide ourselves in the coming years with a force capable of acting in our interest— what one chooses to call a *"force de frappe"*—capable of being operated any time and anywhere. It goes without saying that this force would be based on atomic weapons, either developed by us or purchased, but which belong to us: and since one will be able eventually to destroy France from any point in the world, our force must have the capability of being able to act against every part of the world.[16]

This emphasis on global capability was repeated throughout de Gaulle's tenure in office. In the *Revue de Défense Nationale* of December 1967 an article by General Charles Ailleret, known to reflect the policies of the Élysée Palace, in effect updated de Gaulle's address, calling for a military policy directed against all points on the compass (*"tous azimuts"*).[17] In reviewing the range of threats that France might one day confront, the article made no distinction between the United States and the Soviet Union.

Within NATO de Gaulle could never aspire, even if he had wanted to, to be more than a brilliant second to Washington, a role he would first have to seize from London. Thus, his intention was never for a single moment to reform NATO, but rather to bury it. In an unguarded moment during the legislative election campaign in 1967 Maurice Couve de Murville, the Gaullist Foreign Minister, may have offered a glimpse of this determination. Replying to a question put to him in a public meeting by a celebrated member of his district—When had he first become aware of de Gaulle's intention to withdraw from NATO?—he said he had known about it since 1958.[18]

It was against this murky, somewhat Byzantine background that de Gaulle launched his tridirectorate proposal. A largely spurious proposition was received on its merits and viewed as a serious matter everywhere, not least in France.

Among de Gaulle's virtuoso gifts was a knack for linking various notions and giving them a push in some oblique direction but aimed always toward his great, unchanging goals. The particular track might not go very far, but for a time it extended his maneuverability. When the dead end loomed ahead, he would change course, taking yet another oblique angle. Whatever happened, he held attention, the other players were thrown off balance, a good deal of confusion was sown, and the world was kept guessing as to what he was up to. The years of the Fifth Republic can be divided into periods when de Gaulle was following one or another track; none was to take him far beyond Square One, but together they successfully blocked the paths marked out by the other players—the Americans, the British, the European federalists, and so on.

In the world of politics, diplomacy, and the press, people either were attracted by what they thought de Gaulle was doing to restore France's place in Western councils, were vigorously opposed, or fell somewhere in between. The point is that only a handful understood him. These were people who *had* read *The Edge of the Sword* and the first two volumes of memoirs, and who recalled de Gaulle's penchant during the war for playing the Anglo-Saxons off against Moscow. One such person, a Western diplomat based in Paris, wrote a prophetic dispatch on October 19, 1958, which said in part: "Some may hold* that the General would go 'neutralist,' in other words that he would end by making advances to the Soviet Union and that he would at any rate become a passive partner in NATO. This may be the

---

* This phrase indicates that a few sharp-eyed diplomats understood de Gaulle. But these were connoisseurs who may have influenced their immediate superiors but seldom the high political figures.

eventual outcome; but it will not happen, I suggest, before he has tried another course. This other course is to organize Europe, in conjunction with the German Chancellor, against the Anglo-Saxons." These were the two courses de Gaulle was successively to follow.

In September 1958, four months after returning to power, he was starting down the first track. In the space of a few days three important events occurred: first, the Quai d'Orsay was instructed to notify the West Germans—and Defense Minister Strauss personally—that France considered the so-called Strauss–Chaban-Delmas agreements to be null and void, at least in their military aspects; second, de Gaulle's first meeting with Adenauer was held on September 14 at Colombey-les-Deux-Églises; third, de Gaulle's memorandum proposing the tridirectorate, dated September 17, was delivered to London and Washington on September 25.

Strauss, furious—he later denied the existence of the Chaban-Delmas agreements—sought unsuccessfully to see de Gaulle. The Quai d'Orsay, which had bitterly opposed these shadowy arrangements, was delighted and reassured. Clearly, it was no part of de Gaulle's purpose, and never would be, to have West Germany a candidate for membership in the nuclear club. According to one of the General's entourage, de Gaulle told Adenauer frankly that West Germany must never seek atomic weapons, for it would risk jeopardizing the unity of a Western Europe that France and West Germany must build together. Adenauer is said to have agreed, but affected to know little about the Strauss–Chaban-Delmas affair. (Probably this was true: the best guess is that Strauss, while not concealing the negotiations from the old Chancellor, had told him only enough to protect himself.)

De Gaulle clearly took satisfaction in liquidating these arrangements. In his last meeting with Macmillan more than four years later he told him how, after coming to power, he had vetoed arrangements whereby the Germans and Italians had been asked to share in the cost of building France's isotope-separation plant at Pierrelatte in return for technical advantages.

The second critical event, de Gaulle's meeting with Adenauer, went brilliantly, from de Gaulle's point of view. The Chancellor was captivated by de Gaulle, of whom he had been highly suspicious. Not surprisingly, he had looked on de Gaulle as an old-fashioned Maurrasian French nationalist, a disciple of Poincaré and the right-wing, incontestably Maurrasian historian Jacques Bainville. Both Maurras and Bainville were prominent advocates of the theory of "the Germanies," and de Gaulle's own writings in this vein, as well as his postwar policies, were cause for concern, if not alarm, in Bonn, viz.:

> This Germany should be a federation of states, certainly not a Reich, and the Ruhr should be Europeanized.[19]

> Europe will appear strong and valid on the day when Germany is organized not as a Reich; the day when she is composed of states, doubtless linked to each other by federal ties, but each having sovereignty; the day when the Ruhr is Europeanized, which will degrade no one.[20]

> I have always said and always believed that Europe's base would be a direct agreement between the French people and the German people without intermediary, supposing, of course, that such an agreement were possible. This is not the path that has been taken. One has sought not to bring Germany organized as a confederation into a European grouping . . . but one has instead given West Germany the shape of the start of another Reich. This policy is not good.[21]

But de Gaulle set out to allay Adenauer's concern, to charm him, and to make him an ally—perhaps even a Gaullist. The degree of his success is aptly described by the French political scientist Alfred Grosser: ". . . they met, they liked each other, and after several hours of meetings, it can be said that they formed a tie of friendship that has not failed to this day: General de Gaulle's affection for Chancellor Adenauer was largely a function of the Chancellor's admiration for the General. At the root of the relationship between the two men lay the kind of constant and faithful, and at times unbounded, admiration of the Chancellor for the General, and the General's satisfaction at inspiring such a sentiment in so extraordinary a man." [22]

The conquest of Adenauer had presented no real difficulty for de Gaulle, whose brilliance was matched by charm when he chose. After all, de Gaulle and Adenauer had much in common. They shared a common faith; moreover, Adenauer was a Rhinelander with a profound contempt for the Germans to the east, especially the Protestant aristocracy and most especially the Prussians.* Here he was on common ground with de Gaulle, whose early antipathy to France's privileged classes had hardened during the war, when he identified most of them with Vichy. And they shared a basic mistrust of the German people, as well as an acute sense of Germany's responsibilities for two world wars.

This all conspired to convince Adenauer that he should follow France on the European scene, provided France were strongly and reliably led. The men of the Fourth Republic had been pasteboard figures, bobbing up and down, none of them ever securely or even long in power. De Gaulle seemed clearly the leader of strength with whom Adenauer could deal on equal terms. But *was* de Gaulle reliable? The meeting at Colombey convinced Adenauer that he was, that de Gaulle was another great "European." Meeting later with a group of German jour-

---

* Unlike de Gaulle, Adenauer was not a man of broad culture, not much of an intellectual, and he read little. Yet he was deeply attracted to French culture and had a passion for painting, of which he considered himself a connoisseur. (On a visit to Washington, he once told the Director of the National Gallery, in a tone as proud as it was facetious, that if he were not Chancellor of Germany he could snatch away the Director's job.)

nalists, he was jubilant: "General de Gaulle was very frank, and I found him to be a completely different man from the one presented to us in recent weeks by the German press, and not only by the German press. . . . He is not a nationalist. He showed a perfect understanding of the international situation and the importance of French-German relations." [23]

Astonishingly, Adenauer was also to reveal that de Gaulle had written in his own hand the first three paragraphs of the joint communiqué, which emphasized "cooperation" as opposed to "integration" (that most pernicious of notions in the Gaullist optic) in referring to the "European construction." [24] *Le Monde* reported that the two statesmen had agreed that there was no question of establishing new political institutions within the framework of the Common Market. [25]

A distinguished diplomat recalls being summoned by Adenauer the day after his return from Colombey-les-Deux-Églises. The Chancellor, he says, could not contain his elation that the meeting from which he had expected so little had gone so brilliantly. Adenauer, according to this diplomat, was not "seduced" by de Gaulle but, rather, was "captivated" by him. Whatever the degree of de Gaulle's conquest, Adenauer in time became obsessed by what he felt he could achieve through de Gaulle. Together they would solemnize Franco-German reconciliation and the sacred quest for European unity. Neither Adenauer nor any other German could take the lead; only France could lead. Adenauer was to follow de Gaulle even when an objective assessment of German interests sometimes pointed in another direction.

De Gaulle and Adenauer "discovered" each other on September 14. It was just three days later, on September 17, that de Gaulle's celebrated memorandum was completed and dated. In their supposedly frank and exhaustive discussions, de Gaulle had not even mentioned this monumental gambit to Adenauer, a dereliction that tells a good deal about his style as well as his confidence that he could always reel in Adenauer again at a later date.

The memorandum, drafted in the Quai d'Orsay, expressed de Gaulle's determination that France should take a larger part in world affairs, along with her American and British allies. The document was redrafted and toughened by a then junior official—now an ambassador—assigned to de Gaulle's staff. Various corrections by de Gaulle himself imparted the breath of life to the document, and, with covering letters to Eisenhower and Macmillan, it was delivered to the Department of State and the Foreign Office on September 25.

The memorandum, which has never been published, while faithful to de Gaulle's supposed preference for a trinity of Western powers, went far beyond *anything* that had yet been put forward.

The operative paragraphs were these:

> The French Government does not consider that the security of the free world, or indeed France itself, can be guaranteed by the North Atlantic Treaty Organization in its present form. In its view, political and strategic questions of world, as opposed to regional, importance, should be entrusted to a new body consisting of the United States, Great Britain, and France. This body should have the responsibility of taking joint decisions on all political matters affecting world security, and of drawing up and, if necessary, putting into action strategic plans, especially those involving the use of nuclear weapons. . . .
>
> The French Government regards such an organization for security as indispensable. Henceforth the whole development of its present participation in NATO is predicated on this.

It was further proposed that the new body "should be responsible for the organization of the defense, where appropriate, of individual operational regions, such as the Arctic, the Atlantic, the Pacific, and the Indian Oceans." And it was suggested that tripartite consultations on this proposal take place in Washington at the earliest possible moment.

Stripped of excess verbiage, de Gaulle was demanding—not requesting but *demanding*—a veto on the use of American nuclear weapons anywhere in the world. (De Gaulle was really addressing himself to Eisenhower and Dulles; he assumed that Macmillan's response would be conditioned by theirs.) The language—"joint decisions on all political matters affecting world security . . . drawing up and, if necessary, putting into action strategic plans, especially those involving the use of nuclear weapons"—lacked a cutting edge, but it was clear enough to those who read it. "Joint decisions" meant veto power, and the reference to a "new body" meant formalized, institutionalized new arrangements.

The sense of the blunter paragraphs was that Washington must either meet de Gaulle's remarkable terms or risk a gaping hole in NATO caused by France's withdrawal.

Acceptance was inconceivable. It was unthinkable that Washington could say yes to de Gaulle's terms, certainly not to a veto on the use of American nuclear weapons, even if France were strong enough to play a global role. Britain had such a veto, but *only* on the "double-veto" weapons deployed in Britain. De Gaulle would surely be the first to recognize that no great power would ever allow its hands to be tied by another government in this fashion. And then, apart from all else, France was still teetering on the edge of chaos; her army was tied down in Algeria; the threat of civil war remained; devaluation of the franc loomed ahead.

In the annals of modern diplomacy few if any episodes have been misted over by as much confusion and misunderstanding as this one—or for so long a time. To label de Gaulle's proposition a fraud would be overstating the case, but not by much. Not only did he know perfectly well that Washington could not agree to his terms, he seems to have set out to sabotage even the marginal possibility that his old associate and admirer, Ei-senhower, might accept some of what he seemed to be asking for. Indeed, de Gaulle's handling of the affair astonished even the people closest to him (who were as much in the dark as anyone).

It is first of all axiomatic that if de Gaulle had entertained any hope of a favorable response or if he had regarded his memorandum as negotiable, he would have kept faith with his celebrated passion for secrecy; nobody would have known about his proposal other than the recipients; leaks, if any, would not have come from Paris. In fact, they all *did* come from Paris—and on de Gaulle's instructions.

On September 24, the day before the memorandum was de-livered, de Gaulle gave a copy to Paul Henri Spaak, then Secre-tary-General of NATO. Through this prominent Belgian de Gaulle would be certain to generate strenuous opposition to his *directoire à trois* in the smaller NATO nations. Spaak's reac-tion was strong and visceral. After brief reflection he drew up a memorandum in reply which he communicated to the French government and to nobody else. The key phrases said: "It must be realized that this conception, if it were realized, would mean the end of the Atlantic Alliance. . . . It is necessary, forgive me for speaking so frankly, to abandon the idea of three-power world organization, which seems to me dangerous and unat-tainable."

De Gaulle instructed the Secretary-General of the Foreign Ministry, Louis Joxe, to give a résumé of his memorandum to the West German and Italian Ambassadors in Paris. They were not told about the "veto" aspect of the French proposals, but were able to report the gist of what de Gaulle was demanding to their governments.

The reactions in Bonn and Rome were predictably hostile. Later, on October 3, an Italian ambassador declared that his government would be obliged to re-examine its entire foreign policy if America and Britain agreed to a tridirectorate, which Italy, in any case, was not prepared to accept. But it was Adenauer who reacted most splenetically, with the cold rage and frustration of the deceived. It had been just two weeks since he and his great fellow-European had attained the outer reaches of mutual understanding and agreement. And never even a hint from de Gaulle.

Europe's foreign ministers were all in New York at this moment—for the opening of the UN General Assembly session. Dulles and Foreign Secretary Selwyn Lloyd conferred at length on the afternoon of September 25; their immediate concern was the current crisis in the Straits of Formosa, but it may be assumed that de Gaulle's "hot particle" was also discussed. On the following day, Dulles and Couve de Murville met for an hour. Although the matter was by then operative, it is far from certain that the French Foreign Minister knew precisely what the final version of the memorandum said.

The confusion was general, and no less in Paris than in any other NATO capital. Couve de Murville was plainly disconcerted. On October 2 he said that while he must not be quoted, it was clear the General had made a great mistake. Geoffroy de Courcel, then in de Gaulle's entourage (and as close to him—at least on these matters—as anyone could be), suggested that the affair had been mishandled by the General. A prominent French ambassador remarked that in Couve de Murville's absence the General might have been led into error by others around him. The theme that de Gaulle had bungled runs through much of the diplomatic cable traffic. For example, in mid-October one government dispatched the following advisory message to certain of its embassies: "Our tactical objective in this whole operation must be to help General de Gaulle as gently as we can to get himself out of this impossible position which he has created for himself." And, some days later, an ambassador in Paris was taking the line that de Gaulle had badly mismanaged things "and it is going to be terribly difficult to save his face."

On October 8 Macmillan went to Bonn for informal discussions with the irate Adenauer and listened to an unrestrained denunciation of de Gaulle. Adenauer was especially enraged by the knowledge that the memorandum must already have existed in draft *before* his talks with the General. He told Macmillan that he had guessed wrong about de Gaulle—that the old-fashioned French nationalist in de Gaulle was dominant, as he had earlier suspected.

A fine, pure irony marks this occasion. Macmillan—the most worldly, even the most gifted of all the Anglo-Saxons and Germans with whom de Gaulle was to deal after returning to power —was to become a tragic victim of that strange blend of iron purpose and deep hostility that often animated de Gaulle. But here in Bonn, still very early in the game, Macmillan spent the better part of an afternoon trying to reassure Adenauer—soon to become de Gaulle's great confederate—about the unfathomable figure of the war years, whom he now trusted implicitly. He reminded Adenauer that he had known the General for a long time. Granted he was hard to deal with; still, he was a Christian gentleman with whom one could work to the common good. In any case de Gaulle was not one who would ever do a deal with the Russians. This build-up of de Gaulle—as poignant, in retrospect, as it is ironic—took up the better part of the conversation. Macmillan sought to persuade Adenauer to look upon the memorandum in a less tragic light. He may perhaps have calmed the Chancellor, but he left behind a West German government no less hostile to de Gaulle's proposal.

Meanwhile, Couve de Murville on October 1 confirmed in diplomatic channels that de Gaulle was in fact asking for a veto on American nuclear weapons. Courcel, according to other diplomatic dispatches, told General Norstad the same thing. Norstad, it should be added, says that he doesn't remember any one conversation with Courcel on this subject. But he *does* remember numerous conversations with French officials, some of whom offered the "veto" interpretation while others gave a "narrower" one. Norstad adds that while his memory may be fallible on this point, he recalls that his first impressions of the affair were drawn from those pressing the veto line, his second impressions from others presenting the less dramatic version. Norstad's recollection squares with as much of the diplomatic record as I have been able to piece together.

As October wore on, Couve de Murville and others began to take a softer line: it wasn't a veto on American nuclear weapons that de Gaulle wanted, but closer consultative arrangements among the "Big Three" on world problems. At one point Couve de Murville said the proposal did not *really* contemplate an institutionalized three-power directorate, although that is what the memorandum said; he may have meant not within NATO. A key figure on the French side confided that, believing de Gaulle had made a major mistake in linking the idea of a world tridirectorate with tripartite control of NATO, he and others tried to make this point to the General, who had drafted the operative language himself; de Gaulle agreed—later on—to limit his sweeping design to the world beyond NATO.* From Washington's point of view it was, of course, still wholly unacceptable.

Although Whitehall and the State Department were in close contact on the memorandum, their responses to it were not identical. The Americans refused to negotiate on de Gaulle's communication as it stood; Whitehall—continuing to reflect Britain's wartime role as buffer between Roosevelt and de Gaulle—hoped to find some suitable compromise that would assure de Gaulle's commitment to NATO.

Dulles and Couve de Murville were both in Rome during the

* The same French source says that when de Gaulle met Kennedy in 1961 he told him that the tridirectorate proposal did not apply to NATO itself.

weekend of October 18 for the funeral of Pope Pius XII. Dulles lunched with Italy's Premier, Amintore Fanfani, at the American Embassy and discussed the problem with him. He then conferred privately with the West German Foreign Minister; Bonn seemed ready to accept a watered-down arrangement of close cooperation among certain NATO members on specific problems.

Couve de Murville lunched with Cardinal Feltin and other Church dignitaries at the Villa Bonaparte, the French Embassy to the Holy See. Afterward he, too, called on Dulles at the American Embassy. Dulles proposed that the French government reduce its proposals to more negotiable form (this was the line the British were also taking). Although noncommittal, Couve de Murville seemed to agree.

En route back to Washington Dulles's aircraft made a fueling stop at a military airfield in England. Selwyn Lloyd, spending the weekend at Chequers, drove to meet him, and the two spent an hour and a half in the officers' mess. By this time, the written replies to de Gaulle's memorandum were due to be delivered in a matter of hours. Dulles reported his conversation with Couve de Murville, and Lloyd took the view that everyone must help to spare de Gaulle the consequences of the great error he had committed.

The British Ambassador in Paris, Sir Gladwyn Jebb, delivered Macmillan's reply on October 21, taking the occasion to request that France reformulate the proposals. De Gaulle was noncommittal and distinctly unresponsive. He again linked French participation in NATO to the response to his initiative and said, in effect, that all the unpleasantness might be avoided if only Dulles would agree to discuss the plan he had proposed in a friendly and sensible manner. De Gaulle was reminding Britain where the real power lay.

The American response, dated October 20 and drafted by relatively low-level officers in the State and Defense Departments, was sent out after a routine clearance by General Andrew Goodpaster at the White House. It sought to deflect rather than meet head-on the thrust of de Gaulle's initiative: Washington had a tendency to smother de Gaulle's claims for France by disregarding them. It stressed the virtues of consultation within NATO and envisaged "very serious problems, both within and outside NATO, in any effort to amend the North Atlantic Treaty beyond the areas presently covered."

Actually, Macmillan replied twice. An earlier interim reply had been telegraphed to the British Embassy in Paris in the form of a personal message from the Prime Minister to be transmitted to de Gaulle. This early note had pointed out that Macmillan would be meeting with Chancellor Adenauer and asked (a) whether Adenauer had been informed of the proposal; and (b) whether de Gaulle would authorize Macmillan to discuss it with him. De Gaulle replied in the affirmative to both questions. The second reply of October 21, which has never been published, did meet the issue head-on, unlike the American response. It took full account of the French proposals, noting the obvious bearing they would have on other NATO countries, especially West Germany. Adenauer's distress was specifically noted. De Gaulle was asked point-blank whether he was seeking a veto on American nuclear weapons, and it was suggested that he and Macmillan should meet to explore these questions. The reply also admonished de Gaulle to pay less attention to the institutional forms of cooperation than to the cooperation itself. De Gaulle had never been impressed by such advice, either during the war years or after 1958. Still, Macmillan, unlike Eisenhower, had not closed the door on the directorate; yet de Gaulle never even replied to his proposal for talks.

On October 24 the American and British had their answer. It was predictably negative—based, according to Couve de Murville, who delivered it, on France's concern that in the event of

negotiations the Italians would publish the text of the memorandum, putting de Gaulle in an awkward position. The next
day Couve de Murville observed that it had never been in
de Gaulle's mind to seek a veto on American nuclear weapons;
that he had sought only a measure of three-power consultation
and cooperation—nothing, really, much beyond what the West
Germans were ready to concede.

In the tangled history of postwar Western diplomacy this exchange of memoranda was a turning point. An issue had been
born. De Gaulle had asked for more than could possibly have
been granted.

It was a spectacular gesture, but well within the Gaullist pattern. It was neither the first nor last time that de Gaulle would
ask for something unattainable which, once refused, would permit him to deploy the alternative policy he actually preferred.
He in fact ensured that this would happen by promoting resistance to his own initiative by leaking advance news of it. All the
while, he confused people about his purpose through conflicting messages sent out through aides. In establishing that London and Washington had denied France's insistence upon playing a global role, he would legitimize the tough, independent
policy designed to revive and expand French influence, to free
France, and thus, by his lights, restore her soul: "I was trying
to find a means of leaving the Atlantic Alliance and reclaiming
the freedom lost during the Fourth Republic at the time of the
signing of the North Atlantic Treaty. Thus, I demanded the
moon. I was sure that they wouldn't give it to me. There was no
point in expecting anything. They would always refuse me that.
. . . What they want is to dominate us." [26]

De Gaulle, in short, was setting up the context for his long-
range dealings with the Anglo-Saxons. Meanwhile, he was at
grips with his more pressing difficulties in Algeria, and he often
tended to favor a quarrel with Washington and London in

order to gain support at home. Whatever he did about Algeria was certain to arouse troublesome passions, but rejection of de Gaulle's tridirectorate, even if only vaguely understood by the public, would awaken the sympathy of all Frenchmen sensitive to the issue of Anglo-Saxon discrimination against them.

Throughout the West, above all in France, this incident is widely believed to lie at the heart of de Gaulle's dispute with the Anglo-Saxons. If only Eisenhower had obliged him, or gone part of the way . . . (A legend even developed that Washington never replied to de Gaulle's memorandum. This is why Eisenhower's reply was finally leaked to C. L. Sulzberger in 1963 and eventually published in Congressional hearings in 1966.) But, as we have seen, efforts *were* made to persuade de Gaulle to moderate his demands, to meet Eisenhower half way, and so on, and they failed. And the record shows that at least for a while, de Gaulle's own entourage was as baffled as everyone else.

Suppose the move had succeeded. Suppose that de Gaulle did not exclude the possibility that Eisenhower's and Macmillan's good will and nostalgia in the end would lead to some sort of institutionalized global role for France. So much the better, at least for the short term. This would have strengthened de Gaulle's hand domestically and enabled him to deal more easily with the explosive issue of Algeria. At a single stroke he would seem to have restored France to her former eminence. The great quarrel with the Anglo-Saxons would, in that case, have been postponed until the Algerian war was settled.

But the real state of affairs in the autumn of 1958 is best illustrated by de Gaulle's self-defeating management of the entire matter. And one may also well ask why he canceled the Strauss–Chaban-Delmas arrangements just a few days before sending aloft the directorate balloon. There was no real urgency in liquidating this shadowy enterprise; nothing had been solemnized in a precise, formal sense. To have kept it alive at least for a few weeks would have strengthened de Gaulle's hand with the British and Americans, who were known to be appalled at the prospect of West German participation in France's nuclear-weapons program. Yet the great tactician and student of *Realpolitik* tossed this card away.

Most French officials, when discussing the tridirectorate memorandum, now say that a French veto on American nuclear weapons—world-wide!—was unthinkable. Nothing so sweeping was in de Gaulle's mind, they contend. Yet, leaving the surpassing confusion of the autumn of 1958 for the somewhat quieter spring of 1959, the record still shows that de Gaulle was insisting on this unattainable goal. A very senior and experienced American diplomat recalls that early in the Foreign Ministers' meeting at Geneva, the marathon conference with the Soviet Union on Berlin which lasted from May 11 through August 5, Couve de Murville went back to his first stance and "made it clear" to the Americans that de Gaulle sought a veto on their nuclear weapons. In late June Couve de Murville said publicly: "All that we are asking for is closer cooperation on the general ground of politics and strategy in the world." [27] But in a background news conference for a small group of American journalists he put the French position more precisely. The best account of what he said reads as follows:

A high official has explained privately that by "close cooperation" General de Gaulle means that France should share in the decision before the United States could use nuclear weapons anywhere in the world.

The official confirmed that France is seeking a greater say than Britain has over the use of nuclear weapons by the United States. Britain holds a veto only over the use of American weapons deployed on its territory.

If this condition is met and if France is admitted to the councils of the great powers, the official said, there will be prompt approval of missile ramps and weapons stockpiles in France and the nation's other difficulties with NATO will disappear.[28]

Between October 1958 and June 1959 de Gaulle met twice with Dulles, first on December 15 when Dulles was in Paris for the winter NATO Ministerial meeting. De Gaulle's mood was one of studied hostility: gone was the cordial and philosophical tone of the July 1958 meeting. As is usually the case, a communiqué had been worked out by their aides prior to the meeting. But a senior American official recalls having been awakened early that morning by a call from his French opposite number and told that no communiqué would be issued. And when Dulles arrived at the Hotel Matignon de Gaulle did not leave his office to meet him at the entrance. (*Le Monde* explained that such a gesture is normally extended only to a chief of government; still, Dulles had been met at the entrance in July.)

A reporter for a pro-Gaullist afternoon paper, obviously well briefed, began his account of the meeting as follows: "Never, perhaps, has any Franco-American meeting been so spirited as the one that took place this afternoon in General de Gaulle's Louis XVI office at the Matignon." He went on to list the grievances put to Dulles by de Gaulle: an Afro-Asian resolution in the UN General Assembly demanding independence for Algeria on which the United States had abstained and which had failed by only one vote; American support for Guinea's membership in the United Nations, described as "inadmissible"; a pronouncement Dulles had made with Premier Fanfani against the tridirectorate idea; the presence of four American officials at a reception in New York for Algeria's National Liberation Front; and American visas granted to members of the Front.[29] The crisis over Berlin, now a month old, was Dulles's abiding concern, and de Gaulle pointedly remarked that it was unreasonable to be allies in one place and not in another.

De Gaulle himself had never personally been pressed on

what precisely he was trying to obtain for France by means of the tridirectorate proposal. Dulles now raised the question and, by one account, was told that the phrase in de Gaulle's memorandum about "joint decisions" did mean veto.[30]

Seven weeks later de Gaulle and Dulles, already mortally ill, met again for the last time. Dulles, still deeply troubled by Berlin, was making his final voyage to London, Paris, and Bonn. According to an experienced and trusted aide, he told Eisenhower that he might exceed his brief somewhat when he saw de Gaulle, if Eisenhower would back him up later in Washington. Eisenhower agreed. So, after first conferring with Couve de Murville, Dulles (accompanied by the American Ambassador to France and a senior State Department official) saw de Gaulle (who was attended by Prime Minister Michel Debré). It was a more orderly, less recriminatory encounter than in December, possibly because the main agenda item—Berlin—was an urgent and worrisome problem. They were in general agreement on standing firm in Berlin, with some differences on how to engage the issue with Moscow.

Then, at some point, Dulles and de Gaulle spoke privately (in French, which Dulles apparently spoke without distinction but adequately). According to the same Dulles aide, who recalls seeing the Secretary of State immediately on his return to Washington and hearing him describe his tête-à-tête, Dulles held out the possibility of a French veto on American nuclear weapons deployed in Continental Europe. He did not use the word "veto" but spoke of "advance authorization" or some equivalent; his aide's recollection of the precise phrase is not certain, but about Dulles's intent it is. In return for cooperation in NATO (and probably on the issue of storing American nuclear weapons on French soil as well) Dulles was offering de Gaulle a long step toward what he apparently wanted.

De Gaulle did not respond, Dulles told his aide; "he didn't

seem to grasp the significance of what I was offering." His aide's interpretation is that de Gaulle may have been so astonished that he was unable either to frame a reply or to take Dulles's proposition at face value.

Another interpretation is possible. De Gaulle may not have wanted to cooperate on any other terms than those he had proposed; in short, he may have preferred having the issue of Anglo-Saxon nuclear hegemony to receiving a half-loaf— and some would argue that he regarded a veto on American nuclear weapons in Europe alone as nothing more than that. Most of 1958 had been occupied by non-European crises, after all, in the Middle East and in the Formosa Strait. It was a great issue of the day, in fact, whether de Gaulle had been adequately briefed on the American landings in Lebanon, made just two weeks after the de Gaulle-Dulles meeting in July 1958. The French claim they were neither consulted nor informed, that after the landings Couve de Murville had had to telephone Ambassador Alphand in Washington to find out what was going on, as he could learn nothing in Paris. George Ball has this to say: "Lebanon, Dulles mentioned [at the July 5 meeting], was in the midst of crisis and it might be necessary for the United States to intervene. De Gaulle asked that France be allowed to participate in any Western intervention, but Dulles argued that the intervention of France, the ex-colonial power in the Levant, would hardly be welcomed by the Lebanese." [31] But it is doubtful that de Gaulle received any further word prior to the landings.

This kind of thing was understandably vexing for the French government; compared to the Berlin crisis, however, Lebanon was a marginal and short-term issue. Berlin and Europe, not Lebanon and the Middle East, were the issues that animated de Gaulle's and Dulles's last meeting. And Dulles's proposal must be seen in that light.

The history of the tridirectorate affair set the tone for de Gaulle's relations with the British and Americans in the years to follow. Proposals with hidden purposes would issue from the Élysée Palace which were wholly unacceptable to Washington and London but which were offered on a take-it-or-leave-it, non-negotiable basis. In turn, de Gaulle relentlessly blocked Anglo-American initiatives, mainly for reasons other than those he stated. During much of the period, Washington and London sought means of "reaching" de Gaulle, adducing arguments directed to his stated positions (seldom understanding his real ones). Thus, the prospect of any American President or British Prime Minister doing serious business with de Gaulle was doubtful. His purposes and theirs were by and large mutually antagonistic. It was from the start a limited adversary relationship.

4

Allies at Cross Purposes

Couve de Murville may have begun to understand, but probably few if any of the other French ministers could see the vertiginous path that now lay ahead. The most eventful, most episodic, decisive part of the history was starting. It would last four years, from 1959 to 1962, the first two years setting a pattern that would be emulated in the second two. Both were periods of high tension; in both a Berlin crisis was the central focus; and in both de Gaulle took the hardest public position of any Western leader vis-à-vis the Soviet Union's demands and ultimatums on Berlin, although during both he was withdrawing French units from the NATO command and seeking methodically to weaken the organization. And two American Presidents were strongly tempted—in Kennedy's case even tried—to make a deal: in effect to give de Gaulle the nuclear help that would advance his political claims. That each drew back was due less to resistance in Washington than to de Gaulle's glacial disaffection.

Throughout the four years de Gaulle did his best to turn Adenauer away from Washington and to start a process that would end with Bonn looking to Paris for its security. The other strand of his foreign policy—to prevent an American-Russian dialogue—was served to the modest extent that his granitic Berlin position further reduced the chance of agreement between Washington and Moscow. After an opening gambit of insisting on an inner Western bloc de Gaulle soon resumed his normal posture as a sworn enemy of East-West bloc politics.

His government, naturally enough, was preoccupied with the business at hand; Algeria aside, there was no higher priority than France's nuclear program. Construction of a French nuclear submarine at Cherbourg had been suspended in late 1958 in expectation of the American propulsion system offered by Dulles in July.

Dulles had always been troubled by this offer, fearing that it was not enough to gain de Gaulle's cooperation but that it might strike the Joint Atomic Energy Committee as too much. He was right on both counts. In any case de Gaulle took the matter out of his hands. On March 7, 1959, precisely a month after his final talk with Dulles, de Gaulle revealed that France's Mediterranean fleet "would no longer be available to NATO in time of war"—obviously the only time it would be called upon. The submarine deal fell apart at that point.* Under the amended atomic-energy law, the President must determine that assistance to a foreign country of so sensitive a nature "will promote . . . the common defense and security," that the other country "is participating with the United States pursuant to an international arrangement by substantial and material

---

* Bertrand Goldschmidt, a distinguished French scientist and a director for many years of France's Atomic Energy Authority, believes that the history is somewhat different. In his book *Les Rivalités Atomiques* he says that in February 1959 a French mission came to Washington to negotiate the submarine offer. He says that Washington was prepared to make available only the enriched uranium the vessel would require, and that providing the propulsion system itself had been ruled out chiefly because of resistance from the Joint Atomic Energy Committee. American civil servants with whom the author has discussed this say flatly that Goldschmidt is mistaken. Some believe that the agreement could have been made if de Gaulle hadn't withdrawn the naval units and if Eisenhower had been willing to take on the Joint Atomic Energy Committee himself.

contributions to the mutual defense and security." In time no American President would feel free to make this determination; by chipping away at NATO the French tied the hands of the White House.

Two weeks later, on March 25, de Gaulle held his first press conference as President of France. To a question about the "withdrawal" of the French Mediterranean fleet from NATO, he replied:

> . . . I merely state that the zone of possible NATO action does not extend south of the Mediterranean. The Middle East, North Africa, Black Africa, the Red Sea, etc. are not a part of it. Who can deny that France may possibly find herself obliged to act in these different areas? She would therefore have to act independently of NATO. But how could she do so if her fleet were not available?

It was a strikingly misleading answer. Algeria, at France's behest, was specifically covered in Article 6 of the North Atlantic Treaty. More to the point, the French fleet was French-controlled and in time of peace could be used however de Gaulle saw fit. He had no need to "withdraw" the fleet, and that was not what he was doing. Rather, he was "de-earmarking" his fleet(as Washington jargon put it) in the event of a general war.

It is anyone's guess whether the arrangement to provide France with the nuclear propulsion system could ever have been steered through the Joint Atomic Energy Committee. Powerfully influenced by Admiral Rickover, "father" of the nuclear submarine, the Committee felt highly protective about the submarine propulsion system; rightly or wrongly, its members were convinced that the United States had a big lead over the Soviet Union in this technology, and they were reluctant to "pass it around." Some officials in Eisenhower's Administration thought the Committee could be persuaded, others did not. In the end it would have depended to a great extent on Eisenhower himself. He sometimes remarked in National Security Council meetings that "you can't arm one set of people with firearms and another set of people with bows and arrows." But he believed the Joint Committee was a barrier to all nuclear cooperation with allies other than Britain, and Dulles encouraged him in this belief, demurring on this or that proposal for nuclear aid to France by saying that the Joint Committee would not go along with it.

In fact, while the Committee *was* the ultimate source of resistance—a point of pride to its senior members and staff—Dulles, too, was against helping France. But since Eisenhower's viewpoint was somewhat different, Dulles found it convenient to shift responsibility to Capitol Hill. In taking this position he may have been influenced by the Regional Affairs, Europe (RA) section of the State Department, which traditionally opposed helping *any* country's nuclear-weapons program, including Britain's. Dulles and RA were supported by Livingston Merchant, then Under Secretary of State for Political Affairs, and the Counselor of the State Department, G. Frederick Reinhardt. All these men were leery of the submarine offer; still, they were ready to go along if the Joint Committee said yes, since the good faith of the United States was involved. (The Dutch also wanted a submarine-propulsion system, and, while State Department opinion was more sympathetic to the Dutch request—the Netherlands was a cooperative, if not positively compliant, NATO ally—it, too, came to nothing.)

Another early casualty of the winter was a system of trilateral consultation inspired by Macmillan as a means of giving de Gaulle a part of what he had seemed to demand in his tridirectorate memorandum. It had been agreed late in 1958 that the British and French Ambassadors in Washington should meet regularly with Robert Murphy, at that time the American Under Secretary of State. Elaborate agendas were prepared, covering problems everywhere in the world. These meetings proceeded at a leisurely pace, occurring perhaps once a month, until February or March 1959, when the arrangement collapsed for lack of interest on all sides. The French, who sent Louis Joxe to one of them, claimed the idea was a useless pretense for seeming to meet de Gaulle's conditions. The Americans and British complained that Ambassador Alphand was never instructed and could contribute little. A good guess is that de Gaulle had no interest, let alone patience, with subcabinet discussions of issues on which he took full and solitary responsibility.

The French suspected—correctly—that the West German Embassy in Washington was getting a good account of what went on in these meetings. Yet the West Germans believed their briefings were only cursory, a sentiment that perhaps best reveals how little of interest or value was accomplished by this pioneer venture in trilateralism. Some have said that de Gaulle could have used it as an opening wedge toward his stated goal. But in fact, this dispirited exercise was speedily overtaken by the need for real diplomacy directed to a real problem, Berlin.

For the next four years most events had to be seen in relation to Berlin. Eisenhower would enter his lame-duck period still embroiled in this, the greatest of Nikita Khrushchev's gambits. Kennedy, in turn, just four months after the brave words of his inaugural, was to find himself and his untested administration burdened with an even graver Berlin crisis than the one that faced Eisenhower. Berlin was more than the last great issue of the Cold War: it was a test of the will, determination, and maturity of the Western Big Four—Washington, London, Paris, and Bonn.

In November 1958, Khrushchev launched the "Berlin Crisis," first with a menacing speech and then an ultimatum: a diplomatic note declaring that Western violation of the postwar agreements on Germany rendered these agreements null and void and, with them, the right of the Western powers to maintain troops in Berlin. The words of the ultimatum, although slightly ambiguous, seemed to say that if the Western powers could not reach agreement with the Soviet Union within six months on converting Berlin into a demilitarized free city, the Soviet Union would transfer to the East German government full sovereignty "on land, on water, and in the air." American, British, and French access to Berlin across East German territory, therefore, would be controlled by the East German regime instead of Moscow.

Berlin had a purifying quality; in the harsh light of a showdown with Moscow the real attitudes and purposes of the four Western capitals were revealed. American policy in response to the ultimatum was more ambiguous than some, the West Germans especially, would have liked; yet it was hard enough to alarm advocates of disengagement. Principally, Eisenhower wanted to maintain a firm Western position while minimizing the risk of nuclear war and making certain that the issue of war and peace was clearly set forth in political terms. This meant that Washington would not, say, declare war if Moscow delegated to East Germany the right to stamp Western passports.

West German policy was characteristically paradoxical. Adenauer's real concern was to preserve Bonn's sovereign preeminence vis-à-vis East Germany; he was in no case prepared to risk a war over the status of Berlin. Franz-Josef Strauss was equally reluctant to risk war. He lacked confidence in the Americans' judgment and frankly feared they might use tactical nuclear weapons on German soil. He felt that maintaining a position in Berlin, a city far from Western defenses, suited an offensive strategy but not the defensive strategy imposed by geography. Together, Adenauer and Strauss sought to harden the Western position while discouraging plans to keep open by force the Autobahn linking Berlin to the Federal Republic, as Washington was prepared to do if it became necessary.

For de Gaulle, Berlin was an opportunity—he never really saw it as a crisis. From the start he assumed—doubtless correctly—that Khrushchev was bluffing; and he arrived at a tacit understanding with Adenauer. In return for Adenauer's support for French policies favoring limits on the development of the EEC and France's pre-eminent role in it, de Gaulle would back Adenauer's position vis-à-vis East Germany.* This understanding served as an ideal means for turning Adenauer against Washington and London; at the same time, de Gaulle was trying to catch Moscow's eye.

Great Britain was chiefly concerned with defusing the situation, and to accomplish this Macmillan was willing to pay a higher price than the others. In the end he held firm, but he wobbled often. The role of peace-broker attracted him strongly —and not just because it suited the British political climate. So in December Macmillan arranged to have himself invited to visit Khrushchev in Moscow, and he notified Bonn, Paris, and Washington of his plans without specifying his intentions.

It was this gesture which inspired Dulles's final voyage to Europe; he felt obliged to test the firmness of Macmillan's position and to reassure the West Germans, for whom the British initiative was an unwelcome surprise, to put it mildly. And, of course, as we have seen, Dulles met with de Gaulle. Nobody can

* Alfred Grosser thinks the understanding was reached in their first meeting. "Without being able to prove it in any way, I believe that as early as Sept. 14, 1958, there was a sort of gentlemen's agreement between the General and the Chancellor—not explicit, unsigned, undrafted, based on reciprocity: the Federal Republic would aid France in her Atlantic and European ambitions, and France would give firm support to the Eastern policies of the Federal Republic. On reunification and Berlin, France was never to take any initiatives that did not first emanate from Bonn. Since no initiatives ever emanated from Bonn in this domain, likewise none emanated from Paris." (Grosser, *French Foreign Policy Under de Gaulle* [Boston: Little, Brown, 1967], p. 66.)

say for certain, but it seems at least possible that de Gaulle's hard Berlin position, in contrast to the ambiguity at 10 Downing Street, might have been the factor that moved Dulles to go as far as he did in offering de Gaulle a de facto veto on American nuclear weapons in Europe. (One of his advisers believes it was simply a "fortuitous" gesture, inspired by the pressure of events.)

Dulles suffered a great deal on this last voyage of his remarkably peripatetic tenure as Secretary of State. His meeting with Adenauer was a drama: two strong old men, each greatly admiring the other, meeting for the last time to reconcile their thoughts and fears on the gravest threat to peace yet thrown up in the nuclear age. On Berlin each was firm and unyielding, but not necessarily on the same issues tormenting the problem; and they were far from having reached that harmony of viewpoint the world ascribed to them. On some points Dulles had become more flexible. He had just said publicly, for example, that free elections in both West and East Germany might not be the only way to achieve reunification of the country,[1] and he had suggested in a news conference that perhaps the West might deal with East German officials after all, considering them as agents of the Soviet Union.[2]

This possibility, which soon became known as the "agents doctrine," aroused deep hostility throughout West Germany. Although the Foreign Ministry diplomats in Bonn took a fairly relaxed view of it, the Foreign Minister himself, Heinrich von Brentano, labeled the notion "incomprehensible." In fact, the issue was to be a source of tension and misunderstanding long after the "agents doctrine" itself had been edged out of the planning on Berlin. Should the margin between peace and war, after all, rest on so banal a technicality as which authorities at the frontier would stamp Western passports? Why should arrangements of this sort be construed as diplomatic recognition of East Germany any more than West Germany's trade and other arrangements with Pankow? These questions were being asked in informed Anglo-American circles—rather indignantly at that.

Even more indignation was roused by Bonn's reluctance to commit West German forces in the early stages of a fight over Berlin. But on this point, Bonn was right; a small incident or skirmish could escalate much more swiftly into a third world war if the Bundeswehr itself fought on East German soil. Still, it seemed as if the West German government was seeking the best of both worlds: it rejected any and all concessions regarding East Germany, a position on which it was prepared—in the view of its critics—to fight to the last American; but it was softer than the Americans would have liked on the grittier issues, such as whether to use force to keep the Autobahn open.

Dulles was on the edge of collapse when he saw Adenauer in Bonn. He was obliged to lie on a sofa throughout one small dinner, and speech was difficult for him. Adenauer, deeply distressed, ordered a kind of gruel brought, hoping it might be something Dulles could eat. Under these remarkable circumstances a discussion nonetheless was held. Dulles sought to convince Adenauer that the Berlin issue turned not on the city's ties with the West German government but rather on the rights and obligations of Britain, France, and America in West Berlin as established in the wartime agreements. He made it clear that a conflict with the Russians on a technical point was unthinkable; if conflict was unavoidable, let it be fought on a clear political issue.

In this strained and emotional last meeting neither was much moved by the other's argument. Adenauer was sustained by de Gaulle's tough, uncompromising line; although France did not take direct issue with the "agents doctrine," Bonn had obtained quiet assurances of French support.

Still, he was deeply disturbed, first by Dulles's refusal to press the issue on purely technical grounds affecting only Germany; then, Britain, America's "special" ally, seemed to Adenauer wobbly and unreliable (an opinion vigorously encouraged by de Gaulle), and now the American he had always relied on was, he knew, bidding him farewell. Who in the future could be counted on to guarantee a hard United States position? Strauss was equally disapproving and skeptical—contemptuous of Macmillan's peace-brokering, dubious about Washington's talent for crisis management, alarmed by the threat of a conflict on German territory (and unable to explain to his aging Chancellor that tactical nuclear weapons were something serious—something other than a modish new form of field artillery. Tormented by the worst of prospects—Pankow gradually acquiring the trappings of legitimacy—Adenauer sought to match Washington's view with his own and inscribe them both in concrete. This he could not do.

It was against this somber background that Harold Macmillan went to Moscow. The gloom was relieved only by a few hints the Russians gave—specifically, Anastas Mikoyan, during a visit to Washington in January—that the ultimatum on Berlin had no fixed time limit.

Macmillan, characteristically playing a close hand, was bent on achieving an agreement of genuine importance with Khrushchev. He arrived with a hastily improvised proposal for an inspected freeze, or limitation, on nuclear and conventional arms within an agreed zone on either side of the Iron Curtain. Eisenhower, de Gaulle, and Adenauer had no knowledge that Macmillan was going to propose this. Since the Americans had just consented to a revival of Anglo-American nuclear-weapons cooperation, this bit of evasiveness was not going to go down well in Washington. In taking final leave of Macmillan Dulles had admonished: "I see nothing to negotiate over Berlin." [3]

It began catastrophically. What had been planned as a ten-day visit nearly broke up in a shambles at the outset. First, Foreign Secretary Lloyd was drawn into an angry row with Khrushchev over Berlin. Lloyd said flatly that if the U.S.S.R. pressed the issue, the West would resist. Khrushchev became angrily theatrical and accused Lloyd of threatening him with war. This was followed by a "toothache" ploy; Khrushchev, who had been scheduled to accompany his guests on a side trip to Kiev and Leningrad, announced instead that he would visit his dentist. Macmillan went off to Leningrad anyway, having virtually made up his mind to return speedily to London afterward. Then tempers began to cool. Mikoyan and Andrei Gromyko were dispatched to Leningrad to mollify the British, and the British Ambassador, Sir Patrick Reilley, persuaded Macmillan to meet Khrushchev again. It was at this second meeting that Macmillan put forward his arms-limitation proposal. Khrushchev responded swiftly, and a joint communiqué, while acknowledging Anglo-Soviet differences over Berlin, noted the two nations' agreement "that further study could usefully be made of the possibility of increasing security by some method of limitation of forces and weapons, both conventional and nuclear, in an agreed area of Europe, coupled with an appropriate system of inspection." [4]

With one eye on the forthcoming general elections (certain to be called in fall 1959 or spring 1960), Macmillan became a moth to the flame of Berlin. One of his senior and most influential ministers recalls that Macmillan believed he had "broken through" with Khrushchev—that he had "come within an ace" of gaining an important agreement. At the very least, he was persuaded that the groundwork had been laid for an eventual settlement of Berlin and other Cold War issues. An intensive round of high-level conversations, capped by a summit conference—*et voilà*, the worst would be over, perhaps forever. The image of Macmillan going before the British public as "Supermac" the peace-broker is perhaps a trifle unfair. He was convinced that somebody had to play the role, and who else could offer the necessary experience and perspective? Which nation but Great Britain could moderate the United States' possible excesses and negotiate with Khrushchev as something other than a "Cold Warrior"?

Yet Macmillan achieved nothing by his solitary maneuver in Moscow other than to strengthen the Franco-German diplomatic axis and to deepen Adenauer's doubts about British intentions and their pernicious effects on the Americans. Curiously, he was trying to make a virtue of what was in fact becoming a great defect in British diplomacy—a relentless tendency to discredit himself and his government in Bonn. Adenauer's long and unconcealed anti-British bias had been fortified by London's refusal to join the Common Market and then by its creation of a rival organization, the European Free Trade Association (EFTA). And now Macmillan seemed to be playing into Khrushchev's hands by undermining the unflinching line set forth by Adenauer and de Gaulle. For Adenauer and others around him this was more than just mischievous; it was anti-"European," an attitude arising from an impulse (common to both the Tory and Labour parties) to play the dual role of Washington's junior partner and the catalyst of a greatpower dialogue. Within this quite real British attitude lay the seeds of future difficulties not just for Macmillan but for his successor.

Just a few days after Macmillan's return from Moscow de Gaulle began fitting a second string to *his* bow. While complaining bitterly to Washington and Bonn (especially Bonn) about Macmillan, he took the occasion of his first formal press conference, on March 25,* to acknowledge the Oder-Neisse line as Germany's eastern frontier, something no other Western statesman had (or has) done: "The reunification of the two

---

* The same press conference in which he discussed withdrawal of the French Mediterranean fleet from NATO.

parts into a single Germany which would be entirely free seems to us the normal destiny of the German people, provided they do not reopen the question of their present frontiers to the west, the east, the north, and the south." This was the first of several gestures designed to catch Moscow's eye. It seemed a curious defection from his usual "hard line" toward the Soviet Union; Adenauer was caught off balance, and he wrote de Gaulle privately asking him not to raise the issue of the frontier again; rightly or wrongly, the Federal Republic has regarded the unsettled matter of the Oder-Neisse line as a card for future bargaining with Moscow. De Gaulle agreed to this and never again mentioned Germany's frontiers while the old Chancellor remained in power. (The Gaullist newspaper *La Nation*, however, did on occasion note the "permanence" of the Oder-Neisse line.)

Throughout 1959 and much of 1960 the Big Four of the West were preoccupied by the ascent to the summit meeting and by the problem—more a riddle than a problem—of "nuclear sharing." The first was visible, while the maneuverings over the nuclear dilemma were largely obscured from public view. (These became, in fact, a drama played out mostly within the American government bureaucracy.)

Moscow, having pressed for a summit meeting, had first to cooperate on lower-level discussions, and these, as noted, tied down the foreign ministers from May 11 to August 5. Adenauer's fears that the Americans, with Dulles now replaced by Christian Herter, might make undue concessions to the U.S.S.R. proved groundless. The marathon conference budged neither East nor West. But two days before it ended the world was startled to learn that Khrushchev had accepted an invitation from Eisenhower to visit the United States in late September.

Eisenhower opens the chapter of his memoirs on "personal diplomacy" with this remark: "The news of Chairman Khrushchev's impending visit to the United States was received with consternation by Chancellor Adenauer and President de Gaulle." [5] And indeed, Eisenhower went off to London, Paris, and Bonn to reassure the Europeans, especially the West Germans, that no changes in American policy on Berlin or NATO were contemplated. The Russians and the British had hoped that a summit meeting might be possible in the fall, but de Gaulle (with support from Bonn) managed to get it postponed for a few months, mainly because he too wished to have precisely the bilateral conversations the other "greats" were indulging in. In short, if Khrushchev were to visit Washington, he would have to visit Paris as well; if Eisenhower could come to Europe, de Gaulle could as easily go to North America; in the meantime, he and Macmillan would exchange visits. All of this would make clear France's restoration to the "first rank." Moreover, wedged between the endless tête-à-têtes, a Western summit meeting would be held at the Château de Rambouillet in late December. The path to the hectic Paris summit conference of May 1960, then, was festooned with lesser events which made up in pomp and ceremony what they lacked in substance.

Despondency is a mood that comes easily to Bonn, and never more so than during a Berlin crisis. Adenauer's regime did not object in principle to the American and Soviet chiefs sitting down together. But the Germans were disturbed by the Americans' typical failure to give them advance warning and, still more, by doubts about Eisenhower as a precise negotiator. What the Germans feared was either an inadvertent concession, or that Ike, perhaps spurred by Macmillan, would be tempted to "do something for peace" before leaving the White House.

For a time—months in fact—it appeared in Bonn and Paris that Eisenhower *had* gone too far. On September 28, the day after the joint communiqué at Camp David, he set off tremors by seeming to accept Khrushchev's celebrated claim that the

Berlin situation was "abnormal." He was asked in a news conference whether during new Berlin negotiations

> we will be guided by the same standards and principles that we had before, namely, that any solution must guarantee Allied rights there, and protect the freedom of the West Berliners?

> Reply: I can't guarantee anything of this kind for the simple reason, I don't know what kind of solution may finally prove acceptable, as I say, but you must start off with this. The situation is abnormal. It was brought about by a truce, a military truce, after the end of the war, an armistice, and it put strangely a few—or a number—of free people in a very awkward position.[6]

Indeed, not only in Bonn and Paris, but in every Western capital—Washington included—and almost certainly in Moscow as well, Eisenhower seemed to be softening his Berlin line. The foreign offices were flustered; fears of a major American concession increased. And it all promoted de Gaulle's efforts to delay the summit meeting and to solemnize his link with Adenauer.

Little attention was paid, except by a few diplomats, to the other and more typical Gaullist attitude, now just beginning to surface. In August, shortly before Eisenhower's European trip and after the announcement of Khrushchev's upcoming visit to America, de Gaulle's Prime Minister, Michel Debré, had evoked the danger of France being "crushed" between the two superpowers.[7] In October the third volume of de Gaulle's memoirs appeared, with its famous evocation of France as "arbiter between the Soviet and Anglo-American camps." A month later came the École Militaire address with its reference to France's need for nuclear forces that can "act against every part of the world."

On November 10 de Gaulle held his second formal press conference, during which he stated that "first-hand knowledge of France" was a "precondition" to any summit conference that might be convened. Khrushchev would visit France on March 15. De Gaulle cited the "great importance" he attached to this meeting. And he also allowed the issue of Germany's frontiers to come up again simply by choosing to answer a question about it. (Technically, he had not broken faith with Adenauer, since a journalist had raised the matter, not de Gaulle himself. Still, anyone at all familiar with de Gaulle's press-conference style knew that he answered only those questions he wished to answer.) In replying, he noted that he had covered the point in his previous press conference: "You need only know that I have not changed my mind."

Nuclear-club members are prone to link nuclear or missile events, like a series of tests (or a space probe), with political happenings. De Gaulle was no exception. Khrushchev's visit was preceded by the testing of France's first atomic bomb—at Reggane, in the Sahara, on February 13, 1960.

De Gaulle's exultant "hurrah for France" found no echo in Washington. Eisenhower did not send a congratulatory telegram, and the State Department managed to say only that the event was "not expected." In fact, the Eisenhower Administration was pondering whether to qualify France as a nuclear power under the terms of the amended atomic-energy legislation, and to extend to de Gaulle the kind of nuclear assistance Britain would receive. But, as we have seen, this would have required a *démarche* on the forbidding senior figures of the Joint Atomic Energy Committee, none of them blind to de Gaulle's hostility to NATO or to the steady and rapid deterioration in Franco-American relations since his return to power. Just nine days prior to the French test Eisenhower seemed to be edging in this direction. Asked in a press conference about nuclear aid to France, he replied:

> As far as giving away the bombs, this cannot be done under existing law. Now, I do believe this, that where we are allied with other nations and we're trying to arm ourselves in such a

way as to make certain of our defense, we should try to arm them in such methods and ways as will make that defense more strong and more secure.

I would not ever give any information even if the law permitted—give away information that was still, in our opinion, withheld from the Soviets themselves. But when the Soviets have the information and know-how to do things, it's pretty hard for me to understand why we don't do something with our allies, as long as they themselves stand with us firmly in defending against the probable aggressive intent of Communism.[8]

On February 18, after the French test, another press-conference remark offered further insight:

Now, I think it's only natural that first Britain and then France have done this, in the circumstances of life as we now understand them and know them. . . . We must realize that this spirit of nationalism of which we hear so much is not felt by the underdeveloped nations the one that the people want to be suddenly independent; it's felt by all of us.[9]

Khrushchev arrived in Paris to confront a French leader bent on becoming a nuclear power and, in time, the *independent* spokesman for Western Europe. Past and recent utterances should have made that clear. Furthermore, de Gaulle was the only Western leader who had gone on record as accepting the Oder-Neisse line as Germany's eastern frontier. They should have quite a lot to talk about.

Still, de Gaulle found it no easier to impress Khrushchev in March 1960 than Stalin in December 1944. The problem was the same—France's limited power. De Gaulle exploded a second French atomic device while Khrushchev was resting at the Château de Rambouillet, but two nuclear shots could not erase doubts as to whether an independent nuclear force of any plausibility lay within France's grasp. Khrushchev, like Stalin, had contempt for those who lacked power, especially those who seemed to lay spurious claims to power. He was to remain contemptuous of de Gaulle to the end, deriding him in his conversations with other Western men of affairs. To one prominent personage he described de Gaulle as "an emperor with no clothes."

While no less sensitive to French limitations, de Gaulle played whatever cards he was holding in his game with the Russians as best he could. Never an optimist, he could only try to make a dent; he would continue to point up his vision of a France holding the balance between Germany and Russia in Europe and between the two blocs in the world; with a bit of luck and skillful manipulation of events, one day perhaps . . . And by then the Cold War might be subsiding and France's hands might at last be free.

On Germany de Gaulle had two policy lines, one hard, the other soft. The hard line, for which he got credit, was public, and intended to reassure the French, the West Germans, and the Western allies. The soft line turned up occasionally in tête-à-tête conversation; it was intended to remind the Russians of the Gaullist vision and the West Germans of the political weapons France could use against them—recognition of East Germany, dismemberment of the Common Market, and so on.

Khrushchev, perhaps for the first time, was now presented with de Gaulle's soft line. He was told, for example, that a divided Germany did not necessarily collide with French interests. And in the cryptic language often employed in conversations at this level de Gaulle suggested that if Khrushchev did not insist on some points, France might be more accommodating on others. No hint of this conversation reached Washington, London, or Bonn. In 1967 Jean-Raymond Tournoux's *La Tragédie du Général* offered a sensational quotation from the Khrushchev-de Gaulle tête-à-tête: "To Mr. Khrushchev, the President of the Republic indicated that he was in no hurry, not at all, with regard to [German] reunification. 'You understand me, the problem is not current. We will see later. And who knows? If one allows time to pass, one could have two Germanies, if not three, with Berlin!' " [10] This author can attest to the accuracy of the passage.

Probably de Gaulle didn't assign great importance to this small trial balloon. He was far from ready to make his "opening to the East"—that would come later. Still, the Russians were being put on notice that de Gaulle was a man who meant what he said—and wrote. It was a loaded moment, and it must have been carefully noted, if not by Khrushchev, by other Soviet leaders and future leaders.

In March, before Khrushchev arrived in Paris, the Harold Macmillans had spent the weekend with de Gaulle and Mme. de Gaulle at Rambouillet. Little had emerged from the conversations; each was warily exploring the other's "pre-summit" position. But a few weeks later, just before going to North America, de Gaulle, spending three days at Buckingham Palace on a state visit, received Macmillan and during a conversation suggested that England join the Common Market. Macmillan is reliably reported to have answered "unthinkable," although he and a few other senior Tories, together with some Foreign Office officials, were shortly to begin maneuvering Britain toward precisely this goal.[11] De Gaulle, though, was only fencing. He almost certainly did not believe that Britain would or could accept the discipline of the Common Market or the political consequences of such a choice. And if this *should* change—well, de Gaulle, like most people, tended to deal with a problem only when it became actual.

Ten days later de Gaulle arrived in Ottawa, on the first leg of his North American voyage. The visit went badly, whether in protocol or in political terms. At a luncheon in de Gaulle's honor the singularly heavy-handed Canadian Prime Minister, John Diefenbaker, took pointed exception to France's nuclear-weapons program, citing the financial burden of such projects, the dangers they posed for peace, and his firm conviction that this was no path for Canada. The questions put to de Gaulle by Canadian journalists at a post-luncheon press conference were in the same vein, clearly reflecting Canadian hostility to France's nuclear testing.

From Ottawa, de Gaulle went to Quebec, where the welcome, while predictably warmer, was "modest," as *Le Monde* later described it; and the brief visits to Montreal and Toronto were also disappointing. De Gaulle was upstaged by the arrival of the first transatlantic cargo traversing the St. Lawrence Seaway, opened just 48 hours earlier, an event which "led" the local newspapers. And then, the airport-terminal authorities had not suspended airport traffic at the time of de Gaulle's arrival, a protocol lapse that sharpened tensions. The pro-Gaullist *Paris-Presse* noted that the General seemed "tired and sulky" at Toronto, where the reception was "cold and not enthusiastic." [12] One may wonder whether the famous *"Vive Québec libre"* excesses of 1967 were not in part inspired by de Gaulle's remarkably cool reception in Canada seven years earlier.

By contrast, the Americans lavished on de Gaulle a welcome almost without precedent. New York was described in headlines as "delirious." It was San Francisco's "greatest welcome ever." Apparently, not since MacArthur's return had a public figure so touched America's imagination. Newspapers were prone to note that of the great wartime cast, soon only de Gaulle would remain. Roosevelt, Churchill, and Stalin were gone; Eisenhower would leave the scene in 1960. But de Gaulle, a man already tested, would be there, a reassuring figure. André Fontaine, foreign editor of *Le Monde* and traveling with de Gaulle, compared the atmosphere of Canada with Washington: "The contrast was striking between the paucity of flags and smallness of crowds in these recent days and the massive demonstration of sympathy in the American capital." [13]

And a joint session of Congress was described as "over-whelmed" by de Gaulle's address—elegant, direct, impeccably delivered, with only two brief glances at his notes.

At the other end of Pennsylvania Avenue the visit found a truer balance. Eisenhower, as always, was glad to see de Gaulle. Their last conversation—in Rambouillet in December—had been brief (only 45 minutes, much shorter than Eisenhower's talk with Adenauer). So little had been achieved—the room for agreement so narrow*—that everything on the Franco-American agenda had been pushed to this pre-summit meeting in Washington. But nothing had changed. On Berlin both could agree that the rights of the Western powers could not be bargained away. But on the modalities, or some of them, Eisenhower seemed ready to negotiate; not so de Gaulle. On disarmament he took his standard position that it made no sense to suspend nuclear testing so long as weapons stocks continued to grow.

As for American nuclear aid to France, Ambassador Alphand had taken some soundings a few days before and had learned that the support for helping France found here and there in the Administration was still more than balanced by the resistance of the Joint Atomic Energy Committee and its various State Department allies. The combination of the Berlin crisis and a rapidly deteriorating situation in Laos preoccupied the White House to the degree that there was no question of a major initiative with regard to aiding de Gaulle at this time. The matter was bogged down in the bureaucracy (just where those who opposed helping France wanted it).

Eisenhower *did* tell de Gaulle, doubtless with a straight face, that the next United States nuclear submarine (Polaris type) would be christened the Lafayette. And he presented his guest with a 30-inch scale model of one of the latest in the Polaris

* A second scheduled tête-à-tête at Rambouillet had therefore been replaced by an Eisenhower-Debré talk.

series. The model had a cutaway cross section showing the tubes in which the Polaris missiles were stored, plus numerous interior features of the submarine.[14] De Gaulle's reaction to the gift is not recorded.

The White House conversations ended with the issuance of a joint statement, described by *Le Monde* as one of the shortest in international annals.[15] Yet it had taken Herter and Couve de Murville an hour to produce the brief comment that the two leaders had been able to define more precisely the positions to be taken by the West at the summit conference.[16]

Probably the most, if not the only, important event of de Gaulle's trip was his appearance at the National Press Club in Washington. During a question period he said he doubted that the "U.S.S.R. could be represented by a man [Khrushchev] who better represented the Russia of today, which in my opinion is already no longer the Russia of yesterday nor even the Russia of 10 years ago." [17] Even more pointedly, he called attention to a passage in his memoirs saying it is in the natural order of things for France and Russia to be allied. "Between France and Russia," he added, "there is no conflict of interest." [18] One wonders how many noted and remembered this revealing and succinct assertion before an assemblage of American newspapermen and much of the diplomatic corps. De Gaulle, although for the moment an apostle of the hard line, was reminding the Americans and anyone else listening that his long-run thinking had a distinctly eastward pull.

The summit conference was now less than three weeks away. In every Western foreign office, including the State Department, concern over Eisenhower's intentions was sharpening. With Dulles gone, could Eisenhower be counted on to resist making concessions to Khrushchev? Nobody knew, including the senior officials and civil servants in Washington. The anx-

iety in Bonn was echoed in the Quai d'Orsay. The growing
hostility of many French diplomats and civil servants to Gaullist
foreign policy was for the moment matched by their support for
his tough Berlin line. Quite a number saw that the latter was
something of an optical illusion—a tactically useful position—
camouflaging a softer line and a quite different long-run policy;
still, they backed it vigorously in dealings with Whitehall and
the State Department. What de Gaulle was tampering with was
the future; Berlin, on the other hand, was immediate and urgent.

Not that people at the Quai had any illusions about their
influence at the Élysée Palace. Nobody, including Couve de
Murville, had influence. Policy was dictated by de Gaulle, as
often as not at the last minute. Frequently, foreign diplomats
noticed that Couve de Murville, however skillful at concealing
the awkwardness of his position, was as much in the dark as
they were. But France's pre-summit line on Berlin was clear.
Eisenhower and Macmillan might be willing to conciliate the
Russians, but de Gaulle would not be budged from his stance as
guardian of the Franco-German—the "European"—position.
A French diplomat who fully approved de Gaulle's position on
this if not on other matters has self-mockingly described himself and his colleagues at the Quai d'Orsay at this time as
mouches du coche (stagecoach flies) who, as in the la Fontaine
fable, busily buzz around the horses and urge greater effort as
the coach mounts the hill and then, as the ascent is achieved,
take the credit.

One might suppose that such officials would have sought to
harden the Anglo-American position by working through their
like-minded opposite numbers in Whitehall and Foggy Bottom.
In fact, this was not the case. Threading Berlin policy through
the Washington labyrinth was by itself so complex a task that
outside pressures could not have influenced the result very

much. Many of those who were closely involved on the American side still disagree on what Eisenhower ultimately would have done.

The British thought he would bargain, but in a way that would not undermine basic Western rights of access to Berlin and maintenance of troops. As a senior Foreign Office diplomat has put it, "Ike would not have agreed to a summit without wanting to speak seriously—to negotiate, in effect." Numerous people in the State Department agreed, though much less approvingly. Just a few weeks earlier Eisenhower had bowed to a long-standing Soviet demand to limit Western aircraft flying in the Berlin corridors to a ceiling of ten thousand feet, although Washington had once rejected the idea of such a limitation. Eisenhower decided, on March 8, that high-altitude flights would not be resumed, and on the following day Herter explained that there was "no operational necessity" for flights above the low ceiling.[19]

But other measures directed to "firming up" the United States position were then set in motion. In early April Herter gave a speech which, while moderate in tone, did rule out arms-control agreements with Moscow in the event of Soviet violations of Western rights in Berlin. Later in April Under Secretary Douglas Dillon delivered what could only be called a warning—indeed, with the summit just ahead it was a brutal one. Khrushchev, he said, was "skating on very thin ice"; the so-called German Democratic Republic was "one of the outstanding myths in a vast communist web of prodigious mythology"; the aim of the summit meeting was "to minimize the risk of war of miscalculation."[20]

Five days later Khrushchev answered at Baku with an angry reading of the Moscow litany on Berlin.

That *both* sides were now hardening was a source of great comfort to most Western diplomats, since they were unable to imagine that any concessions by Eisenhower and Macmillan would be matched on the Soviet side. Sill, nobody was quite certain what would happen when the principals finally met. Would Macmillan manage to throw up some sort of span between Eisenhower and Khrushchev? Or would the combination of de Gaulle and the State Department hard-liners keep Eisenhower out of trouble?

The question was to remain open forever, thanks to the Soviet air-defense unit which winged the U-2 reconnaissance aircraft of Francis Gary Powers and forced it to earth in Siberia. Still, Khrushchev did not have to use the incident as a pretext for wrecking the summit conference. But from Moscow's point of view, Berlin had apparently gone sour—for the moment at least—and was no longer ideal terrain for Cold War skirmishing; the balance of risks seemed to rule it out. Eisenhower's *gaffe* about the city's "abnormal" status and his acceptance of a ceiling in the air corridors had set off a fair amount of confusion, but by May, if not before, the Soviet leadership was disabused, and the optimistic notions fostered by the "spirit of Camp David" were put aside.

When the heads of state finally convened in Paris in May 1960 de Gaulle was superb, both as conference host and conscience of the West. The occasion perfectly suited his magisterial style. (When Khrushchev complained about the U-2 overflights, de Gaulle haughtily reminded him that Soviet reconnaissance satellites were photographing French territory every three hours or so.) And, at one point, he may have saved Macmillan and Eisenhower from doing something foolish. Khrushchev wanted an apology about the U-2s, didn't get one, and stormed off to the countryside outside Paris while Eisenhower and Macmillan went to the Élysée Palace to confer with de Gaulle. An American who was present says that the chaos into which Khrushchev had plunged the conference had left Macmillan in a highly emotional state. He proposed that he go as an emissary to Khrushchev; world peace, he pleaded, hung in the balance. Eisenhower "was in between and probably could have been moved either way. Then, abruptly, de Gaulle said no and killed the idea." [21] De Gaulle's entourage was proud of this moment. One of them says that Herter took de Gaulle aside and told him, "You saved the day." (The same French official believes—probably wrongly—that Herter meant not just de Gaulle's veto of Macmillan's quixotic notion, but all his efforts, right up to May 1960, to shore up the Western position.)

The luminaries left Paris. Eisenhower faced a seven-month lame-duck period, which in addition to further disappointments, would take his Administration to the edge of a debacle in Laos. Macmillan departed bitter. His great venture in peace-brokering lay in ruins; it had, in his view, plunged to disaster on the wings of Captain Powers' U-2. He, who had given the Conservative party a 102-seat parliamentary majority in the October elections, had turned a corner but could not know it. The future held even greater disappointments. Two and a half years later he was again to leave a conference in France—this one a tête-à-tête with de Gaulle at Rambouillet—an even more bitter figure and fully disabused.

Khrushchev returned to Russia via East Berlin, and the world wondered anxiously what he would do. It was a predictably boisterous and abusive performance, but the message was heartening. The Soviet Union was not ready to sign a peace treaty with East Germany—not yet. "We are realists," Khrushchev said, and "we shall never follow an adventurous policy." The question of a German peace treaty would be pushed back for "six to eight months." Berlin was off the boil, at least until a new administration arrived in Washington. Events had vindicated de Gaulle's hard line.

De Gaulle's credit in Washington was now remarkably high, considering his hostility toward NATO, test-ban talks, and other projects close to the heart of both the Administration and

Congress. With France moving toward a nuclear capability, however slowly, support for de Gaulle mounted in the Pentagon, both among civilians and military services. In the State Department, Under Secretary Dillon was sympathetic. Resistance in the AEC was lessening, reflecting perhaps a notion that in return for military assistance de Gaulle might not go forward with the isotope-separation plant at Pierrelatte. And, of course, Eisenhower was friendly to the idea, albeit at the same time wary of the irascible Joint Atomic Energy Committee.

De Gaulle understood all this but was unwilling to make any of the concessions that might have disarmed his critics. On the contrary. Whenever Eisenhower seemed to be edging toward the French side of the argument de Gaulle took some step that only widened the gap between Paris and Washington. An example is Couve de Murville's gratuitous reminder to a few American journalists in June 1959 that the tridirectorate proposal amounted to a veto on American nuclear weapons everywhere (and his similar statement to American colleagues at the Foreign Ministers Conference at around the same time). Yet this was also the moment when the United States agreed to supply France with nuclear fuel for a research reactor, an agreement which, while obviously not of the first order, did require the Presidential determination noted earlier.

Nobody, perhaps including Couve de Murville himself, knew *why* he had been instructed to revive the "hard" interpretation of the tridirectorate proposal. What seems clear is that far from wanting to improve Franco-American relations, de Gaulle had decided to maintain, perhaps widen, the gap between the two countries. To accept nuclear assistance would run counter to this purpose.

In the spring of 1959 Dulles died, to be replaced by a figure who could never have the same influence with Eisenhower. The last six months of 1959 were confusing, with the new Secretary of State, Herter, tied down for eleven weeks at the Foreign Ministers Conference and much of the rest of Washington absorbed by the disintegrating situation in Laos and other trouble spots. Anxiety in Washington created a sentiment in favor of strengthening ties with the European allies, especially France. Yet this was one of the moments de Gaulle chose for returning to his futile demand for a veto on American nuclear weapons. Why did he do it? One possibility is that he consciously sought to undermine the efforts of those Americans, including Eisenhower, who would have liked to help him. If, as I think, the original tridirectorate proposal was largely bogus, it is conceivable that he might have decided to continue in this pattern. The aim, as always, was to take France out from under Anglo-American domination. And for that de Gaulle needed an issue.

Yet the case for extending nuclear aid to France was gathering strength throughout 1959 and early 1960. The argument that it would favor the United States' balance of payments was backed up by the notion that if "we don't sell it to them, eventually somebody else will." Only slightly more persuasive was the argument that assisting a nation's advanced-weapons program encourages that nation's technological dependence upon the donor. Some (though not all) of the flaws in the "technological-dependence" argument were becoming clear in 1959. The conflict with arms-control considerations, for example. Apart from the immediate problem of how West Germany would react to this sort of Franco-American link, advancing the date when France would acquire a nuclear capability would also mean advancing the date when France—its foreign-policy interests not necessarily consistent with those of the United States—could sell advanced-weapons systems to the less developed countries. This was—and will be, whatever happens—a restraint on those who have pressed for giving nuclear aid to France. Finally, de Gaulle's government was determined *not* to depend on Washington, and its quest for help was pursued selectively.

Although nuclear aid for European allies was advanced most strongly in the Pentagon, the categorizing element was to be found in the State Department's Bureau of European Affairs. A bureaucratic struggle was beginning; at first it would be fought out in the State Department—which then as now also harbored the first-line opponents to helping France, or any other country, acquire a nuclear-weapons capability.

The issue of "sharing" nuclear weapons with allies of the United States tended to split the Washington bureaucracy into three schools. The first, concentrated in the Pentagon, wanted close bilateral cooperation, not just with Great Britain but with France and some of the other West European nations. A second, located in Regional Affairs and the Policy Planning Council in the State Department, wanted a "multilateral" formula which would guarantee a United States veto on decisions to fire NATO nuclear weapons, while permitting some European ownership and participation. A third school, drawing on people in all parts of the national-security apparatus (and in Congress), favored doing nothing—that is to say, maintaining the status quo.

The low-key interdepartmental drama over this general issue continued for some months and, because of it, the United States' position on the nuclear issue was opaque as the December 1959 NATO Ministerial meeting approached.

In fact, there was no United States position. The Defense Department, pushed by both the balance-of-payments argument and military politics, was far from ready to stifle its impulse to sell weapons systems to the Europeans. And the State Department, still divided, was unable to impose its more cautious view. So a rather unruly, if not anarchic, tone tinged the American performance at the December NATO meeting. State and Defense—that is to say, Christian Herter and Thomas Gates— were still in deep disagreement when the plane carrying the American delegation landed in Paris, and a telephone call to

Eisenhower was needed to bring the two agencies together, if only for the moment. In addressing his European counterparts Herter proposed more integration and more cost-sharing within NATO, while Gates spoke of "potential European reinforcement for the American missile family."

Gates also said that a missile project for Continental Europe's defense was under study and could be put into production through the appropriate NATO agency.[22] In fact, Gates and his colleagues were talking to the Europeans about the possibility of putting quick-reaction ballistic missiles on barges and railroad cars in Western Europe. The Navy and Air Force each had candidates for the missile to be selected. The Navy was committed to Polaris, and some Navy representatives were pushing the system at the Europeans with little regard to the vital questions of control, and so on. (The Navy had installed a small model of the Polaris system at the conference headquarters, and any curious delegate, by pushing a button, could witness a miniaturized missile take-off.) Meanwhile, an Air Force colonel was hawking the Minuteman, then scarcely out of the design stage. The Air Force was also seeking a home for its as yet undeveloped "Missile X," a mobile medium-range ballistic-missile system suited for deployment on trucks or rolling stock. Since it could be argued that West Europeans required MRBMs (to counter Soviet missiles targeted on their cities), the Air Force hoped to be able to share Missile X development costs with them. And so on.

Shortly after the December meeting the proposal for offering missiles to the Europeans, which elements in the European Bureau had been trying to nudge through the State Department labyrinth, sprang up in only slightly modified form as the "Gates proposals" (named after the Secretary of Defense). The bureaucratic skirmishing began again—this time, though, as a more direct Pentagon–State Department clash. The "Gates proposals" amounted, in effect, to a plan for offering the Polaris (or some other comparable quick-reaction ballistic missile) to European allies either for purchase or manufacture under American license. This idea was strongly backed by Pentagon officials (especially in the Navy and Air Force) and by the civil servants in ISA. But the question of who would control the warheads was more than a little disconcerting. A "two-key" system was implicit—that is, with responsibility shared by both the United States and the host government technicians—but the fallibility of such a system (at that stage of its development) was becoming apparent. The proposals thoroughly alarmed numerous figures in the State Department, some of whom put forward an alternative: the Europeans could purchase the delivery systems for themselves or manufacture them under license, but the weapons themselves must be under NATO control in such a way as to prevent any diversion for national use.

Eisenhower's two press-conference statements about aid to France quickened the tempo of the debate. Those in the State Department who took the Pentagon side of the argument did what they could. (De Gaulle's tough line on Berlin helped the European cause.) At the April NATO Ministerial meeting Secretary Gates discussed plans to modify the Polaris system so that it could be land-launched as well as submarine-launched, and he proposed deployment of hundreds of them on barges and flatcars when they became operational a year or two later. He also proposed modifying the system of dual control by giving NATO's Supreme Commander the authority to join the nationally controlled missiles with the jointly controlled warheads and fire the weapons.[23]

Pressures on the other side were also gathering strength. By now Washington "had come out of the shadow of Sputnik," in the words of one State Department official. America's fear of being second-best in weapons development was declining. Sputnik and the Soviet ICBM would not turn the strategic balance against America.

In May 1960 the State Department activists, backed by their ISA allies, revived the idea of giving France a nuclear-submarine-propulsion system. But Eisenhower said no. The Joint Atomic Energy Committee had again come down against this sort of thing,[24] and the Navy and AEC also opposed diffusing the propulsion technology. The issue of helping France with her nuclear program was, effectively, shelved for the remainder of the Eisenhower Administration. Equally, the Gates proposals were stalled. The worrisome ambiguity that seemed to leave open the possibility of national missile capabilities in Europe (briefly, the Gates proposals seemed to permit any Polaris residue remaining after a European production line had met NATO requirements to revert to national ownership) had never been resolved. Moreover, West Germany's lively interest in accepting Polaris delivery systems (without the warheads) had aroused concern not only in the State Department but in London, where American assistance to de Gaulle had until then been viewed in a generally favorable light. Now, Whitehall took a clear position against the Gates proposals, as did de Gaulle, for the same reason. Lastly, it was at this point that de Gaulle abruptly decided to escalate his difficulties with the lame-duck Administration of his oldest and best American friend.

Stonily ignoring the warm feelings his performance at the summit conference had inspired in Washington, de Gaulle sent a letter to Eisenhower on June 10 reviving the most sensitive and divisive items on the Franco-American agenda. World-wide strategic cooperation and—yes—joint decisions on American nuclear weapons were called up again.[25] The General's letter provoked a lively exchange of correspondence, pithily summarized as follows by the State Department, for Congressional hearings held six years later:

The two Presidents met twice in the fall of 1959 and twice in the spring of 1960, and agreed that political consultations would continue regularly at their level, at the Foreign Minister level and at the sub-secretary level. General de Gaulle wrote to President Eisenhower on June 10, 1960, that this system of political consultations was fine but that cooperation in "the field of strategy" was also required. President Eisenhower replied on August 2, recalling that the offer of military talks on Africa the year before had not been followed up by the French. He suggested another approach that would not contemplate formal combined staff planning, but rather talks among military representatives on all strategic questions of interest to France in various parts of the world, primarily outside the NATO area. General de Gaulle did not respond to this proposal. Instead he suggested a tripartite meeting at the heads-of-government level, to work out a joint plan for organizing united action on world problems and for reorganizing the Atlantic Alliance. President Eisenhower replied on August 31 that in order to prepare for such a meeting the General should set forth his views on NATO in a memorandum. General de Gaulle had twice before promised to circulate such a memorandum. He responded to this last request only in his press conference on September 5, 1960.[26]

This was the third of de Gaulle's formal press conferences, held semiannually at the Élysée Palace. Asked to put some light on his concept of NATO, de Gaulle made two points. First, the "world powers of the West" must be able to organize "their political conduct and, should the occasion arise, their strategic conduct outside Europe." (The example of the Congo was invoked. If the United States, Britain, and France had taken a single position on the Congo crisis from the beginning, de Gaulle said, "the result would have been better than the bloody anarchy now existing in this new State." In fact, Eisenhower had proposed joint three-power action in Africa, the State Department summary noted. But de Gaulle, after first agreeing, had never named a French representative, although urged to do so.) Second, "the defense of a country, while being of course combined with that of other countries, must have a national character. . . . That is why France keeps her fleet directly under her own orders. . . . Furthermore, France feels that if atomic weapons are to be stockpiled on her territory, these weapons should be in her own hands. . . . This is what France understands by the reform of the Atlantic Organization."

There was nothing new in this recital of by now well-known positions. As for what precisely de Gaulle wanted, this was made clear in various of his communications to his Anglo-Saxon colleagues; it amounted to unconditional acceptance of his sweeping claims for France. As before, there was nothing to negotiate.

After retiring, Eisenhower often said that it was the Joint Atomic Energy Committee's opposition that prevented him from assisting de Gaulle's nuclear program. He even said that the Atomic Energy Act should be repealed in order to relieve the President of its restrictions.[27] And obviously, the Committee, along with the NATO buffs within the American defense community, was a chief source of resistance. Indeed, the success of the latter in turning aside most of the proposals for aiding France showed that a small group of bureaucrats, if persistent and if assured of some high-level support, could normally block the initiatives of larger and more powerful lobbies within the government.

But these obstacles could probably have been overcome had de Gaulle taken a more moderate line. Eisenhower offered him quite a lot—perhaps as much as he could within the limits of the law and the limits imposed by Washington politics. Yet de Gaulle never responded. In fact, *he* was and would remain the greatest obstacle to the achievement of the global role he professed to want.

As time ran out on the Eisenhower Administration de Gaulle

served notice on its successor. France's budgetary debates in the autumn of 1960 were the occasion for Couve de Murville to tell the National Assembly: "Participation in atomic strategy, participation in the supreme decision, that is our aim." [28] But rarely can an old and tired administration convincingly pass on its insights to a successor. Every administration learns by its own experience, mistakes, and disappointments.

5

The Education
of John F. Kennedy

John F. Kennedy's first few months in the White House were tumultuous, with crises everywhere but in Europe, where it seemed he might be given a period of grace. The initial impulse of the new Administration was to find some area of agreement with the Soviet Union. The American Ambassador in Moscow, Llewellyn Thompson, was charged with exploring the possibilities of a nuclear-test-ban agreement; after some delay he managed to see Khrushchev in Siberia in early March. Agreement in principle was reached on a Kennedy-Khrushchev meeting, which both sides wanted, but Thompson got nowhere on the test-ban issue. The Soviet leadership was in fact already preparing to break the informal moratorium that had existed since 1958; Russia was to resume nuclear tests in the late summer.

Some weeks later President Kennedy made the crucial decision to extricate the United States from the impossible, even ludicrous, situation in which it found itself in Laos. The Eisenhower Administration had ill-advisedly sought to make an anti-Communist redoubt of this primitive little kingdom. Laos was an "arrow aimed at the heart of Southeast Asia." Thus, the neutralist Prince Souvanna Phouma, perhaps the only leader of stature among the Laotians, was twice toppled from power by the American "country team" and replaced by various right-wing characters. France and Britain strongly backed Souvanna Phouma, while the Communist bloc supported his vigorous and able half brother, Prince Souphannouvong. Kennedy's hope was, at best, to move the parties toward a neutral, albeit possibly chaotic, solution; at worst, he was buying a few years of non-Communist rule. Yet the decision also deepened the American commitment to defend Vietnam south of the 17th parallel, since, in political terms, a neutral Laos meant a re-emphasis of South Vietnam as the point from which the United States would resist Asian Communism. The consequences of this involvement were to dislocate America's foreign relations for years to come.

The pressures and anxieties with which the Kennedy Administration was seized from the first day were shared in other Western capitals, where officials were frankly worried about the American performance in foreign affairs and the prospect of a young, untested President. Kennedy thus devoted a good deal of time in his first months in office to taking the measure and acquiring the confidence of his peers, Macmillan, Adenauer, and de Gaulle. Of the three, de Gaulle was the one who fascinated him and aroused his admiration, a sentiment shared by many of those who made up the new Administration. Macmillan interested Kennedy, but he was wary of Adenauer. Kennedy and his advisers were determined that American policy in the 1960s would not be subject to a veto in Bonn, as many thought, somewhat extravagantly, had been the case in the 1950s.

Not that it would matter, but Kennedy did get off on the wrong foot with de Gaulle. Everyone had expected him to name Charles Bohlen as his Ambassador to France, and the prospect of Bohlen, a highly regarded and trusted professional with experience in France as well as the Soviet Union, pleased the French; he was thought to be an excellent choice. Eventually Bohlen did come, but not until October 1962. The initial nominee was General James Gavin. Now it is no reflection on Gavin to say that the French would have preferred Bohlen. No matter that Gavin was highly regarded in America for his intellectual flair and independent spirit.* His lack of diplomatic experience and uncertain command of the French language contrasted unfavorably with Bohlen. Kennedy was believed to be sending one general to deal with another, when everyone knew, or should have known, that de Gaulle had little time for professional soldiers. *France-Observateur*, in noting the Quai d'Orsay's lack of dispatch in communicating the inevitable *agrément*, observed prophetically: "Everything points to the belief that General Gavin's mission should be one of rather short duration."

Kennedy met twice with Macmillan before seeing either de Gaulle or Adenauer. The first meeting, a rather desultory 90-minute conversation, took place in Key West at the end of March while Macmillan was on a tour of the West Indies, the United States, and Canada. The Laotian crisis was the sole topic. Macmillan and the Foreign Office were no less distressed than Kennedy by the United States' involvement in the land-locked little monarchy. But, since Washington had not yet obtained the cease-fire that would set in motion a real effort to reach a settlement, Macmillan had no choice but to promise to support a limited American intervention if the cease-fire efforts collapsed.[1]

The two men met in Washington a week later for longer and more formal talks. But it was all too ceremonial, and didn't go well. The dinners were on a large scale, and Kennedy and Macmillan were continuously flanked by large numbers of advisers

---

* Gavin's fidelity to his own convictions was perhaps intended to impress de Gaulle, who extolled disobedience in a good cause. Gavin had resigned in 1958, when he was in charge of the Army's research and development program, rather than continue to take part in a military policy he regarded as harmful to the Army's and the country's interest. He was offered a fourth star at the time, but turned it down.

during all the meetings (which on one day lasted a total of seven hours). The British met everyone in the new Administration but could not get a clear impression of Kennedy, who felt defensive with Macmillan and somewhat put off by the subtle Edwardian manner of the older and more experienced man. At one point he tried to break the stiffness and ritualism of the meetings by moving them to his yacht, the *Honey Fitz*, but the quarters were too cramped for the number of people involved in the *tour d'horizon* that had been scheduled, with the result that senior officials on both sides found themselves virtually sitting in one another's laps while listening to the bureaucrats' briefings on such knotty questions as Laos. Macmillan found the young President difficult to comprehend, uncertain, and overly dependent on his advisers; Kennedy said little, and the British couldn't tell whether the more assertive (and sometimes disconcerting) attitudes of certain of his advisers had his backing. The close friendship later to bind Kennedy and Macmillan was far from predictable in April 1961.

Still, a key point was nailed down. Macmillan told Kennedy that he planned to take Britain into the Common Market, provided this would not jeopardize the "special relationship" with Washington. Kennedy gave the necessary assurances but, contrary to widely held belief, never pressured Macmillan to take this step. Whatever their feelings on the subject, Kennedy and his advisers were not yet so sure of themselves as to attempt to twist Macmillan's arm. Every American administration has strongly favored Britain's involvement with the EEC, but Washington's views have never been decisive on this issue, and sometimes not even significant.

Adenauer arrived in Washington a week later, on April 12, and again, the encounter was not a success. Kennedy had difficulty communicating with the old Chancellor, whose suspicions of the new Administration were already hatched and would grow. Perhaps at that stage only another Dulles, a kindred spirit of his own generation, could have removed Adenauer's doubts about the strength and durability of the United States commitment to West Germany. All successor custodians of American foreign policy have found themselves endlessly reassuring the West Germans, as a husband must reassure a doubtful or jealous wife.

Kennedy was scheduled to see de Gaulle on May 31—in Paris, the French noted happily, whereas Macmillan and Adenauer had traveled to Washington. Since de Gaulle had last met Eisenhower in Washington protocol, strictly applied, required that the American chief of state now go to Paris, and this suited the White House, since Kennedy hoped to meet Khrushchev afterward.

On April 23, a little over a month before Kennedy was due to arrive, de Gaulle suddenly found himself backed to the wall by a cabal of mutinous French generals in Algeria who appeared to control the bulk of France's army and air transport capability. General Maurice Challe, the nominal leader of the *Putsch,* was former chief of the French air force and had had long NATO experience. An invasion and seizure of the *métropole* under his command appeared imminent. De Gaulle broadcast an appeal for the help of the people of France, and Prime Minister Debré made an even more dramatic request for popular support against invading air-borne units. The Interior Ministry was preparing to pass out arms to private citizens.

In this moment of crisis Kennedy transmitted two messages offering broad support to de Gaulle; the first was delivered to the Élysée Palace on the very evening of the expected invasion. According to one well-informed account, Kennedy, in addition to offering any assistance that might be requested, warned American commanders in France that unauthorized elements might try to seize United States installations and ordered them to block such efforts by all means short of armed action. Landing fields would have been covered with obstacles to prevent use by air-borne units.[2] But this unequivocal support for de Gaulle failed to discourage rumors that the CIA was in some way involved in the attempted *Putsch*. C. L. Sulzberger, trying to silence these rumors, reported (doubtless correctly) that they had started in Moscow and were spread by certain anti-American French officials. Even *Le Monde*, he noted, was saying, "It appears well established that American agents more or less encouraged Maurice Challe." [3] Alain Peyrefitte, a Gaullist deputy, a future minister, and already an important mouthpiece of official thinking, also wrote in *Le Monde*: "It is probably that the insurgents hoped for at least the benevolent neutrality of the government in Washington, if not its active support. Doubtless, certain conversations, perhaps even advances—harshly denied by Kennedy's message—made the rebel generals think the United States would welcome with satisfaction the installation of a government that was not only 'resolutely anti-Communist,' but above all more pliable than General de Gaulle's." [4]

As before, the supreme issue between de Gaulle and the Americans was the nuclear aid he would refuse to seek directly and for which he would make no concessions. His expectations very low, de Gaulle intended to keep alive France's claim to parity with the United States. (Thus, in March, Couve de Murville had returned to the question of de Gaulle's directorate proposal and vetoes on American nuclear weapons. "I am not sure that to use the term 'veto' is exactly appropriate. Its use in the U.N. Security Council has given the word a derogatory meaning. One speaks disapprovingly of the word 'veto', but one speaks with approval of the necessity for agreement." [5])

In the first year or so, Kennedy's Administration understood de Gaulle no more than its predecessor. And like Eisenhower, Kennedy soon found himself pulled in different directions by the "Francophiles," the "multilateralists," and the "stand-patters" in the foreign-policy establishment. By instinct he was himself a "stand-patter," but the pressures to do *something* were strong, and not all of them arose in the Potomac basin. At least once, and probably twice, during 1961 Macmillan wanted to sell de Gaulle certain technology and material that Washington continued to embargo. The French were still seeking nuclear-submarine technology and inertial-guidance components. The White House, strongly backed by the State Department's protectionists in the Regional Affairs section and relying on the Anglo-American agreements that prohibited nuclear help to third countries, said no. Around this same time the National Security Council took the contradictory position of deciding to make available inertial-guidance components and technology to the West Germans, who were procuring and manufacturing under license advanced tactical American combat aircraft. This distinction in Bonn's favor was carefully noted—and resented—in Paris. Other elements in the State Department—those who had before supported nuclear aid to de Gaulle—sought to revive the plan to give France a nuclear-propulsion system for submarines, an offer that had been the victim of so many false starts in the preceding two years. As before, the initiative was blocked, chiefly by the regionalists whose chief concerns were NATO and the Common Market.

This group was deeply involved in a broad interagency review of NATO and European policy; its anti-Gaullist bias infused the exercise and sharpened the tension already developing between the White House and State Department. Never a great admirer of the State Department, Kennedy now worried that its European regionalists were gaining the upper hand within the bureaucracy and would force his. (They were strongly backed by Under Secretary George Ball and their point of view was tacitly endorsed by Secretary Dean Rusk, who bore no affection for de Gaulle.) While Kennedy was attracted to their vision of a strong and united Europe, large and untested ideas offended his pragmatic instincts.

Briefly, he felt that the State Department was trying to crowd him into an adversary relationship with de Gaulle, whose hostility to a supranational Western Europe—Monnet's Europe—was well-known. Thus, early in his Administration Kennedy was becoming uncertain, even ambivalent on European issues. This ambivalence was to mark his performance on such issues as nuclear sharing almost to the day he died.

Kennedy was disconcerted by more than a mere clash of viewpoints within the bureaucracy. He had equipped himself with weighty and prestigious advisers on European affairs. Dean Acheson was on the scene. The able and experienced Paul Nitze was serving as Assistant Secretary of Defense for International Security Affairs, after having functioned as Kennedy's consultant on national-security issues in the period between his election and inauguration. There were also McGeorge Bundy, Walt Rostow, Adlai Stevenson, and Chester Bowles to be taken into account, as well as Rusk and Ball, whom Kennedy knew less well than he did the others. Robert McNamara made an immediate impact. Last but hardly least, the British Ambassador, David Ormsby-Gore (now Lord Harlech), was closer to Kennedy than *any* of them, as later chapters will show. In short, the normal problem of shaking down a new administration was complicated by the glittering array of talent Kennedy had assembled; only through experience could he assay these personalities and usefully relate their various qualities and insights to the taxing and dangerous problems for which he bore ultimate responsibility.

Although Eisenhower's people had left behind a good deal of unfinished business, notably the Laotian crisis, they had managed to spare their successors a commitment of any sort on the "Gates proposals." The NATO Ministerial Conference in Paris in December 1960, a last hurrah for the outgoing administration, marked the end of the Gates proposals and the beginning of something else—the multilateral nuclear force (MLF).

Gerard Smith, Chairman of the State Department's Policy Planning Council (which had always strongly opposed the Gates proposals), on behalf of Herter, put forward as an alternative suggestion to the Gates plan a sea-based nuclear force assigned to NATO, provided a system of multilateral control could be worked out. The gesture was frankly designed to get the incoming Administration off the hook with regard to earlier proposals for quick-reaction land-based missiles in Europe. Among other considerations, it would clearly be easier to assure American control of weapons on submarines or surface vessels than on bases operated by allied military forces.

Shortly thereafter Herter, Douglas Dillon, and Gates briefed a member of the incoming administration on the MLF. He in turn also talked to Spaak, Secretary-General of NATO, about it. His feeling, as he recalls it, was that the MLF was "not a clear proposal on its face and that it would be improper to prejudge it." And that was his recommendation to the President-elect.

On May 17, 1961, shortly before seeing de Gaulle, Kennedy repeated and embellished the MLF proposal in a speech in Ottawa by offering to "commit to NATO . . . five . . . Polaris submarines" as a forerunner to a jointly operated and jointly financed sea-based NATO nuclear force. At the time it was not a very significant gesture; the vastly complicated system of control remained to be worked out, and this in turn required a strong expression of European interest. Few people in Washington expected much response from the Europeans. Thus Kennedy was committing himself to very little. As before, the real issue was whether to help de Gaulle.

Just after Kennedy's forthcoming visit to Paris was announced de Gaulle received C. L. Sulzberger, a highly favored outlet to the world beyond the Élysée Palace. Over the years Sulzberger's frequent *New York Times* columns based on private audiences with de Gaulle provided guidance of no little importance to the foreign offices of the world. The message for Washington, Sulzberger reported now, was that it would be up to Kennedy to broach the questions of Big Three political direction and nuclear sharing; de Gaulle would not raise them.[6] Sulzberger also warned of de Gaulle's aversion to American power moving into areas of Africa vacated by France, as well as his sensitivity to American activity in Southeast Asia.[7]

Nuclear sharing, then, was still the great unstated issue, while American influence in former French colonies was an emotional issue, no less important for being so close to the surface. De Gaulle's feeling about places once under French control or influence was unimaginably strong. It involved more than just the issue of preserving and promoting French political influence, although that was crucial. Equally vital was the other side of the coin—preserving the world vocation of the French language and culture. (A visiting political leader who spoke some French would often find a more sympathetic ear in the Élysée Palace than one who spoke none, de Gaulle's normally hard-headed view of things notwithstanding.)

The suspicion that imperial America is poaching in French preserves runs deep in France, on the right and on the center right, and it found its purest expression in de Gaulle and Debré. American efforts to put this suspicion to rest by supporting de Gaulle vigorously in Algeria—indeed, by not undertaking any military and cultural programs in French-speaking Africa that were not cleared through his government—never impressed him. The United States had, after all, moved into the political vacuum left by France in Laos and Vietnam.

This ritualistic disapproval of American policy found in the Élysée Palace sharply curtailed the ability of working-level diplomats to coordinate Franco-American activities in Asia and Africa. Almost anything that involved French-speaking Africa, say, or Southeast Asia, and which required de Gaulle's O.K. would be blocked. French diplomats, by and large, tended to take a more balanced and tolerant view of American policies. But de Gaulle's message to his Foreign Office was that coopera-tion with Washington in faraway places really meant acquiesc-ing in their drift into the American orbit. Thus was launched a great bureaucratic game of trying to keep various matters at so low a level as not to require Élysée approval. If this meant a failure to move forward, as often it did, it was also a means of preventing de Gaulle's veto on various items of joint concern. As one French diplomat observed: "We supply the sticks and stones of French policy; we have nothing to say about whether the structure will be neoclassic or flamboyant."

It was the Congo, once Belgian, now independent, French-speaking, and bordering the French Congo, which fiercely di-vided Paris and Washington in the spring of 1961. The UN peace-keeping efforts, from which de Gaulle withheld French financial support, angered him. The UN, he said in his fourth press conference (his first since Kennedy's advent), was:

> a scene of disturbance, confusion and division. . . . The result is that it carries to the local scene its global incoherence, the personal conceptions of its various agents and the individual partiality of each of the states which send their contingents with their own orders—send them, then withdraw them.
>
> Under these conditions, France does not see how she can adopt any attitude toward the United, or disunited, Nations, other than that of the greatest reserve. In any case, she does not wish to contribute her men or her money to any present or future undertaking of this organization—or disorganization.

De Gaulle refused to allow Congo-bound UN planes to overfly French territory, and he persuaded French African countries to follow suit.[8] A glance at the map shows quickly the extraordi-nary inconvenience this hostile gesture produced.

Four days before de Gaulle's press conference, Alain Peyrefitte (an unofficial Gaullist voice, as we have noted) observed in another newspaper article that for de Gaulle, Africa was a sphere of Western influence; to introduce the UN there was to invite disorder, subversion, and Soviet penetration. The Congo difficulty, he concluded, would have been resolved by the concerted action of the three great Western powers.[9] *Le Monde*'s André Fontaine noted America's support for the UN action and observed correctly that de Gaulle's preference for a Franco-British-American joint action was regarded as "chimeric" in Washington.[10]

Aside from Berlin, then, Kennedy and de Gaulle were going to have little if anything to agree on. Moreover, it was clear that, despite Kennedy's high admiration for de Gaulle, his stay in Paris was to be little more than a stopover on the way to the more important meeting with Khrushchev in Vienna. Doubtless, de Gaulle was more sensitive to this than anyone. A press campaign, among other things, was stimulated to blur this point. French newspapers of all political colors pointed up the distinction between de Gaulle receiving JFK in Paris and Macmillan and Adenauer being obliged to do the traveling.

The Élysée Palace was also letting it be known that de Gaulle would play the role of Adenauer's advocate. This would impress Bonn. Some of Kennedy's advisers held views on the German problem which, rightly or wrongly, thoroughly alarmed the West German Embassy in Washington and in turn Adenauer. De Gaulle was soon to exploit German doubts about Kennedy, if he hadn't started already.

Among the endless press speculations on Kennedy's trip, an article by Fontaine was more prescient than most. Nobody could say what Khrushchev had in store for Kennedy, he remarked, and wondered "if he isn't for a starter going to pull a Berlin bomb out of his bag on arriving in Vienna. The majority of experts, for the moment, are inclined to think the contrary. The Soviet press has seemed for several days to be preparing its readers for a new thaw rather than an imminent test of strength." [11]

The Paris conversations with de Gaulle—on May 31 and June 1–2—seemed to be Kennedy's most successful thus far with any Western political leader. Whatever their differences, Kennedy felt he had achieved a rapport with de Gaulle, and they swiftly and publicly reached agreement—at least in general terms—on holding firm in Berlin. The ceremonial part of the Kennedys' visit, to no one's great surprise, was a glittering success: the poignancy of the meeting between the weathered old lion who embodied so much of the history of the first half of the century, and the young President who embodied so much of the hope for the second was lost on no one.

As was so often the case in tête-à-tête meetings with de Gaulle the two nations' interpretations of the conversations on the grittier issues varied sharply. On the tripartism issue, for example, a French official who was present says, "Kennedy's reaction to the proposal was not responsive, not warm. He was very evasive." And on nuclear sharing the same official says, "Kennedy was more negative than either Eisenhower or Norstad [NATO's Supreme Commander] had been." But actually it was Kennedy who took the initiative on tripartism, knowing as he did that de Gaulle would not bring it up himself; he had asked Paul Nitze, between a morning and afternoon session, to draw up a suitable proposal. This amounted to high-level three-power military contingency planning for Laos, the Congo, and Berlin—all three being trouble spots that fell in what de Gaulle regarded as spheres of French influence. De Gaulle responded favorably, promising to take a number of steps to implement the proposal. In fact, he took none, though he was urged to do so. De Gaulle was clearly no more intrigued by joint military planning now than he had been by the three-power ambassadorial meetings in Washington in 1958–1959. Kennedy was beginning to repeat some of Eisenhower's experience. Nothing short of the original directorate would be acceptable, yet no one put a lower estimate on its prospects than de Gaulle himself.

In a report to the American people some days later on his trip Kennedy said, "My talks with General de Gaulle were profoundly encouraging to me. . . . No question, however sensitive, was avoided." This was perhaps technically correct, but some questions were taken head-on, others not quite so frankly. Probably the best-informed account of what happened was by Sulzberger, who had had a private talk with Kennedy after the latter bade de Gaulle farewell at the Élysée Palace. The President [Kennedy], he wrote, had wisely avoided the tougher questions at first, and had begun with Berlin,

> where it was known in advance that full accord existed. In fact, subtracting time for interpretation, this discussion took little more than a quarter of an hour. Then slowly Kennedy moved the exchange to other areas: Africa and Asia, South America, our support of the European Common Market.
>
> It was only after this harmonious background was created that attention was turned to the two essential causes of Franco-American difficulty—consultation and the atom. . . .
>
> [Kennedy] seemed to have settled the first and helped smooth injured feelings on the second. All this is a great deal. The terminal communiqué describing this three days' colloquy is even more laconic and useless than is customary. Furthermore, at de Gaulle's behest, little background information was disseminated. Nevertheless, despite this paucity of information, one may say that Kennedy's first trans-Atlantic venture in diplomacy has shown positive results.[12]

Almost a year later, when relations between Kennedy and de Gaulle were visibly disintegrating, Sulzberger wrote that "both men thought relations had been improved by an implied agreement [at the 1961 meeting] that Paris would be treated by Washington on the *same degree of intimacy as London*" [13] (italics added).

Kennedy, apparently, played the Paris visit by ear, and left believing the affair had gone off well, far better than he and his party might have expected. But the glow of satisfaction they took with them lasted no longer than the few hours to Vienna. There, on the second day of his talks with Khrushchev, Kennedy was confronted with a Soviet ultimatum that relaunched the Berlin crisis. Unless he would agree to sign a treaty recognizing the existence of the two Germanies, Khrushchev would conclude a separate treaty with East Germany before the year's end, at which point the Western allies' legal position, stemming from World War II—occupation rights in Berlin, access to the city, and so on—would be treated as null and void.

The stormy meeting with Khrushchev was perhaps useful, as chroniclers of the Kennedy years claim, in giving the new President a sharp sense of what he was up against. Nonetheless, Kennedy had gone to Vienna bearing the burden of the Bay of Pigs disaster and the Laotian difficulties; his administration was far from having completed its shakedown period. He arrived not knowing what to expect from the Russians, and he left apparently on collision course with his blustery interlocutor.

It was at this sober moment that the warm (and politically consequential) friendship between Kennedy and Macmillan was born. Returning to the United States via London, Kennedy stopped to brief Macmillan (and attend a family christening). They met at Admiralty House. A large conference had been arranged, with numerous advisers, in the earlier pattern, but the two men decided to talk privately instead and spent an hour and a half together in the Prime Minister's small study. They emerged friends.

The 1958–1960 Berlin crisis had inspired the creation of allied contingency planning conducted in Washington by the American, British, and French Ambassadors. The contribution of this working group was to present everyone with the same factual evaluation of the threat. In July 1961 the group was enlarged to include West Germany, and then was split into several subgroups dealing with the various political, military, and economic aspects of the Berlin problem. Special military arrangements for handling a Berlin crisis were established outside NATO in a little-known command called (then as now) Live Oak. Its chain of command ran through the Big Three governments, and the commanding generals—one each from Britain, France, and the United States—were and are responsible to NATO's Supreme Commander *only* when a military contingency plan has been set in motion by the governments.* Live Oak works alongside SHAPE, but has separate communications and so on.

All these arrangements suited de Gaulle perfectly. They offered him precise and reliable estimates of the various problems, but committed him to nothing. It would remain so. Never during the anxious weeks and months of the 1961 Berlin crisis did de Gaulle agree to a predelegation of authority to an allied military commander. He was no more impressed by Khrushchev's threats in this second round than he had been during the first. His real concern lay in the possibility that Berlin would in the end draw Washington and Moscow closer together bilaterally. This, of course, would conflict with de Gaulle's own plans, and it reinforced his implacable hostility to any Soviet-American contacts on Berlin. His private line was that the United States should provide a nuclear guarantee to Western Europe, but should otherwise not meddle in European affairs.

Some weeks before going to Europe Kennedy had asked Acheson to draw up some Berlin contingency planning, and Acheson had preceded Kennedy to Paris in order to explain Washington's current thinking on Berlin "crisis management." James Reston, who covered the Kennedy trip, reported from Paris:

---

* The *primus inter pares* is always the British general, with two stars. The other two are brigadiers.

It is understood that he [Acheson] proposed, first, that the North Atlantic nations be placed on an emergency basis. Second, he is said to have urged that a U.S.-British-French military task force be ready to convoy supplies through the West German-East German checkpoint at Helmstedt, if necessary, to demonstrate the West's determination to carry out its commitments on West Berlin.

General de Gaulle is reported here to have been impressed by Mr. Acheson's presentation, but he did not commit himself to it at that time. . . .

"Whether he did so today [with Kennedy] is not known.* Some of General de Gaulle's aides believe that the West should use an airlift to avoid a Communist blockade, as was done in 1948, before risking war by running an armed convoy through Helmstedt. Washington is known to feel this is impractical for the following reasons: New electronic devices have made it more possible for the Communists to interfere with allied planes. The standard of living in West Berlin is now much higher and, to be maintained, would require a much heavier supply of goods than in 1948. Modern jet aircraft do not have the landing facilities in West Berlin available to propeller aircraft of 13 years ago.

The French concede all these points, but argue that, if an airlift is used, the Communists would be obliged to take the first act of war to stop it. The use of an Allied armed convoy would be interpreted by the world as the first act of war, they contend.[14]

The airlift worked in 1948, but in the summer of 1961 another airlift was out of the question.

Still, the Americans found little if any support when they insisted that the Autobahn to Berlin must be kept open. Franz-Josef Strauss was no less leery of the plan to use force, if necessary, to keep the Autobahn open than he had been in 1958–

---

* He did not. And, as noted by Sulzberger, Kennedy and de Gaulle disposed of Berlin in about fifteen minutes.

1959; the British were plainly reluctant; and de Gaulle was committing himself to very little. Yet de Gaulle's line also created a fair amount of bureaucratic concern in Bonn and Paris. West German resistance to any scheme that might unnecessarily or prematurely expose the Bundeswehr to actual fighting with East Germans was by now understood on all sides and accepted. But France's refusal to be more constructive was harder to forgive. Macmillan, given his past performance, inspired little confidence in these circles. The reporting from the West German Embassy in Washington, excessively influenced by the less orthodox thinkers around Kennedy, probably caused still greater concern, if not alarm. The danger seemed to be that the American position would again show signs of wobbling, thus possibly tempting the Russians (who might not perceive that in the end Washington, and London in tow, would do whatever was required to hold Berlin) to provoke the West. In short, a number of experienced Continentals feared that the threat of nuclear war was becoming more than a mere abstraction for war-gamers. For the Élysée, predelegations of authority were nevertheless out of the question. "It is enough that America shows she is prepared to make nuclear war," was the message from Olympia.

Not surprisingly, the French were always fully cooperative in Live Oak, however. And their representatives on the Berlin contingency planning group in Washington usually cooperated fully in diplomatic planning, although they were always the last to receive instructions. (The West German side was top-heavy with lawyers who taxed the patience of the other delegations with their single-minded devotion to the legal nuances of every piece of paper. Some of the Americans aroused mistrust with the other three delegations; as individuals, their grasp of the problems seemed less sure. Among the notable exceptions was Nitze, who chaired the military contingency planning committee and had the respect of his European colleagues and the three foreign offices as well. He was considered both tough and able.)

Contingency planning for the Autobahn might have led to sending a patrol to assist a blocked vehicle, then a company to relieve the patrol, and so on. Gradual escalation by probing was Washington's preference; this obviously required swift reaction at the decision-making levels. On this score, to some Americans the British were more of a problem than the French, since sometimes they dawdled over measures to which the French made no objections. (They once, for example, refused to run a convoy to one of the checkpoints, although the French did run one along with the Americans.) The French agreed to predelegate authority in preparatory stages, but no further. If it came to a question of committing combat aircraft to the air corridors, for example, formal governmental approval would be required. On this as on many other matters, the British, in the end, accepted the tougher American position, though often not without having an argument. One of the senior British representatives recalls: "The French were not far apart from us [on military contingency planning]. We, like the French, wanted to reserve military questions for a governmental decision. The Americans, on the other hand, wanted to shorten the reaction time. Our point was that it would be difficult to anticipate with precision what might be involved in any one of the various contingencies."

A rising hostility between the British and the West Germans is sharply expressed in the reminiscences of this same official: "It was always," he says, "a question of getting the Germans to agree to something constructive. They tended to hide behind the others—to let the others do the running with Moscow— while always scenting betrayal. We sought constantly to explain the British position to Adenauer, who would grasp it for a time, and then get it wrong again a few weeks later." In fact, the British position was the most advanced in the sense of

being the most flexible, while the West Germans were the least
flexible on any point that even remotely touched on the issue of
East Germany's legal status. De Gaulle appeared to sympathize
with Bonn's sensitivity to the less rigorous Anglo-Saxons, while
siding with Britain on the issue of predelegations of military
authority. These tactics irked many in Washington. In a
military sense it mattered little; then as now the United States
supplied the bulk of the force, and the British a good deal more
than the French, whose contribution would have been distinctly
marginal. But de Gaulle was taking credit for the hardest declaratory position.

Remarkably enough, the Berlin planning group, however
chafed by the dissonant voices of four governments, managed
to play its role with distinction. More precisely, the group
performed an historic, possibly unprecedented, function. Besides doing much to stabilize the Berlin situation, its continuing, patient, and arduous efforts taught the governments
quite a lot about joint crisis management.

The autumn of 1961 was an agonizing period. The Berlin
wall had gone up. Castro's influence seemed to be spreading in
the Caribbean. And in South Vietnam the government of Ngo
Dinh Diem was unwilling either to prosecute the war against
the Viet Cong realistically or to undertake any of the basic political and military reforms that Washington believed essential.
Indeed, the situation in Vietnam had deteriorated to the point
where some responsible officials in Washington contemplated
withdrawing a measure of America's support for Diem, thus
encouraging his adversaries to do just what they were to do in
October 1963. The Administration shrank from this option,
however, and instead began a military build-up. Apart from
other considerations, Kennedy was unwilling to make any gesture that Khrushchev might mistakenly interpret as a sign of
weakness and that would further aggravate the Berlin problem.

The Berlin wall shocked the world, but while its human consequences were appalling, the officials in Western capitals were privately relieved. The pressure that had been built up by the steady stream of West-bound refugees had become intolerable. Adenauer was the slowest of the West's leaders to react; involved in a political campaign, he appeared at the wall only after a week. None of West Germany's leaders, of whatever party, favored a military response. Two or three days before, the Soviet Ambassador had called on Adenauer with a private message from Khrushchev known to have contained certain assurances. The two talked for nearly three hours. The wall was a political fact.

Franco-American relations were taking a sharp turn for the worse. During the summer things hadn't gone badly. The United States had managed a slight build-up of its French-based forces, to which the Élysée raised no objection, possibly because Washington wisely avoided seeking formal approval at that level. Also at this point, French air units based in West Germany were equipped with American tactical nuclear weapons. De Gaulle, of course, had always refused to accept such weapons on French soil unless he could control some or all of them, but a distinction was made for his units in West Germany, perhaps because the French government simply wanted to know as much about these weapons as, say, the West Germans did. For Kennedy to make them available required the same mutual-security determination that Eisenhower had once made in de Gaulle's favor during the Berlin crisis in 1959.

After his visit to Paris Kennedy welcomed suggestions from some of his advisers on how to move closer to de Gaulle. But the effects of the Berlin wall and the implied face-down with Khrushchev tended to shunt Franco-American relations to one side. In September some State Department officials proposed inviting de Gaulle to Washington. Rusk and a few others were opposed, but had Berlin not claimed so much of Washington's attention the visit might well have taken place. Also, the nuclear-submarine issue arose again and again, though never formally. French officials were not getting a really satisfactory answer as to why the original Eisenhower-Dulles offer of the propulsion system could not be advanced. They were told that it was at the moment "inopportune" or that it would set off pressures in Bonn. The latter argument simply irritated the French. It seemed a weak alibi, the more so since Washington was selling non-nuclear components of advanced-weapons systems to the West Germans that were denied to France on the grounds that such material would assist the French strategic-weapons program. Finally, Washington and Paris were beginning to compete for a big share of West Germany's advanced-weapons market. Rightly or wrongly, the French felt that the United States, by putting heavy pressure on Bonn, was claiming a disproportionately large share of this rich market. The issue of arms sales, especially with regard to combat aircraft, would become an eternal sore point.

Yet something positive was in the wind. A number of things were coming together. By autumn Great Britain had applied to join the Common Market, which seemed to have played a role in the exuberant growth rate of its member countries; negotiations would start in the spring. Kennedy, meanwhile, faced a growing balance-of-payments deficit and a lackluster performance by the American economy. Current trade legislation was due to expire in June 1962; Washington was aroused by the outline of a broad solution to these interrelated problems: Britain, in joining the European Community, would impart balance to the Continentals and perhaps serve as Europe's interlocutor in Washington; a new and liberalized American trade law would promote greater transatlantic commerce, and this in turn would lighten America's financial difficulties while strengthening political ties. Europe might one day even be encouraged to take larger responsibilities in world affairs. But too little thought was given in Washington and London to de Gaulle's reaction to this "Atlantic partnership," as it later became known. As the autumn wore on he was withholding support for the Russo-American conversations on the Berlin question and warning Adenauer of a sellout. His reaction to Britain's formal application to join the Common Market was known in diplomatic circles to be glacial.

From mid-September to mid-November Adenauer, after narrowly winning his elections, was unable to form a government, an embarrassment to him and a cause of still greater confusion within Bonn and between Bonn and Washington. When he did form his government, he went immediately to Washington. His talks with the Kennedy people showed that the American and West German positions were closer than Bonn had feared. The West Germans acquiesced, though far from cheerfully, in what became known as the Rusk-Gromyko conversations on Berlin, but very specific limits were set on their scope. Nor was the visit without its stormy moments, which included burning by mutual consent the minutes of one Adenauer-Kennedy conversation.[15]

Almost simultaneously, de Gaulle was spending the weekend at Macmillan's estate at Birch Grove, in Sussex. The undercurrent of stiffness and tension that marks even the most informal of these occasions was in this case slightly relieved, or flavored, by the sort of incident one can imagine occurring in the English countryside, if never in the forest of Rambouillet. A few moments before the talks were to start in the late afternoon of Friday, November 24, Macmillan's gamekeeper appeared and made a vigorous protest about the numerous police and plain-clothesmen in the adjacent woods. All the pheasants were departing, and, he reminded the Prime Minister, there was to be a shoot in a few days' time. (The Algerian war had, of course, inspired numerous plots against de Gaulle's life, and such protection was to be expected, although Macmillan had been startled the day before his guest's arrival to receive a large quantity of bottled blood of de Gaulle's blood type. He and his house-keeper argued over whether it could be permitted to displace a supply of herring in the only refrigerator on the premises.)

Birch Grove was one of three critically important meetings between de Gaulle and Macmillan—their last three—and in some ways it was the most interesting for what it revealed about de Gaulle's thinking and intentions. His attitude was very hard and very gloomy. He had yet to make a breakthrough in Algeria, and the prospect of the Rusk-Gromyko talks greatly disturbed him.

The meeting began with just two aides present—Sir Philip de Zulueta, Macmillan's bilingual private secretary, and Geoffroy de Courcel, de Gaulle's Chief of Staff. Macmillan began by observing that during their last meeting (at Rambouillet in January 1961) de Gaulle had asked if Britain was prepared to join the Common Market. Macmillan said it seemed to him possible that Britain could enter the Community on a confederal basis. He noted that Britain had been put off for a time by the European federalists.

De Gaulle, in reply, described the EEC as a fragile structure; it was difficult to see how Britain could be fitted into it. Shifting the conversation to the Cold War, on which he made a lengthy statement, he observed that nothing thus far had been lost to the West; in time Western Europe would learn to live with the Russians as it had learned to live with the Americans. One day, he said, the four powers would sit down and discuss various *faits accomplis*. Germany was divided, he noted, and he could not say that he found this regrettable. But there was no need to leave Berlin; this was a false issue the Russians had created. A treaty was possible on the basis of the division of Germany and of Germany's frontiers. Since the status quo in Berlin was favorable to the West, why negotiate? On the other hand, the frontiers were more or less favorable to the Russians. As for the division of Germany, de Gaulle recalled that while France might have yielded Alsace and Lorraine in 1871, she had not, under the Treaty of Frankfurt, renounced her claim to them. So, he ended, one might conclude a treaty accepting the existence of the German Democratic Republic (East Germany), but there was no reason to do it prematurely.

What de Gaulle seemed to be saying was that he was ready to sign a treaty with Moscow based on the division of Germany, if and when the Soviet leaders stopped issuing threats and ultimatums. Here Macmillan was abruptly confronted with de Gaulle's tempting soft line.

He chose to respond to de Gaulle's unwillingness to negotiate on Berlin. He noted the possibility of the moral and economic pressure that Moscow could bring to bear on that city. De Gaulle objected that it wasn't possible to negotiate under these conditions. He went on to say that Adenauer disliked Prussians and was not worried about Berlin itself; France, he said, would not take part in a Berlin settlement. Adenauer had not won a large majority in the elections, and this, de Gaulle added, argued for making haste in building Europe and for refusing to negotiate with Russia. After Adenauer he foresaw a succession of German chancellors (Ludwig Erhard, Strauss, and so on) in the style of the Weimar Republic.

Macmillan stressed the need for joint Western action. He said they were faced with the choice of doing nothing and going to war, or negotiating. Negotiations could be kept narrow, confined to the technical point concerning the West's rights of access to Berlin, or they could be enlarged to cover the main German questions. He said he would not object to narrow negotiations and, noting the importance of maintaining West German morale, added that these would be more difficult if Britain but not France joined the United States vis-à-vis Moscow. He agreed that it was annoying that Adenauer had not received a clear majority. Instead of negotiations de Gaulle preferred the idea of a joint statement from the Western powers to the effect that none of them was willing to change something that had lasted fifteen years.

The same restricted group met the following morning. Macmillan now argued strongly for British membership in the Common Market. After a good deal of talk about agriculture and the preferences enjoyed by Commonwealth countries in their trade with Britain, Macmillan reminded de Gaulle of the special arrangements under the Rome Treaty which France had secured for her former African dependencies. De Gaulle retorted that his Africans, unlike the dominions, had nothing to sell.

As the conversation took a more political turn, Macmillan suggested that if Britain could not enter the Common Market in 1962, the moment might not recur. A failure of the negotiations would dictate another course for Britain, a course nobody could predict. He, de Gaulle, and Adenauer were men of destiny; the disappearance of Adenauer would indeed be dangerous. He cited the famous "there is a tide in the affairs of men. . . ." The Greek city states, he noted, were able to come together only for the occasional marathon.

De Gaulle replied that he and the French people wanted Great Britain in Europe but did not want to change the character of Europe. The United Kingdom and her Commonwealth would dissolve Europe in the Atlantic sea. British membership was desirable, since France alone could not contain West Germany (nor perhaps even Italy) by herself. Europe had everything to gain from Britain's membership. But Europe must have an economic, a political, and a defense base. This reference to defense was a signal, or warning, and Macmillan did not miss it. He noted his agreement: the Commonwealth could not be abandoned, but one must not destroy the political and economic equilibrium of Europe. De Gaulle observed that none of these things could be settled quickly. He concluded, somewhat ambiguously, that in the end all the problems would be solved.

It had not gone well. De Gaulle seemed to accept in principle the idea of eventual British participation in Europe—he had, after all, twice suggested it to Macmillan—but he was distinctly bearish on the short-term prospects. He was saying that the impact on Europe of Britain's entry at this point was not acceptable. Yet Macmillan chose to rely on the lofty assurance that in the end all the problems would be solved.

On Berlin de Gaulle had been even harder. Kennedy, too, was discovering this. At the December NATO Ministerial meeting France refused to agree to any language endorsing contacts with the Soviet Union on Berlin. Fourteen foreign ministers supported such language, but Couve de Murville was adamant, and progressively softer versions failed to budge him. At various points the negotiators asked Couve de Murville to telephone de Gaulle for less rigorous instructions. He refused. This unprecedented behavior shocked most of his colleagues—from the veteran NATO buffs like Spaak to the newcomers like Rusk, who used to describe the foreign ministers as the "world's smallest trade union." In fact, the foreign ministers do have a sense of forming a club, one with certain implicit rules. For one of their number to refuse such a request from his colleagues was unthinkable. Couve de Murville ignored the rules, and the temperature of the proceedings went up sharply. Finally, the Secretary-General of NATO's international staff managed to find language that could be interpreted as meaning something or nothing. The amenities had been observed. What none of the foreign ministers knew was that Couve de Murville went that evening to de Gaulle to see if he couldn't obtain some flexibility for the French position. The General had not budged.

In the midst of this wrangle Kennedy placed his first and last telephone call to de Gaulle. The Presidential gorge was rising rapidly, and Kennedy's interpreter, a man whose political sense easily matched his linguistic gifts, apparently struck a nice balance between the strong sentiment that inspired the call and propriety.

This all coincided with a story in *Paris-Presse l'Intransigeant*, a pro-Gaullist mass-circulation newspaper which bore the subheadline: "De Gaulle Suspects Kennedy More Than He Fears Khrushchev." The story recalled Yalta—how with what lightness the "division of the world [was] decided by the giant nations"—and raised the specter of an agreement between Moscow and Washington on Berlin in the same pattern. De Gaulle's "painful memories" of Yalta were also cited. The article noted that de Gaulle would not give Washington a blank check by permitting military integration, and concluded that one couldn't even be sure that the Americans would use their forces to defend Europe.

A few weeks later de Gaulle told the French people that by "refusing to negotiate on Berlin or Germany so long as the Soviet Union does not stop its threats and its injunctions and bring about an actual easing of the international situation, we believe that we have spared our allies and ourselves the catastrophic retreat, dramatic rupture, or tragi-comical engulfment in which the conference would obviously have ended."

Kennedy and Macmillan had a problem that de Gaulle didn't share. Berlin appeared to bear the seeds of war with the Soviet Union; public opinion in Britain and America simply could not be led to such a confrontation without prior contacts or negotiations of some kind being made to prevent it. History would bear out de Gaulle's assumption that Khrushchev was bluffing —but he was far from alone in taking this view even at the time. To many Americans and British who worked on the Berlin problem, it seemed most unlikely that Moscow would abandon control of so explosive a situation by giving the East German regime control of the West's lines of access to Berlin. Still, the possibility had to be reckoned with, which meant taking the responsibility for defusing the problem. De Gaulle, much less troubled by public opinion, was able to play Berlin by ear, since he bore none of the real responsibility.

Kennedy's first year had been hard, perhaps unfairly hard. Still, he was learning. The December NATO meeting, some people in Washington felt, was the beginning of Kennedy's education on de Gaulle. Probably that was true. But much remained to be learned. The Gaullist view of European politics as revealed at Birch Grove and throughout the month of December might well have aroused concern, if not alarm, in London, Washington, and Bonn. But it did not. Too much else was happening. Khrushchev's aggressive diplomacy, after all, was the absorbing problem, not de Gaulle. In the space of a year that would change.

6

Nuclear Aid to France—
the Great Temptation

Kennedy's inaugural year had reached its somber end. In gaining the confidence of a large part of the electorate, much of it hitherto skeptical, the President had made an auspicious start. But his great enterprise of fostering a less irrational world order was going badly, or seemed to be. The Administration sensed that its grip on events, whether in Europe, Southeast Asia, or Latin America, was at best uncertain. The President's State of the Union address, delivered on January 11, reflected the anxiety: "It is the fate of this generation—of you in the Congress and of me as President—to live with a struggle we did not start, in a world we did not make. But the pressures of life are not always distributed by choice."

In fact, things were less grave than they seemed, though no one could have demonstrated this and few, if any, tried. Berlin was the crucial issue, but here at least contact had been made with Moscow, and the likelihood of major Soviet provocation had declined.

Not even the most wildly optimistic estimate could have foreseen that before the end of 1962 the Berlin crisis would be off the boil for good, and that prospects would develop for a nuclear-test-ban treaty and, beyond that, a limited *détente* with the Soviet Union. No one could then know that Castroism was not to have great resonance in Latin America. A settlement of the conflict in Laos lay ahead, and, contrary to what many in Washington expected, it was not to lead to a Communist takeover of that country—certainly not in the next few years. The war in Vietnam was still a struggle waged primarily between South Vietnamese. In fact, among Kennedy's major problems, only de Gaulle was to prove to be more remote from reason and moderation than had been anticipated. Arthur Schlesinger has written that Kennedy's one meeting with de Gaulle "increased his understanding of the clarity and tenacity, though not yet of the ferocity, of de Gaulle's vision of Europe and the world." [1]

Kennedy had come to office predicting (correctly) that his foreign-policy efforts in the Atlantic area would depend on his relations with de Gaulle. Now, as 1962 began, he saw Franco-American relations disintegrating and, in the background, a still acute Berlin problem and worsening relations with Adenauer as well. In probing the Soviet position on Berlin, he needed the support of his allies—Great Britain, France, and Germany. De Gaulle, for whom, as we have seen, the Berlin crisis was an opportunity, busily exploited the weak spots in everyone's position: with Macmillan, he pointed to the "realities" of the German problem and outlined a softer stand than even London would accept; with Adenauer, he probed the ambiguities in the Anglo-Saxon position and warned of a sellout. Although his tough public position on Berlin was not matched by support for the tough military contingency planning pressed by Washington, his arguments fully persuaded Adenauer, whose Anglo-Saxon phobia had become obsessive.

Some in Paris can recall that when Pierre Mendès-France traveled to Baden-Baden as Prime Minister in January 1955 he was subjected by Adenauer to an attack on his foreign policy delivered in the bluntest of terms; the complaint was that Mendès was not cooperating sufficiently with the Americans, who, after all, must "lead the West." In February 1962, seven years later, de Gaulle made the same trek and listened to Adenauer deliver a blistering attack on American leadership; de Gaulle, it may be recorded, "opened like a flower."

He and Kennedy were on a collision course. De Gaulle understood this—it was, after all, his destiny—but Kennedy did not, although he perhaps had begun to sense the scope of their differences and de Gaulle's unbending hostility to any notion or proposition that bore Anglo-Saxon fingerprints. The contrast was arresting: Kennedy, burdened with responsibility, seeking to inject some stability into a chaotic world, partly by reconciling somewhat contradictory propositions such as Atlantic cohesion and European integration on the one hand and centralized control of nuclear weapons on the other; de Gaulle, playing on the contradictions, turning instability to his own advantage, whittling away at the Alliance by withdrawing sea and air support from NATO, and silently preparing implacable resistance both to the notion of integration and to British membership in the Common Market. Kennedy and Macmillan were fixing their goals, if none too clearly; de Gaulle set himself squarely in their path. He would destroy their hopes with what one of his ministers has called "the explosive liberating force of his solutions."

Despite the apparent collapse of communications the year 1962 was the most eventful in de Gaulle's relations with the Anglo-Saxons. It included two memorable meetings with Macmillan and the re-emergence of strategy as an issue. And, of higher importance, that eternal nonquestion of aiding France's nuclear-weapons program was posed, not once but twice, each time in its sharpest form to date. For habitués of the theater of international politics, it was a good year, offering, *inter alia*, the greatest Anglo-American crisis in memory and the Cuban missile affair, the nuclear confrontation that perhaps had to happen once. But for de Gaulle, it was a decidedly mixed year. On the plus side, his hands were to be freed by a settlement in Algeria and a political success at home. On the negative side, diplomatic initiatives rested entirely with the Anglo-Saxons. Kennedy, after all, was dealing alone with Moscow; perhaps even worse, he was making a pernicious effort, in de Gaulle's view, to consecrate American dominance of Western Europe. Kennedy's "grand design" would gain plausibility by the passage of a sweeping and liberal Trade Expansion Act. And Macmillan, preparing Britain for entry into Europe, was busily doing what he did best—maneuvering his party and constituencies behind the application, re-forming his cabinet to the same end, and disarming Commonwealth opposition. Much worse for de Gaulle, the Cuban missile crisis was to solemnize Kennedy's pre-eminence among world statesmen and clear the way for a Washington-Moscow dialogue.

In early 1962 de Gaulle began returning the bulk of his Algerian army to the *métropole;* he would not reassign them to NATO, from whose clutches—always more hypothetical than real—he had already withdrawn the French fleet. Then, in March, at precisely the moment when de Gaulle's negotiating team was settling the Algerian war at Evian, the nuclear issue arose.

The Kennedy Administration was firmly opposed to nuclear proliferation, and more sensitive to the issue—at least in a declaratory sense—than its predecessor. But Kennedy was beset with the chronic balance-of-payments deficit he had inherited, a large part of it traceable to America's overseas military expenditures. Kennedy had complicated the problem somewhat by (justly) revoking Eisenhower's ban on dependents of American military personnel stationed in Europe. Other, more rational measures were sought to stem the flow of dollars, and Robert McNamara was already trying to "offset": that is, to offset the dollar cost of deploying American military forces in

Europe with sales of military equipment. At the end of 1961 he had obtained a commitment from the West Germans—specifically from Defense Minister Strauss—to buy annually $700,-000,000 worth of military hardware, over and above normal purchases, from the American shelf. This was considered a great breakthrough. (A somewhat similar offset initiative taken by the Eisenhower Administration in its waning days had been rejected by the Germans.) The agreement was for two years and would later be extended into 1967. An agreement with Italy fell into place, and Great Britain soon began to spend progressively larger sums on American hardware—probably too much in terms of the pressure this put on her own international account. France was the last of the big markets. Contact between McNamara and Pierre Messmer, France's Defense Minister, had been established; Messmer, in fact, had agreed at the end of 1961 to buy $50,000,000 worth of American hardware that would normally have been procured elsewhere.

This was a beginning, but Washington was thinking in grander terms. A new shift in American strategic thinking was about to be formalized into doctrine. Its thrust in Europe, where the balance of power was centered, was to be on qualitative and quantitative improvements in non-nuclear forces, so as to give the United States the broadest possible range of military options. France's battle-hardened Algerian army would admirably fit this strategic design; it was, by any military measure, an important asset; in NATO, it would reduce the pressure on American forces as well as the growing dependence on West German units. Numerous elements in the Pentagon, civilian and uniformed, were determined to find some means of overcoming de Gaulle's reluctance to assign these units to NATO.

Put briefly then, most of the key Washington agencies were looking hard at the alluring French military market and the returning French hoplites. Also, a few skeptical souls in Washington and London by now suspected that de Gaulle's hard line on Berlin camouflaged his unsuccessful earlier efforts to make a private deal with Khrushchev that would have softened his line on East Germany.* This perception of de Gaulle's penchant for the double game may have fortified the resolve to anchor France more securely to the Western Alliance. But how? With what means might de Gaulle's cooperation be purchased? The apparently self-evident answer—to remove the prohibition on aiding France's strategic-weapons program—was an illusion. De Gaulle could not be purchased at any price, as Kennedy would discover. His Administration would try even harder than Eisenhower's before it learned that no deal was possible with de Gaulle; that viewed from the Élysée, any joint arrangement with the Anglo-Saxons was tantamount to submission. Not until France had returned to the first rank among world powers— until she could deploy *credible* strategic forces of her own— could she even contemplate joint nuclear targeting. For the time being, nothing was possible.

Kennedy was deeply ambivalent about the General. To the historian in him, de Gaulle's brooding presence dignified the present and linked great events of the twentieth century; the ending of the war in Algeria further dramatized the legendary figure. But political instinct and judgment warned him to be careful. By March 1962 Kennedy's ambivalence toward de Gaulle had found strong expression in his Administration, all of whose senior officials, excepting Rusk, had entered office pro-Gaullist. General Maxwell Taylor, Chairman of the

---

* On January 8, 1962, C. L. Sulzberger, always reliably informed about these matters, wrote in *The New York Times* that for the first time the Kennedy Administration was "beginning to question the sincerity of de Gaulle's refusal to participate in negotiations with Russia. The argument ran: 'If you really mean business about going to war on Berlin, the first thing is to have contact with your enemy so that we, as well as you, will know you mean business.' Does de Gaulle's refusal even to have contact indicate a serious intention to go to war if necessary? We are serious and know what we must do. Is de Gaulle serious? . . . And the Americans are adding up previously muted doubts. . . . Is France's NATO obstinacy part of some private Russian deal aimed at settling Algeria?"

Joint Chiefs of Staff, had just returned from Paris, apparently convinced by French defense officials that if the United States lifted the embargo on aid to France's strategic-weapons program, de Gaulle's government would be more cooperative on NATO matters. Military politics, always close to the surface of Franco-American relations, began to assert a commanding influence.

Taylor felt that it was nonsense to continue the prohibition. He was supported by the Under Secretary of Defense, Roswell Gilpatric, and by Assistant Secretary Nitze. With the Algerian incubus gone, they argued, de Gaulle would doubtless be willing to resume normal participation in NATO if he got something in return. It was a perfectly plausible calculation, whatever might have gone before.

Looking back, Nitze says that it was necessary to "smoke out the French" on NATO; that he had doubted that de Gaulle's cooperation could be obtained at any price, but that it was essential to prove this. Thus, he actively supported an initiative that would achieve this purpose. Rightly or wrongly, Nitze was regarded by numerous colleagues as among the strongest advocates of assistance to the French military program. One of them recalls that Nitze consistently pressed for help for France in order to make her less independent and to promote prospects for some kind of interallied nuclear arrangements. Again, viewed objectively, it was a reasonable position.

During his end-of-the-year meeting in Washington with McNamara, Messmer had offered to send his armaments team to explore the possibility of additional French purchases from the United States. But first, the head of military sales agreements in the Pentagon, Henry Kuss, together with a Treasury representative, went to Paris to work out the outlines of an offset arrangement similar to that which had been reached with the West Germans. These discussions led to an agreement that General Gaston Lavaud, director of French military procurement, would go to Washington for higher-level talks. A letter of invitation to Lavaud was drafted for Gilpatric's signature and approved by McNamara. Critics in the State Department, where the letter was not cleared (although a copy was of course referred to Bundy at the White House), say that it amounted to an invitation to the French to come to Washington with a "shopping list."

The Americans were hoping for the greatest possible dollar-volume sale, confined as far as possible to items that would not significantly affect France's strategic-weapons program. The French interest was precisely the reverse. They were not prepared to spend a lot of money, but they wanted to use the opening to obtain items related to the most advanced American systems and designs. Neither Lavaud nor anyone else was authorized to go beyond a military-sales agreement. De Gaulle's government had the task of somehow gaining access to American weapons technology without becoming a *demandeur* and without paying the political price that Washington could be expected to attach.

The French "list," when it arrived, caused a good deal of commotion in Washington. The Pentagon had somehow expected that basic conventional items, unrelated to nuclear weapons or delivery systems, would dominate; and they were thinking in terms of several hundred million dollars. In fact, the French list priced out at about $50,000,000 and treated the great panoply of American weapons systems and technology like a smörgåsbord. "They wanted samples of this and samples of that—samples which in effect embodied hundreds of millions of dollars in research and development," one Pentagon official said. Broadly speaking, the French wanted items of a highly specialized and advanced nature in naval, aircraft, and missile technology. They wanted star-tracker systems, long-range sonar, valve-control technology for nuclear submarines, inertial-guidance parts and data, avionics, and so on. They showed no interest in buying complete weapons systems, only parts and data that could simplify and shorten their own programs.

The Pentagon reviewed the list with other agencies, including the State Department, where it set off a squall, as one high Defense Department official put it. Lavaud arrived and, according to Nitze, was asked to relate the question of purchases to political matters. Would France play her role within NATO or not? Lavaud replied that he was not authorized to discuss such matters.

Whatever else was said or left unsaid, great pressure developed to sell the French a good part of what they were asking, even though neither Lavaud nor his colleague from the Ministry of Finance, according to Kuss, ever indicated that France would be willing to spend any more money than originally contemplated.

Not much of this affair found its way into the press, but *The New York Times* carried a brief article from Paris after the matter had been settled; it surmised that the list included nuclear-submarine data, equipment for a gaseous-diffusion plant, guidance systems, missile parts, and propellants. (A high Defense Department official has said this report is accurate.) The source for this article was almost certainly the American Embassy in Paris; the Ambassador, General Gavin, was another leading advocate of helping de Gaulle. The article concluded that the eventual turndown of the Lavaud mission caused "considerable anger" in Paris.[2]

Lavaud's visit roughly coincided with Kennedy's celebrated remark during his March 22 press conference that, "Personally, I am haunted by the feeling that by 1970, unless we are successful, there may be ten nuclear powers instead of four, and by 1975, fifteen or twenty." At about this same time the State Department drew a bead on the Lavaud mission. A copy of Gilpatric's original letter was sent over from the White

House, together with a memorandum requesting the Department's comments on a number of questions, which, boiled down, asked the following: What would the United States obtain in return from this departure from its antiproliferation policy? More specifically, could this alter General de Gaulle's attitude toward NATO and other matters affecting collective security? The Assistant Secretary of State for European Affairs, Foy Kohler, hastily assembled a small group representing the Regional Affairs section of his bureau and the Policy Planning Council. This group prepared a reply which argued forcibly that the United States would obtain nothing in return for abandoning the prohibition. The State Department case stemmed from its by now traditional view that Washington should not do for Paris what it was not prepared to do eventually for Bonn. And it was a consistent position. A majority of State's key officials all along the line were opposed to helping *anyone's* nuclear-weapons program, including Britain's, and this policy, as we have seen, had scattered support throughout the government, especially among certain civilians in the Pentagon.

Great Britain, with the only clear and current claim to new membership in the nuclear club, had a strike force consisting of 180 long-range bombers rapidly approaching obsolescence. As Albert Wohlstetter, then of the RAND Corporation, had written a year earlier: "England's cancellation of its costly program for the Blue Streak missile marked the conscious transition from a hopefully 'independent deterrent' to the much less ambitious 'independent contribution to the deterrent.' " [3] It seemed to many that the awful problem of nuclear sharing might become more manageable if the British should eventually be obliged either to opt out of the nuclear club or to put their nuclear assets into a jointly controlled NATO force in which non-nuclear European countries would have some participation. To give nuclear help to France would be to sow the seeds of an eventual West German claim for the same aid, just as aiding Britain had given substance to the French claim.

The Lavaud affair reached its denouement toward mid-April. A meeting chaired by Bundy was held in the White House Situation Room. All of the national-security agencies were represented by senior officials, and each, excepting the State Department, supported the initiative to sell de Gaulle the embargoed hardware. Even while serving in the State Department under Eisenhower, Dillon had advocated nuclear aid to France; in his current position as Secretary of the Treasury it was most unlikely that he would be any less in favor of the idea. John McCone, Director of the CIA, had pressed for the U-235 agreement while serving as Atomic Energy Commissioner; McCone's well-known Francophilia survived his passage to the CIA, which, as noted before, had formally withdrawn its traditional reservation about French security (even if the Joint Atomic Energy Committee perhaps had not). McNamara, who bore the "offset" responsibility, favored the sales agreement with France, although with perhaps less brio than his senior associates Gilpatric and Nitze. General Taylor and the other Joint Chiefs did, too. Probably the subtlest position was Bundy's. On every side he is described as having favored the initiative, but only on balance. Doubtless the financial argument impressed him less than the political one, although, like Rusk and unlike some of the others, Bundy had a clear appreciation of the political dangers. He did not take a position as such on the immediate issue of whether to crown General Lavaud's mission with success. His role, as he conceived it, was to provide the President with the clearest possible view of the available options and their implications.

Bundy and the President normally took a pragmatic view of these problems as they arose, although they were necessarily and deeply preoccupied by the nuclear riddle. Some weeks earlier, on February 16, Bundy had begun a speech at Yale University by saying, "An astonishing number of the great issues of international affairs turn on the way men see and value nuclear weapons." Like the President, Bundy was leery of broad schemes intended to discourage the British and French from trying to be independent nuclear powers, however laudable he may have found the purpose. Like the President, he distrusted doctrinal argument.

Britain was a nuclear power and not likely to give this up when France was also establishing a claim and moving as rapidly as possible. France could not be ignored; one day it would be essential, whether in political or strategic terms, to link French nuclear forces as tightly as possible with America's and Britain's. The problem of a West German claim would thus require some solution other than a ban on aid to France. In any case, whatever the merit of the State Department's concern, the question of a West German nuclear role was not current. The French problem was. Such was the thinking of quite a number of what might be called traditionalists in the government, many of whom were officials in the State Department with "country" responsibilities, or intelligence specialists.

Kennedy eventually decided against the senior officials of his Administration save Rusk; the conventional State Department argument had persuaded him; the so-called Kohler Paper was adopted as American nuclear policy with regard to France. The issue had turned on whether helping de Gaulle would promote the stability and coherence of the NATO Alliance by moderating French policy. In April 1962 Kennedy felt compelled to answer the question in the negative. A few days later, on April 18, he seemed to formalize the decision in a news conference:

Q. There are reports that some of your top military advisers are urging the U.S. to help France with the development of its nuclear striking force.

A. . . . The policy of the United States, of course, continues
to be that of being very reluctant to see the proliferation of
nuclear weapons. We are attempting to, in our disarmament
offers that we've made we are attempting to, and in my
speech last September before the United Nations I said that
I thought it would be regrettable if nuclear weapons prolif-
erated or spread. So that our policy continues on that basis,
and will continue unless we feel that security requirements
suggest a change.

Kennedy seemed to be bolting the door on further exceptions
to the stated American position. But the question of aiding
France was far from closed. Remarkably, the official policy
started to melt away almost immediately upon its reaffirmation.
What happened offers a nice insight into the capricious manner in which a big government, especially one as large as that
of the United States, conducts its business.

In early May McNamara and Rusk were in Athens for the
spring meeting of NATO Ministers. The duality of Washington's French policy suddenly—crazily—swam to the surface.
McNamara, with Kennedy's approval, had given himself the
task of explaining America's new strategic doctrine of "controlled response" to his European colleagues. Most of them
were unsympathetic, in many cases because they doubted the
strategy, in others because it was a Pentagon–RAND Corporation concept entirely innocent of European thinking or participation. The emphasis on non-nuclear options at a time when
the Soviet Union had developed nuclear weapons capable of
reaching the United States as well as Western Europe provoked
considerable unease. The credibility of the American commitment to defend Europe with whatever necessary means risked
being compromised. McNamara sought to reassure the Europeans by taking them over the very ground that had convinced
him and his colleagues that a strategy based on central control

of nuclear weapons and non-nuclear options offered the only means of making the use of such weapons even remotely plausible.

Kennedy had told McNamara to open the book and "show them the hardware." That is what McNamara did. He flatly committed the United States to maintaining nuclear weapons in Europe for the defense of Europe. He dwelt on the criteria and procedures which would determine the use of nuclear weapons, citing the will and determination in Washington to employ if it had to, under carefully controlled conditions, nuclear weapons selectively against Soviet military targets, while holding in reserve the retaliatory capacity to devastate Soviet cities. It was —is—a strategy designed to compel restraint on the other side.

For the first time, really, it was explained to Europeans with chilly precision that American strategic weapons were sufficient to defend Europe and the United States, that independent European deterrents were not only unnecessary but dangerous. How could American strategic forces, trying to eliminate a selected list of Soviet military targets, induce restraint upon the Soviet leadership if some uncoordinated European nuclear force was trying at the same time to "take out" one or more Soviet cities? (The American strategy was known for a time as the "no-cities" strategy; France's so-called *force de dissuasion* is a frankly anticity weapon.)

A colleague of McNamara and chronicler of his policy, Professor William Kauffman, has written: "The task he set himself (in Athens) was a burdensome one, perhaps too heavy for a single speech to bear. . . . By all accounts he held his audience enthralled for nearly an hour." [4] "Enthralled" they were, although some, particularly among the French, were hardly happy at being told that there was virtually no acceptable alternative to dependence on Washington for their ultimate security.

But the French were, or should have been, speedily mollified.

Having just completed his virtuoso performance on strategy and the virtues of centralized control, and on only a few minutes' reflection, McNamara abruptly agreed to sell France a squadron of KC-135 jet tankers. This was a matter that had been discussed with the French primarily at a low diplomatic level and quite apart from the Lavaud mission. It had strong backing from the American Embassy in Paris, and Boeing Aircraft, the manufacturer of the jet tankers, was also pushing hard for the sale. Yet the sale would seem to collide directly with Kennedy's explicit ban on aid of a strategic nature to France. Advocates argued that the aircraft would not affect de Gaulle's advanced-weapons programs and technically that was true. Nonetheless, it was these American jet tankers, and nothing else, which gave the French nuclear strike force such marginal plausibility as it presently has; without these aerial refueling stations de Gaulle's Mirage-IV bombers would scarcely penetrate the eastern shores of the Mediterranean.

The prospect of selling the tankers naturally aroused opposition in Washington. A story was floated that the White House had refused to sell the aircraft to France. Advocates of the sale then elicited a White House denial of the story, which in turn cleared the path for McNamara's approval of the deal. Rusk, who was also at Athens, did nothing to oppose McNamara's decision, although it was one about which even members of the latter's own civilian staff had deep reservations. The sale of the KC-135s became the first in a series of gestures by the Kennedy Administration which undermined the strong position taken only weeks earlier.

And even that decision had rested on shakier ground than many who participated might have thought. One among them, for example, recalls going to Paris and raising the matter again with two French civil servants with access to the Élysée.* It was, he says, a matter of putting the question again to de

* I am unable to find confirmation of this recollection on the French side.

Gaulle: if France's NATO position were modified, the United States might withdraw its ban on certain of the export licenses of special importance to the French strategic-weapons program. He recalls that one of the two civil servants talked to de Gaulle and got nowhere. This same American official, together with a still more important colleague, subsequently raised the matter yet again with Ambassador Alphand just as he was planning to return to France for the summer holidays. Whatever Alphand may have said or done, de Gaulle's attitude remained unchanged.

This curious sequence of events had proved once again that within the American government a skillful clutch of bureaucrats (in this case the so-called regionalists of the State Department) could block a major initiative, however potent its backing (and this group had been turning aside such initiatives for years), and in turn be outmaneuvered, especially when the balance of payments was at issue. Together, the two episodes dramatized the sharply conflicting tendencies within the Administration regarding France, as well as Kennedy's vulnerability to both.

Oddly enough, de Gaulle and Kennedy were publicly proclaiming their differences over Berlin within a few days of the jet-tanker sale. On May 15, at a press conference, de Gaulle spoke derisively of the "soundings" on Berlin that Washington was taking in Moscow. Kennedy replied tersely in a press conference of his own two days later: "We wish to have some voice in events in Berlin because if the moment of truth comes it is the United States which is expected to take the very vigorous action which could involve our security as well as that of Western Europe."

De Gaulle's press conference, the first after the conclusion of a peace in Algeria, was a romp across the terrain where he was happiest: European politics; the German problem; the Atlantic Alliance; the Geneva disarmament conference; Franco-African relations—nothing on domestic affairs. It was an indulgence, a form of *volupté*; it was as if a Shakespearean actor, having been condemned to years of idleness and then to uncongenial, mediocre drama, at last had the occasion to declaim the great passages from the tragedies.

By mocking European integration, he provoked the resignation *en bloc* of those of his Christian Democratic ministers, each a good "European," who had served the Fourth Republic.

> Dante, Goethe, Chateaubriand belong to all of Europe to the extent that they were respectively and eminently Italian, German, and French. They would not have served Europe very well if they had been stateless or if they had thought and written in some kind of integrated Esperanto or Volapuk. . . . I have already said, and I repeat, that at the present time there cannot be any other Europe than a Europe of states, apart, of course, from myths, stories, and parades. . . . In this "integrated" Europe, as they call it, there would perhaps be no policy at all. . . . But then, perhaps, this world would follow the lead of some outsider who did have a policy. There would perhaps be a federator, but the federator would not be European. . . . Thus, let us place reality at the base of the edifice and, when we have completed the work, that will be the time for us to lull ourselves to sleep with the tales of "The Thousand and One Nights."

A question on NATO drew a warning that "as regards the defense of France, everything is now in question," because the United States and the Soviet Union are "capable of . . . destroying each other."

> It is not certain that they will take this risk. . . . A French atomic deterrent is coming into existence . . . is going to grow continuously . . . and will completely change the conditions of our own defense, of our intervention in faraway lands, and of the contribution we can make to the safe being of our allies. . . . The gradual return of our military forces from Algeria is

enabling us to acquire a modernized army—an army which is not, I daresay, destined to play a separate or isolated role but which must and can play a role that would be France's own.

This press conference marked a moratorium on one of de Gaulle's favorite constructions, "Europe from the Atlantic to the Urals." For the next three years he was to seek to build his French-led Europe on a Franco-German axis, and his return to the phrase on February 4, 1965, signaled a dramatic shift in the application of his policy.

Two days later Kennedy replied in precise, brisk terms:

> We do not believe in a series of national deterrents. We believe that the NATO deterrent, to which the United States has committed itself so heavily, provides very adequate protection. Once you begin, nation after nation, beginning to develop its own deterrent . . . it seems to me that you are moving into an increasingly dangerous situation. . . . That, however, is a decision for the French. If they choose to go ahead, of course they will go ahead. . . . We do not agree.

He added:

> However difficult becomes this dialogue with General de Gaulle over what I would call the Atlantic Community and the respective roles of each country within it, I would think it would be a far more difficult situation if General de Gaulle were not as stalwart in his defense of the West.

But the real state of affairs was perhaps best revealed when Kennedy, asked if he would see de Gaulle again, said he was not sure there "would be any greater agreement if we met."

A few days earlier André Malraux, Minister of Culture, had visited Washington, and the Kennedys had treated the visit with all the panache of a great event. At the White House dinner honoring this romantic figure and philosopher of Gaullism, Kennedy's after-dinner toast was a model of taste and sense of occasion:

A good deal has been written . . . about the difficulties that have occasionally come up between the President of the United States and General de Gaulle. . . . I know that there are sometimes difficulties . . . but I hope that those who live in both our countries realize how fortunate we are in the last two decades to be associated in the great effort with him. And we are glad to have Mr. Malraux and Madame Malraux here because we believe that they will go back to France and say a kind word for the United States—and its President.[5]

De Gaulle sparred with his adversaries during most of 1962. But, except during a few scattered moments, like the May 17 press conference, the center stage was denied him. For in both Washington and London, the goal of "Atlantic partnership" appeared to join coherent public policy with uncommonly large vision. As Kennedy described it in Philadelphia on July 4, the two pillars of Atlantic partnership, Europe and America, would be, if not exactly equal in power, securely linked by joint political, economic, and social purposes.

I will say here and now, on this Day of Independence, that the United States will be ready for a Declaration of Interdependence, that we will be prepared to discuss with a united Europe the ways and means of forming a concrete Atlantic partnership, a mutually beneficial partnership between the new union now emerging in Europe and the old American union founded here 175 years ago.

The scope of the Independence Day speech, while it excited Europe's imagination, surprised some members of Kennedy's own Administration, certainly the Department of State, where all or most of the officials concerned first read it in their morning newspapers. It had been a White House affair, and given Kennedy's suspicion of large designs and untested political assumptions like European unity, somewhat unexpected.

De Gaulle had earlier in the year defined France's obligation "to build Western Europe into an organized union of states, so that gradually there may be established on both sides of the Rhine, of the Alps and perhaps of the Channel, the most powerful, prosperous and influential political, economic, cultural and military complex in the world."

This wasn't so bad—the reference to the Channel was even encouraging. (Washington's chief interest, after all, was in British participation in the European Community, not as an American Trojan horse, but as a competing and moderating political presence.) But actually, de Gaulle was trying to organize the *"rassemblement des vieux pays autour de moi"* that he had spoken of privately and, of course, adumbrated in his memoirs. The so-called Fouchet Plan negotiations for political union of the six EEC members were soon to collapse after de Gaulle diluted the working group's proposals, already weighted on the French side of the argument and largely drafted in his own Foreign Ministry. He then told the professionals in the Quai d'Orsay that if he couldn't make Europe *"à six,"* he would make Europe *"à deux"* (with Germany). His hopes were probably not high, but until the winter of 1964–1965 he would never cease working at it. And it was no part of his purpose to give Britain a European vocation.

Macmillan's Washington visit of April 27–29 was a curtain raiser to the drama of this tumultuous year. To Kennedy's welcoming remarks, he replied:

> These meetings which we have had [this was the fifth] are becoming not just occasional but I am happy to say, a normal practice, and although they excite sometimes a certain interest in the press, as to what it is exactly that we are going to do, we do, as you say, Mr. President, generally find something to do which may be useful. . . . The real truth of it is . . . there is something quite different in being able just to talk over problems, simply, face to face, in an informal manner. Perhaps it is that that is the very basis of the friendship, partnership, alliance—call it what you will—between your country and mine.[6]

Macmillan was talking about the so-called "special relationship" between America and Britain. Now if the first thing to be said about the special relationship is that it exists, the second is that it has steadily declined in recent years. And it is mildly paradoxical that the decline increased considerably in the Kennedy years. Macmillan and Kennedy had, after all, developed a degree of rapport rarely found between political chiefs. The British Ambassador in Washington, David Ormsby-Gore, had been a friend of Kennedy's since boyhood; his assignment had been requested by the President. "Kennedy told friends that, *next to David Ormsby-Gore*, Bundy was the brightest man he had ever known" [7] (italics added). Sorensen has written: "The Ambassador knew both the President and the Prime Minister [to whom he was related by marriage] so well that he was ideally equipped to interpret or even predict each one's reactions to the other's proposals. . . . The President often consulted with or confided in the British Ambassador as he would a member of his own staff. 'I trust David as I would my own Cabinet,' he said." [8] This does not overstate the case. Indeed, Ormsby-Gore was closer to the President than any member of the Administration except Robert Kennedy, nor was there any mystery about this.* It was generally understood, and Ormsby-Gore, a gifted and highly motivated man, had the respect of "the town."

---

* The closeness of Ormsby-Gore to the President, and the value put on his opinions and advice, is sharply illustrated in Robert Kennedy's account of finding the Ambassador with his brother on the evening of October 23, at the height of the Cuban missile crisis: "I left the Russian Embassy [he had just had a long conversation with Ambassador Dobrynin] around 10:15 P.M. and went back to the White House. I found the President with Ambassador David Ormsby-Gore (Lord Harlech) of Great Britain, an old friend whom he trusted implicitly. I related the conversation to both of them. . . . Ambassador Ormsby-Gore expressed concern that the line of interception for the quarantine had been extended 800 miles. This would mean a probable interception within a very few hours after it was put into effect. 'Why not give them more time,' he said, 'to analyze their position?' The 800 miles had been fixed by the Navy to stay outside the range of some of the MIG fighters in Cuba. The President called McNamara and shortened it to 500 miles." [9]

Still, he was the British Ambassador, in a period when the difference between the real power of Britain and of the United States was growing rapidly, which in fact largely accounts for the decline in the special quality of the relationship. Washington was less and less inclined to consult London, while London had become progressively less responsive to American concerns. In short, the relationship had become too one-sided.

Whether seen from the White House or from Capitol Hill, a special relationship with Britain—even a nuclear partnership —was a normal, possibly even reassuring, state of affairs. It arose from the traditional American view of imperial Britain, politically stable (and, thus, unique in Europe) and exercising her traditional and unique influence in parts of the tumultuous less-developed world. By 1962 this attitude had lost much of its force. For a number of reasons the Kennedy Administration was less vulnerable to British influence than its predecessor. Many of the personal associations, political and military, dating to the war, had been destroyed by death or succession. British military staff had exercised considerable influence on American policy within NATO, primarily because they were better at this sort of thing than their American colleagues. But with the coming of McNamara and the stress not just on central control in Washington but on *civilian* control, this began to change.

Another striking change was also starting to have effect. Years of experience with nuclear weapons and of guaranteeing the security of the Western world affected America's view of itself. For one thing, Americans were beginning to lose their sense of cultural inferiority. For another, a new managerial type was appearing, who, unlike his counterpart in Whitehall, was the product less of the traditional, humanistic culture than of this culture fused with a more purely American experience —especially her growing technological culture. This American, who moved freely around a circuit that included the universities, the Pentagon, and the glamour industries of the postwar years, was predictably less impressed with traditional attitudes and political values upon which so much of policy was based.

For Britain now to turn to the EEC was to acknowledge, first of all, that her role lay less in playing Greece to America's Rome, as Macmillan liked to put it in private conversation, than as political makeweight in Western Europe. To join Europe would not mean abandoning an interlocutory relationship with Washington. Instead it could mean that the privileged bilateral link would be subsumed by a more mature relationship between America and Western Europe, in which Britain's experience and improved position would again permit her to influence large events.

A curiosity of the special relationship is that differences between the two capitals follow a normal pattern; put differently, Anglo-American disagreements are as frequent and as difficult to "fix" as disagreements between, say, Washington and Bonn, or London and Ankara. But however far apart the two capitals might be on a given matter, consultation has normally been intimate and steady. The Suez crisis of 1956 was a notable exception; 1962 would record others.

Ormsby-Gore's presence in Washington and the growing friendship of Kennedy and Macmillan probably prevented the special relationship from collapsing altogether in 1962. What was neither clear nor even understood on the American side is that the character of the relationship—to the degree that it relied on frank and easy communication—had become a mockery of the word "special." For this, the larger responsibility rested with the British. Macmillan was betting heavily on his bid to enter the Common Market, and he was determined to play his hand guardedly. (In the British government, this was not so difficult; on any matter concerning nuclear weapons, for example, only a handful of people were involved—the Prime Minister and the ministers in the Cabinet Defence Committee, their permanent undersecretaries, a few parliamentary private secretaries and specialists. Contrast this with the American government bureaucracy, where internal pressures were such that relatively few issues, however sensitive, could be kept secret for long; add to that the need to keep Congress informed. It is not that Washington is more direct and open than other Western capitals; it is simply "leakier.")

Berlin, a summit conference, NATO force levels—these were agenda items in the Washington meeting, but the key item was Britain's entry into the EEC. Kennedy said that British membership was a political matter to which his Administration attached great importance. Macmillan needed no convincing. The political argument was central to his own thinking; moreover, his talk with de Gaulle at Birch Grove seemed to show that Britain would have to move quite a distance to satisfy the Élysée's "political" requirements. Macmillan was now preparing to move quite a distance.

Of the April meeting, Sorensen wrote:

> They did not always see eye to eye. Macmillan was more eager for summit conferences with Khrushchev and less eager to prepare for war at West Berlin. He was not sure whether his government could go along with American plans for NATO conventional forces and Kennedy knew his government couldn't go along with Great Britain's recognition of Red China. From time to time, the President had to discourage the Prime Minister's temptation to play the role of peacemaker between East and West, and at least once Macmillan was briefly but violently angry.[10]

Throughout these months the Kennedy Administration had been keeping Britain fully informed of any advanced-weapons negotiations, however unpromising, it may have contemplated with the French.* Not so Macmillan. Just a few weeks away from presenting de Gaulle with an important initiative bearing on Europe's nuclear and non-nuclear defense, he said nothing about it to Kennedy. Neither then nor later was anyone in the American government told of what Macmillan was planning, although the joint agreements on which Anglo-American nuclear cooperation is based would eventually have been affected by it.

A few days after returning to London Macmillan announced that he would see de Gaulle at the Château de Champs on June 2–3, a meeting for which he had taken the initiative. The press was told that Britain wanted, first, to clear up the difficulties arising from France's impression that there was an Anglo-Saxon *directoire* in NATO, and second, to obtain some clarification of de Gaulle's attitude toward the British application to the Common Market.

At Birch Grove, as has been noted, Macmillan had chosen to ignore de Gaulle's negative comments and tone and had relied instead on his very general assurance that in the end all the problems would be solved. And he had taken careful note of de Gaulle's emphasis on defense, which seemed to suggest that Britain's eligibility for a European role would depend upon her reorienting her defense arrangements toward Europe. Macmillan was prepared to go a good part of the way. A year or so earlier he had discussed with Kennedy the idea of establishing a closer military connection with de Gaulle. To the degree that this might have involved exchanges of nuclear-weapons data or material—specifically forbidden by the Anglo-American nuclear agreement—Kennedy was negative. But now the climate had changed—somewhat. Kennedy wanted Britain in the Common Market, and the notion of an eventual European nuclear force based on a Franco-British *entente nucléaire* was gaining

---

* Technically, Britain could have objected to these, had they come to anything, under the Anglo-American nuclear agreements.

respectability, if not adherents, in Washington. But what Macmillan envisaged almost certainly more nearly resembled de Gaulle's old tridirectorate proposition than an integrated European command and control structure, even though Kennedy was by now disenchanted with the notion of a triangular arrangement, and de Gaulle never had looked upon it as a serious matter.

Macmillan's preparations for the meeting with de Gaulle were complex and subtle. His strategic ploy was to disavow any intention of playing the high card of nuclear cooperation with France. Thus, on May 4, *Le Monde*'s London correspondent reported (giving as his source "officials close to the Prime Minister"): "The British Government does not envisage for the moment any 'nuclear arrangement' with France with a view to facilitating entry of Great Britain into the E.E.C." A number of similar stories were to appear, some of them inspired by the Foreign Office. The defense initiative had already traveled its course through the Whitehall machinery, with the Ministry of Defence favoring it; the Foreign Office argued that although it would not work, it was perhaps on balance a useful ploy. This skepticism was deepened by a report from the Paris Embassy in mid-May warning that de Gaulle might terminate the negotiations in Brussels with a French veto. This was the first of several such warnings from Paris, none of them ever communicated to the Americans, who right to the end took a bullish view of Britain's chances with the EEC.

France's strategy was laid down in the Quai d'Orsay—more precisely by Foreign Minister Couve de Murville and Olivier Wormser, Director for Economic and Financial Affairs. Wormser, now Governor of the Bank of France, is a highly respected figure who played a large part in the turbulent affairs of the early and mid-1960s. Although widely and justly known as an Anglophile, he was also an *ancien compagnon* of de Gaulle, a skillful executor of his policies, and highly suspicious of the integrationist notions of the "Monnet" Europeans.

The strategy, quite simply, was to exhaust Britain's patience, if not her will, by stretching out the negotiations to the limit and extracting concessions from Macmillan on every conceivable question, small or large. But this strategy would be jeopardized if de Gaulle's coldly hostile opposition to the British application became noticeable.

Georges Pompidou, who had replaced Michel Debré as Prime Minister in May, favored this stretch-out technique; certainly he was against opposing the British overtly—and for domestic political reasons. With the Algerian war ended, a number of political leaders, including some who had helped bring de Gaulle to power, would now feel free to try to topple him. And conservative political opinion, badly traumatized by the Algerian settlement, might play into their hands. Much of the French right and center-right had always considered de Gaulle excessively anti-Anglo-Saxon and dangerously vulnerable to the Communist bloc. Crucial legislative elections were scheduled for November; these would be preceded by a Constitutional referendum on election of the French President by universal suffrage. This was no time for boat-rocking. De Gaulle apparently agreed.

Earlier, de Gaulle had tended to doubt that Great Britain would dilute her privileged American and Commonwealth associations by joining Europe. But the British attitude, as revealed by the tone and pace of the Brussels negotiations together with Macmillan's request for the meeting at Champs, showed disturbing strength of purpose. And if further evidence was needed, it was delivered by de Gaulle's Ambassador in London on the eve of the conference.

Geoffroy de Courcel was the most senior of Gaullists in length of service, having come with de Gaulle to London in

June 1940 as his aide-de-camp. Not long after de Gaulle's return to power in 1958 Courcel became Chief of Staff at the Élysée Palace, a post of immense importance which he held until mid-February 1962, when he was sent to London and replaced at the Élysée by Étienne Burin des Roziers. Courcel, then, was an Ambassador of some consequence and was treated as such by the British—that is, until it was later discovered that, like all of de Gaulle's ambassadors and most ministers, he had no influence and was no better informed about French policy than anyone else.

On the eve of the Champs meeting, after a scant two months in London, Courcel was summoned by the Prime Minister. Macmillan told him that he intended to take an important defense initiative in his conversation with General de Gaulle. He then proceeded to read to Courcel a short paper that embodied the substance of what he was to propose; approved by the Cabinet Defence Committee, the paper covered both nuclear and non-nuclear defense and indicated that Britain would be prepared to Europeanize her defense arrangements.

Courcel, who was to attend the Champs talks, went immediately to Paris and reported to de Gaulle. He told de Gaulle that if the paper meant what it said, something new had entered the picture; this might be a real possibility. De Gaulle agreed but remained skeptical.

On June 2, the day the Champs talks began, *Le Monde* reported Macmillan's announcement that there would be no "nuclear bargaining between Britain and France." He was clearly following the time-honored custom of disavowing in advance what in fact was uppermost in his mind. Secretary of State Rusk had met twice that week with Ambassador Alphand, the reporter noted, and concluded: "It should be recalled that for the first time in months representatives of the United States, Great Britain, France, and Germany met in Washington in

order to harmonize their views on the 'soundings' on Berlin."
De Gaulle, for the moment, was on his best behavior.

The talks began in the late afternoon on Saturday, June 2.
Macmillan was accompanied by Zulueta, and de Gaulle by
Étienne Burin des Roziers and his interpreter, Andronikov.
Macmillan found at Champs a more secure de Gaulle than the
one he had entertained at Birch Grove—the difference being, of
course, the Algerian settlement. De Gaulle was rarely open in
conversation—his negotiating style (like Macmillan's) was
sibylline—but he was even cagier now. At Birch Grove he had
been hard, uncompromising, critical. Now there was more
nuance and shading, an apparent reluctance to commit France
in any direction or to disclose French intentions.

Macmillan declared the United Kingdom's acceptance of
both the Common Market's external tariff on industrial prod-
ucts, and its commercial and agricultural policies. After desultory conversation de Gaulle asked whether Great Britain could
carry out a policy that had been laid down primarily by France
and West Germany—in short, a European policy. Macmillan
answered with a lengthy statement in which he envisaged a
"double-headed" alliance, and concluded with some observa-
tions about the desire of young people to build Europe.

The next morning de Gaulle remarked that he could see that
the Prime Minister and the British government were determined to advance toward Europe. He went on to explain the
rationale for France's independent nuclear deterrent and posed
the strategic issue then beginning to divide NATO. This was an
opening for Macmillan, who proceeded to make a case for a
solid European organization and even used the phrase "two pillars" in postulating Europe's relationship with the United
States. It was ironic, he noted, that European federalists were
strongly committed to British membership in the Community,
while he himself was more attracted to French ideas about or-

ganizing Europe. De Gaulle did not bite at either of these lures, and the meeting was adjourned.

It was resumed briefly before lunch in a *réunion élargie*, with Pompidou, Couve de Murville, Courcel, Sir Pierson Dixon (at the time, British Ambassador in Paris), and Pierre Maillard, de Gaulle's diplomatic counselor, joining the talks. Again de Gaulle noted Britain's evolution toward Europe and implied that France and Britain were in the same "psychological" position on the European question (a concession to the British that committed him to nothing at all). Macmillan returned to his concept of "two pillars" and suggested that after Europe was created—after Britain became a part of it—political and defense questions could be taken up. A European army might be necessary and some sort of European nuclear deterrent as well. He noted the possibility that the American and Russian deterrent forces might be "too large" to be credible. Again de Gaulle did not respond, and the meeting adjourned shortly thereafter for lunch.

The same enlarged group met for the last time in the afternoon. This time Couve de Murville opened by noting that both Britain and France were excluded from the talks that Washington was conducting with Moscow. Pompidou then observed that the Americans were acting as emissaries to their own allies. De Gaulle, reversing the line he had taken at the end of the Birch Grove meeting, said he could no longer see any value in a tripartite heads-of-government meeting. He pursued Couve de Murville's point and cited Kennedy's independent style when he had met with Khrushchev in Vienna.

Macmillan listened to all this and observed finally that he liked the United States but that Americans were a volatile people and tended to become easily excited. De Gaulle disavowed any anti-American feelings, but the United States' leadership was not good, he said. He then voiced two rather disconnected thoughts: first, Britain was progressing in its evolution toward Europe; second, Adenauer's whole policy was founded on American military support and financial and economic strength. De Gaulle was suggesting, perhaps, in his cryptic way, that one European state, Britain, however close its American attachment, was moving in the right direction, while another state, West Germany, however hostile its current relations with Washington, was moving in the wrong one.

These complaints about American leadership and style may well have been an orchestrated attempt to draw Macmillan out on his view of the "special relationship." But this was incidental to the theme of the meeting: France's view of Britain's European credentials. De Gaulle had turned in a performance of immaculate ambiguity. As at Birch Grove, he had responded to Macmillan's urgent argument for speeding toward Europe as quickly as possible by observing that the train had not yet left the station.

And he had said nothing, literally nothing, in response to Macmillan's offer to put Britain's defense forces at the service of Europe. Macmillan raised the matter twice during the formal talks and again during a walk (their longest private walk together), when he tried to link Europe's defense with British membership in EEC and Europe's organization—and got nowhere. De Gaulle would talk only about himself and France, repeating that he would do all he could and then it would be up to others to follow in his footsteps. It was, of course, the same line he had taken during the walk in the Matignon garden in 1958. He would not be trapped.

Britain and France were in tacit agreement on only one point: the meeting must be presented as a success to the public. The French were determined to appear responsive and helpful. Macmillan, too, needed a success, for somewhat more complicated reasons. He was, after all, the head of government in a constitutional monarchy where powers were distributed and the Prime Minister's own authority limited by his Cabinet, his party, and public opinion. (De Gaulle was directing the affairs of a republic in which power was largely concentrated in his own hands and the impression of a plebiscitary monarchy was inescapable.)

In the following week Macmillan would have to lead a foreign-policy debate in the House of Commons—which, according to an aide, accounted in part for his "no nuclear bargaining with France" announcement on the eve of the conference. "He didn't want the other kind of headline," the aide observed. More important, Macmillan was now deeply committed to the idea of joining the EEC; in order to generate momentum for this at home it was desirable to place Britain's prospects in the most optimistic light.

The press comment was well managed. A headline in *Le Figaro* on June 4 read: "The Worst Misunderstandings Have Been Dissipated," and the story spoke of the renewal of an "old friendship," and so on. In *Le Monde* André Fontaine took the same line, giving more detail:

> Macmillan has returned satisfied. He did not find at the Château de Champs the Mr. No depicted by several British newspapers, but an old friend who, relaxed and gracious, extended him the honors of the Château and the park, warmed by a sun for which one had abandoned hope. . . . Macmillan will undoubtedly not be displeased to be able to reply to critics that he found de Gaulle favorably disposed to Great Britain's entry in the E.E.C. —so well disposed that, even beyond the Brussels negotiations, the two men have envisaged future forms of political cooperation . . . and defense policy.

In London *The Guardian* carried Leonard Beaton's more guarded story:

> An official in the office of the French Prime Minister, M. Pompidou, who is normally not available to the press by telephone, personally got in touch with several British correspondents to inform them of how relieved President de Gaulle was by all that

Mr. Macmillan had told him. . . . French officials are almost desperately anxious to convince the British press that there is not, nor ever has been, any question of France's blackballing Britain's admission to the club. "You pay your entrance fee and you're in," one official said to me.

The talks had ended with the release of a communiqué (by no means customary on these *intime* country-house occasions) which had been prepared in Whitehall before the meeting; the British delegation took satisfaction from its ready acceptance on the French side. It noted "agreement on the community of interests between the United Kingdom and France," adding that "they intend that this spirit should animate them in considering the great international problems with which they have to deal. It is in the same spirit that they have embarked upon and intend to continue the negotiations now proceeding in Brussels."

An old associate of de Gaulle's who attended the Champs meeting called on the General in Paris several days later. Macmillan's defense initiative was something new, he suggested, and should be pursued quietly at the highest level, certainly apart from the Brussels negotiations (which dealt mainly with economic and agricultural matters of little interest to de Gaulle). De Gaulle, he recalls, seemed to agree that it might be something new, but "he didn't take my advice." Even old associates who thought they understood de Gaulle's purposes could mislead themselves as easily as the uninitiated.

An associate of Macmillan's says that the United States probably got an account of the Champs talks, but not a full one, and that it was "unlikely" that Macmillan communicated anything privately to Kennedy. Washington, then, was relying on the bullish reports circulated by the French and British governments. Such reports continued to set the tone for some time. Washington and London each took a relentlessly optimistic view of Britain's chances, right up until de Gaulle's veto in

1963. The skepticism found here and there in Whitehall and among astute (and concerned) elements in the Quai d'Orsay was muted. It never influenced Macmillan or most members of his government. For them, the great enterprise of preparing Britain for entry into Europe would only be undermined by talk of possible failure. In the end, they believed, not even General de Gaulle would be willing or perhaps even able to resist a determined British bid, backed by the other EEC members of the Community. Washington concurred cheerfully.

It was not an implausible position. France could make it difficult for Britain—could compel her full acceptance of the Rome Treaty and the accumulated EEC regulations. Britain could and would be forced to end the imperial preferences awarded to agricultural produce from the old dominions as well as the new members of the Commonwealth. But in the end, France, too, would have to acquiesce.

Looking back, it appears that this position might have been vindicated had Britain made an all-out effort in Brussels in June and July. The summer, not the autumn, was the period when de Gaulle just might have felt obliged to make this one enormous deviation from principle. For he was then politically vulnerable. He lacked a majority in the National Assembly (during the Algerian war he had always managed to rally the moderates in opposition to his side, but this was no longer a sure thing), and a veto of Britain might well have been an issue that would bring down the government. Diplomats and government officials in every Western capital had doubts that de Gaulle would survive. "[His position] seemed so shaky, after the loss of Algeria, that much of the State-CIA-White House speculation had been not how he would block Western unity, but who or what would succeed him." [11] Willingness on the British side to end the Brussels negotiations by swallowing everything, together with Macmillan's offer to adopt a European policy in the most sacred of domains—defense—might have been sufficient to capture the General's grudging acquiescence.

A close Macmillan associate believes that Britain could have forced the negotiations to a conclusion in July and recalls that this tactic was considered and rejected; it would have been difficult, he notes, since Macmillan would thereby have exceeded his mandate; he had yet to gain acceptance of his policy among the Commonwealth Prime Ministers, to say nothing of the Tory party congress. "But probably he could have brought it off." He concludes that the Champs meeting, since it had gone better than Birch Grove, lulled the British into complacent optimism, while, on the other hand, it doubtless convinced de Gaulle for the first time that the Macmillan government was serious. Macmillan and his colleagues, continuing to build up support for their European policy, became its victims. By the time they had touched the various bases it was too late; de Gaulle was no longer constrained by domestic concerns.

Perhaps there never *was* a strategic moment—neither in midsummer 1962 nor at any other time. And if there was, it went very largely unnoticed.

7

The Psychodrama of
Skybolt and Rambouillet

On the banks of the Potomac and the Thames a number of serious people began to feel—of all things—optimistic. It would be unfair to say that Washington and London were euphoric in the drowsy summer of 1962; nothing, after all, had changed. But the Kennedy and Macmillan governments were riding high. Kennedy's strength and confidence continued to rise. The Anglo-American troubles with the adversary without, Khrushchev, and the adversary within, de Gaulle, were not less taxing, but something was in the wind. Some of the pieces essential to a more rational Atlantic system seemed to be falling into place. Britain needed Europe and Europe needed Britain. A strong and balanced European Community would offer a large and benign vocation for West German energies and would be a way for Western Europe eventually to look out for itself, instead of relying indefinitely on America. In the nuclear age stability is the cherished objective of a great power. For Washington, Britain in Europe would mean more stability in Europe. And the Pentagon's new strategy seemed to lower the risk that men might actually reach the outer bounds of violence.

In fact, things were not falling into place. The logic of what Kennedy and Macmillan were trying to do lacked the force to clear the obstacles ahead—some seen only dimly, others not at all. And the special nature of nuclear weapons does not necessarily make nuclear politics more amenable to reason and logic than any other politics.

To take a dramatic example. High-level contacts between Washington and Paris took place in the early part of 1962 on the question of joint nuclear targeting—coordinating the budding French nuclear capability (not then deployable) with American forces. The French were reluctant; de Gaulle was not interested in joint targeting as long as he lacked a really plausible nuclear element. But for the Americans, who had (and have) the nuclear responsibility, it was intolerable even to contemplate an uncoordinated nuclear element within the Atlantic Alliance. A very senior member of the Kennedy Administration found himself arguing the point with Pierre Messmer, France's Defense Minister. When Messmer insisted on France's right to target independently, he told him that if it should ever appear that France might even contemplate the independent use of nuclear weapons against *anybody*, the United States *"would not let you."*

Probably too much has been written about nuclear strategy. Throughout the 1960s it preoccupied many social scientists and members of the defense community. At one level the strategic argument was carried on thoughtfully, creatively, and usefully; at another, it became just a polemic. In any case, the transatlantic debate was performed at rather a high decibel level and churned up a good deal of righteous indignation. Many of the Americans who knew about nuclear weapons felt the Europeans understood nothing about controlling them. And there was something in that. Many of the Europeans felt that American strategists either cared nothing or understood nothing about European political requirements. And there was something in that.

The debate did not really impress de Gaulle. He did not

believe—never had believed—in nuclear war, just as he never believed in the Berlin crisis. Yet just as he used the Berlin crisis to build up his credit in Bonn, so he exploited the nuclear-strategy issue to build up his domestic strength and his position vis-à-vis other European members of NATO—especially the West Germans, who were the most nervous about the new American strategy.

In 1962 Raymond Aron said he failed to understand why nuclear weapons could cross the Atlantic (to Britain) but were forbidden to cross the Channel (to France). Numerous generals and colonels in search of a new vocation for the French army embraced the nuclear issue; their objections to an American strategic monopoly went well beyond Aron's moderate position. Some even conceived of a French force as a detonator, the device that would, if used automatically, call American nuclear forces into play. De Gaulle was much too intelligent to contemplate such nonsense himself, but he encouraged and exploited the thinking of his officers,* wanting them to have something to erase the bitterness aroused by the settlements of the Indochina and Algerian wars.

The issue suited de Gaulle perfectly. He knew, even if his general staff did not, that French nuclear weapons, if ever used at all, would be fired only after America's. And because the United States guarantee covered all of Western Europe, France could build her own nuclear forces at her own pace and de Gaulle could do as he pleased without jeopardizing security. He could even throw doubt, as he did, on this guarantee without fear of seeing it withdrawn. Briefly, the strategy issue fasci-

---

* Various persons around de Gaulle also encouraged this "detonator" notion, and tried to persuade the West Germans in particular that this would be a key function of France's nuclear force. Eventually, a senior member of the Kennedy Administration informed the French government in the bluntest language that French nuclear weapons would never trigger the American strike force.

nated those who were drawn to it either intellectually or occupationally. De Gaulle fell into neither group. For him the issue was merely useful. Just how useful the nuclear issue was to de Gaulle became clear in the next six months.

On June 16 Secretary McNamara chose the occasion of giving a commencement address at the University of Michigan to unveil America's new strategy (it became known in the press and in some defense circles as the "Michigan strategy"). The speech was actually a declassified version of the presentation McNamara had made at Athens six weeks earlier. As such, it may be remembered as a classic of that genre of commencement address which, while it says a great deal, unfairly taxes the cognition and attention span of the audience.

In establishing his case for centralized control of nuclear weapons McNamara assaulted in remarkably undiplomatic language the claims of other pretenders. This landmark statement, one of the most important issued by the Kennedy Administration, still deserves to be quoted at some length:

> Relatively weak national nuclear forces with enemy cities as their targets are not likely to be sufficient to perform even the function of deterrence. If they are small, and perhaps vulnerable on the ground or in the air, or inaccurate, a major antagonist can take a variety of measures to counter them. Indeed, if a major antagonist came to believe there was a substantial likelihood of it being used independently, this force would be inviting a pre-emptive first strike against it. In the event of war, the use of such a force against the cities of a major nuclear power would be tantamount to suicide, whereas its employment against significant military targets would have a negligible effect on the outcome of the conflict. Meanwhile, the creation of a single additional national nuclear force encourages the proliferation of nuclear power with all of its attendant dangers.
>
> In short, then, limited nuclear capabilities, operating independently, are dangerous, expensive, prone to obsolescence, and

lacking in credibility as a deterrent. Clearly, the United States nuclear contribution to the Alliance is neither obsolete nor dispensable. . . .

The general strategy I have summarized magnifies the importance of unity of planning, concentration of executive authority, and central direction. There must not be competing and conflicting strategies to meet the contingency of nuclear war. We are convinced that a general nuclear war target system is indivisible, and if, despite all our efforts, nuclear war should come, our best hope lies in conducting a *centrally controlled* campaign against all of the enemy's vital nuclear capabilities, while retaining reserve forces, all *centrally controlled*. (Italics added.)

There was quite a lot more of this, all in the same vein, all directed at the American defense community and at the governments of the Soviet Union and France. To Moscow, McNamara was signaling the depth of American power and the restraint and moderation underlying the control of it; to France, he was stressing the futility and, indeed, irrationality of a middle power's quest for a strategic nuclear capability. It was all supremely rational and fully responsive to American interests—and to the world's interest—in preventing nuclear war.

But the speech was not a success in political terms. Doubtless it communicated some useful signals to Moscow. But it was hardly calculated either to influence or to embarrass the target of so much of the rhetoric.*

It is unlikely that the State Department was able to comment in advance on McNamara's remarks, although they were certain to have a bearing on the Brussels EEC negotiations. A

---

* Any doubt that France was the target was removed a few days later when McNamara issued a clarification excluding Britain from the thrust of his remarks: "What I said at Ann Arbor was [that] separate nuclear capabilities operating independently were dangerous. But Britain's bomber command aircraft with their nuclear weapons have long been organized as part of a thoroughly coordinated Anglo-American striking force and are targeted as such." (*The New York Times,* June 24, 1962.)

Senate Foreign Relations Committee study published three months later said: "The cause of Britain's membership [in the Common Market] can hardly be served by harsh public criticism of the national policy of France, whose President more than once has indicated his concern that the British application is an American Trojan horse intended to keep Europe dependent on the United States." [1]

When Rusk went to Europe on June 19, three days after McNamara's Ann Arbor speech, the disharmony of the Administration's various positions was again in evidence. In Paris, where he saw de Gaulle, Couve de Murville, and others in the government, Berlin was as usual one agenda item, coordination of nuclear weapons and targets another. But why, after all, attempt to reach some accommodation with France's nuclear program only a few days after denouncing it? The fact that Washington sought (unsuccessfully) an agreement on coordination of targeting amounted to implicit recognition that France was, or was becoming, a nuclear power, however modest.*

Governments, serving as they do those cold monsters the nation-states, are normally cautious and skeptical. Curiously, the optimism of Washington and London at this time was hedged with less than the normal caution, which points up the degree of commitment in both capitals to the more rational Atlantic system they envisaged.

The Brussels negotiations recessed in August, having made a great deal of progress. In September Macmillan skillfully engineered Tory backing for and neutralized Commonwealth opposition to his European policy; Kennedy got his Trade Expan-

---

* According to a *New York Times* report from Paris dated June 20, "France politely turned aside today as premature a proposal by Secretary of State Dean Rusk that an eventual French nuclear force be coordinated with United States and British forces. Foreign Minister Couve de Murville was reported to have told Mr. Rusk in the course of a three-hour meeting that the question of coordination of nuclear forces was inevitable but 'not yet current.'"

sion Act, his most notable legislative achievement to that date. In October the world suddenly found itself on the brink of nuclear war. The resolution of the Cuban missile crisis days later changed everything. It meant a formal end to the Cold War, at least in its crudest and most unstable form; it meant an end to the Berlin crisis; and it gave Kennedy's prestige an enormous boost in all capitals, not least in Moscow and Paris.

The trauma of the missile crisis—for a time, at least—obscured other things. Suddenly, in November, the British discovered, or pretended to discover, that the Americans were on the verge of canceling the Skybolt missile program. This was calamitous. Britain's nuclear strike force was to be entirely dependent on the Skybolt missile system in a few years. Macmillan was already in trouble: his fall by-elections had not gone well; the Brussels negotiations, now resumed, were stalled on the vexatious problem of adjusting British agriculture to Common Market regulations; and he must have had some nagging doubts about French intentions, especially after de Gaulle's remarkable victory in the November legislative elections.

The Skybolt weapons system had its origins in the Pentagon politics of the early 1950s. It was to be the Air Force's answer to the Navy's Polaris, at times even being called the "Polaris of the sky." Skybolt was designed as a thousand-mile two-stage ballistic missile to be released from beneath the wing of a large bomber, and its purpose was to help the big bombers reach strategic targets by destroying perimeter defenses. This was a weapons system to quicken the hearts of the air forces of both the United States and Britain: Skybolt would extend the operational life of the American B-52s and the 180 Vulcan bombers that constituted Britain's nuclear deterrent; it would allow the bombers to stand off and attack an enemy well beyond the range of his air defenses.

If that was Skybolt's great virtue, it was also its chief defect, since the future of manned strategic bombers was in doubt, if not in jeopardy. Another disadvantage was the remarkable complexity of the system:

> In many ways it was the most complex ballistic missile system the U.S. had yet undertaken—more so than Minuteman or Polaris. The missile had to be launched over an altitude range of several thousand feet, to be able at high speed to resist shock, vibration, and noise from a hostile environment and to be integrated in a unique way with the mother ship which, with its computer system, contains about 130,000 parts.[2]

A number of sharp images were etched by the Skybolt affair; one was the strength of purpose, tenacity, and bureaucratic ingenuity of a uniformed service engaged in protecting what it regards as a primary mission, in this case manned strategic bombing; another was the curious inability of other agencies of government to oppose effectively a program that is strongly backed by a uniformed service, especially if that service is allied with its British counterpart.

The Eisenhower Administration was doubtful about Skybolt from the beginning and never made any secret of its lack of commitment to the program. The chief doubters were Secretary of Defense Gates and his deputy, James Douglas.

The British position was more complicated. Britain had no strategic weapons other than the V-bombers; a medium-range ballistic missile, the Blue Streak, was being developed, but its costs were soaring and the question of location and hardening of silos had still to be faced. Skybolt, on the other hand, would maintain the effective life of the aging V-bombers until 1970, perhaps longer. Defence Minister Harold Watkinson urged that Blue Streak be canceled in favor of a purchase agreement with the United States for Skybolt—an argument, really, for an act of faith in the "special relationship." Britain would abandon its own missile program and as a nuclear power would become completely dependent on a still-to-be-built American weapons system. The money saved in buying a complementary American system instead of developing a British missile would, presumably, liberate resources for joint Anglo-American objectives east of Suez. Watkinson's thinking carried the day, at least within Macmillan's government. And, indeed, the cancellation of Blue Streak in 1960 was perfectly consistent with the thinking that had animated British foreign policy since 1945. Britain would be a complementary and, when necessary, restraining influence on America—a junior partner wise in the ways of Americans and able to fortify American policy with worldly and mature insights. This, of course, was the *European* role which Washington had urged on Britain for more than fifteen years.*

Still, the Skybolt proposal did not go unopposed in London. Pockets of resistance were found in the Foreign Office and the Ministry of Defence. The Atomic Energy Authority had doubts, too, based on information it was getting from the AEC in Washington. So did Sir Solly Zuckerman, Scientific Adviser to the Prime Minister, although it is unlikely that he did anything about them. And a senior member of the Defence Ministry recalls that he and many of his colleagues began to argue instead for Polaris, as soon as they "saw the Americans putting their money on it in 1959. That is when we should have taken it—as soon as Blue Streak proved that Britain could not build a missile independently. Perhaps we had to go through the Skybolt experience to learn the lesson."

In fact, the U.S. Navy was urging the British to take Polaris instead of Skybolt (the fiercesome figure of Admiral Rickover became involved in the effort to "sell" Polaris to London), and Washington made it clear that Polaris was available. But the alliance between the two air forces was not matched by the

---

* Admittedly, Washington always encouraged a continued strong British preserve east of Suez also.

navies. The Royal Navy simply did not want Polaris. This disheartened the Whitehall bureaucrats who did, and who were counting on the sailors to "do the running" and offset the Air Force lobbying for Skybolt. But the traditionalist Royal Navy feared that Polaris would drain off resources from the classical modes (surface ships). "Who wants to make a career under the waves?" is the way the then First Sea Lord, Casper John, liked to put the question. Watkinson says he never presided over any meetings on the issue in which his service chiefs were divided; and this is doubtless true.

The Skybolt compact was struck in March 1960 at Camp David. In return for Skybolt Britain would swallow the political consequences of granting the United States a base in Scotland for its nuclear submarines (at Holy Loch). It was not a formal understanding, but for both parties it virtually amounted to one:

> It was never referred to by such a vulgar name as a "bargain," and each item was negotiated without specific reference to the other. But it is clear from later evidence (however much confusion and soul searching the question of this link between the two caused the Kennedy Administration) that each side considered the other's commitment morally binding.[3]

America would continue to bear Skybolt's heavy research and development costs (destined to run in the end to $500,000,-000). Britain would pay only for the purchase of the operational missiles it bought, plus the cost of adapting them to the V-bomber fleet.

The ceremony at Camp David had been preceded two months earlier by a working-level meeting at which the main parts of the understanding had been agreed to. After that, further opposition was futile, although the U.S. Navy and elements in the State Department and other agencies continued to argue in favor of substituting Polaris for Skybolt. And by now a large part of the Whitehall bureaucracy was for Polaris and against Skybolt, encouraged in most cases by opposite numbers in the State and Defense Departments. The bureaucratic skirmishing continued even during the Camp David meeting, with Eisenhower's naval aide openly lobbying for Polaris while other Americans discreetly urged their British colleagues to think twice. A member of the British party, then relatively junior but close to Macmillan, recalls having been a target of much of the anti-Skybolt, pro-Polaris American pressure. He himself needed no convincing, but when he tried to make the case for Polaris he was taken aside by two senior colleagues (who had participated in the earlier meeting)* and told bluntly to "shut up."

But by now the issue was not whether Britain should take Skybolt or Polaris, but whether Skybolt would ever reach the production stage. Again, the pressure for it would be applied by the U.S. Air Force backed up by the Royal Air Force and the Douglas Aircraft Corporation, Skybolt's prime contractor.

In June, three months after the Camp David meeting, Watkinson met with Defense Secretary Gates. It was agreed that the United States would make every reasonable effort to develop the missile and could rely on an initial British order for 100. Although this may have been the Skybolt's finest hour, an ominous premonitory shadow appeared shortly after in the form of an unpublished side agreement which provided that either party could terminate its interest in Skybolt at any time, after having first consulted the other party. It was also agreed that if the United States canceled the project, Britain would be free to take over Skybolt's development.

After this it was all uphill. Numerous danger signals were hoisted in the autumn by the outgoing Eisenhower Administration. Various experts were opposing Skybolt; the cost estimates were doubling; London was warned that the prospects were un-

---

* One of them was the late Lord Normanbrooke, at the time Secretary of the Cabinet.

certain; Gates cut back Skybolt development funds in the last Eisenhower budget. The initial recommendations of the incoming Kennedy analysts were bearish, but Secretary McNamara was worried about the famous "missile gap," or the general impression of a missile gap (it turned out never to have really existed), and decided for political reasons to ignore the Skybolt's doubters and to restore the funds Gates had withdrawn.

By April 1961, however, McNamara, too, was taking a pessimistic line when he testified before the Senate Armed Services Committee: "All the development problems have not been solved. Many of them are complex and we cannot predict for certain that the development will proceed so satisfactorily that we will wish to recommend procurement for this system." [4] Yet the Skybolt lobby was operating at peak efficiency. The U.S.–U.K. agreement had provided that Britain could assign RAF officers and British technicians to follow Skybolt's development, and this meant that the gloomy noises coming from the Defense Department were continually offset by stubbornly optimistic reports to London from the RAF team assigned to the Pentagon and Douglas Aircraft. A key British official, who then as now was closely involved in his country's nuclear affairs, says laconically: "The RAF was getting different information than I was getting."

McNamara reached a temporary compromise with the Skybolt lobby: the program would continue into 1962 provided that development funds were held beneath $500,000,000. But the issue was becoming more complicated and reflected the Administration's concern with promoting nuclear stability and more centralized control of nuclear weapons.

In the American armory Skybolt's task was limited to neutralizing the enemies' defences or, as the experts call it, "defence suppression"; while for the U.K. it was purely a weapon of attack. Whenever the British political argument cropped up about the need to maintain an independent deterrent Washington suggested earnestly and with raised eyebrows that defence was a serious business—not merely symbolic.[5]

The phrase "serious business" was really intended to mean that only a great power like the United States could afford to deploy nuclear forces capable of performing a broad range of missions and in sufficient depth to withstand a first strike and still be able to destroy the enemy society.

In short, various parts of the Washington bureaucracy hoped that Britain would be "phased out" of the nuclear club; the British example would be useful to the French and perhaps the Germans. Skybolt, then, might become the means for liquidating the British nuclear deterrent, instead of sustaining it. The British were obviously aware of this point of view but took comfort in the knowledge that it was not shared by the senior members of the Administration—certainly not by the President or Rusk and probably not by McNamara or Bundy. Who *was* drawn to the idea of forcing Britain out of the nuclear club? The British felt that the bias against their "independent deterrent" was concentrated in the State Department and focused perhaps in the office of Under Secretary George Ball. Feeling, it is true, ran highest in the State Department but was by no means confined to it. Impatience with the special relationship had taken hold in most of the agencies dealing with national security affairs.

As a practical matter the "special" quality of the United States relationship with Great Britain by now counted for little (leaving aside the unique role of the dollar and pound sterling in supporting the world-payments system) and consisted in the main of special arrangements for the collection, evaluation, and exchange of intelligence. (A former Defense Department official who observed these intelligence arrangements at close hand describes them succinctly as a "horse and rabbit stew. We put in the horse and they put in the rabbit.")

Throughout much of the last half of 1962 Washington edged

in small, uncertain steps toward the liquidation of Skybolt. The British were warned, but never told outright, of what was now Skybolt's certain fate. (To do so would have been to risk a counterattack by the Skybolt lobby and its Congressional troops.) They tended to ignore these warnings, being convinced that in the end the Strategic Air Command and its allies, plus the moral pressure of the "special relationship," would prevail. This misreading of the signs and portents was a measure of how far the special relationship had declined, a trend that de Gaulle and his colleagues never understood, let alone believed.

In September Watkinson's successor at the Ministry of Defence, Peter Thorneycroft, in Washington for a defense review, was warned by McNamara that Skybolt was flunking the test of cost effectiveness. A number of American officials were convinced that Thorneycroft never transmitted these warnings to the Cabinet.

The hour of truth for Skybolt might well have followed Thorneycroft's visit, but Washington's attention was abruptly and fully claimed by the Cuban missile crisis. It was not until November 7 that McNamara told Kennedy and Rusk that he was seriously considering canceling Skybolt. On November 8 he summoned Ormsby-Gore and drew a clear picture of Skybolt's difficulties, but he said that the final decision would be taken in three to four weeks.[6] On November 9 he telephoned Thorneycroft, repeated essentially the same message, and called Thorneycroft's attention to possible alternatives to Skybolt.

At this point the matter fell into a state of suspension. Nobody did anything. The State Department and the White House, ignoring indications that the cancellation of Skybolt would mean a political crisis with Britain, were content to leave the problem in the hands of the Pentagon, for which Skybolt was not really a political matter—a key element in the special relationship with Britain—but a weapons system that fitted neither the changing American strategy nor the criteria of cost effectiveness.

> Unfortunately, preoccupation with the Cuban and India-Chinese crises (fighting had just broken out on the mountainous Sino-India frontier) postponed all White House decisions on the defense budget until late in 1962, too late for an orderly consideration of the problems created by Skybolt's demise. The President . . . mistakenly assumed that it was largely a technical and not a political problem. He paid comparatively little attention after McNamara promised to see . . . Thorneycroft and "work it out." After Cuba, it seemed a small problem. All problems did. Later Kennedy would wonder about why his Ambassador to London, David Bruce, or . . . David Ormsby-Gore, or Macmillan himself, or Rusk, or someone, had not warned both sides in advance of the storm. But no doubt Macmillan wondered why Kennedy had not called him; and Rusk, after warning Kennedy in November of the possible British reaction, deferred to McNamara.[7]

Actually, Ormsby-Gore had done something.

> About a week later [after the McNamara-Thorneycroft telephone conversation], Sir David Ormsby-Gore saw the President and reminded him that cancellation of Skybolt could stir up a real crisis in Anglo-American relations. But the gravity of his warnings still did not seem to have quite sunk in. . . . It did not sink in perhaps because Washington thought this was London's crisis and London felt exactly the opposite.[8]

One of Kennedy's close advisers, looking back, reflects that his own attention at this moment was absorbed by the problem of "getting those Il-28's out of Cuba." (The Soviets, in removing the offensive missiles from Cuba, had left behind twenty or so light Ilyushin jet bombers. Kennedy was insisting that these, too, would have to go.) "Perhaps if I had known David then as well as I know him now we might have avoided this."

The implication is clear. Communications between London and Washington had fallen into disrepair. Neither the warmth between Kennedy and Macmillan nor the intimate place of Ormsby-Gore in the Kennedy circle managed to head off a full-blown Anglo-American crisis. How to explain the paralysis? Even in retrospect it is difficult. Despite all the warnings the British apparently did no contingency planning for the cancellation of Skybolt, chiefly because they could not envisage —indeed could not accept—the possibility, just as they could not accept the possibility that the Brussels negotiations might fail despite the warnings from the Foreign Office and de Gaulle's obvious resistance. Nor is there a simple explanation for the breakdown of communications. Because the Anglo-American relationship is both the most important and the least formal for Britain, it is in a way the most difficult. The channels of communications between London and Washington are almost too numerous, and this was especially true in the Kennedy days. There was the PM's tie with the President; the close relationship between the Foreign Minister and Secretary of State; and there was Ormsby-Gore's privileged place at the White House. In short, for the working-level people in Whitehall, it was often difficult to know where and how best to proceed with the Americans.

Finally, possibly most importantly, there was Harold Macmillan's penchant for thinking that in the end he could carry the day for Britain by drawing on his wartime associations (with de Gaulle and Eisenhower) and his newer friendships (Kennedy). This effectively froze matters—creating situations that could be resolved only by eleventh-hour interventions from No. 10 Downing Street.

The Macmillan instinct for playing "Superman" with UK foreign policy was more often betrayed than vindicated. During the Suez crisis, for example, "Macmillan (who was then Chancellor of the Exchequer and the strongest figure in Eden's

Cabinet) did not have the resentful view of the USA which marked and ultimately dominated Eden. He seems to have believed that Britain should play the part of the Greeks in a new Roman Empire directed by the President of the USA; he did not hanker for a separate foreign policy. He wished and believed that the USA would always back Britain in the long run whatever they did." Just a few weeks before the invasion, Macmillan returned from a two-week visit in the United States having "apparently convinced himself that 'Ike will lie doggo until after the election.' " [9] Ike, of course, did not "lie doggo," and Macmillan was a chastened man a month later when Washington insisted that Britain would have to agree to a cease-fire before withdrawing capital from the International Monetary Fund to prop up sterling.

At Bermuda in March 1957 Macmillan's faith in old associations was confirmed when Eisenhower agreed to restore Anglo-American nuclear collaboration. Now, in the autumn of 1962, Macmillan was counting on Kennedy to salvage Britain's heavy investment in the special relationship, and on de Gaulle to make possible Britain's admission into Europe.

After some postponements McNamara arranged to go to London on December 10. By now the Skybolt affair was in the public domain—on page one actually, where it was to remain for quite a while. "Suez to Skybolt," said *The Daily Herald,* "it has been a pretty rotten road." [10] All that was missing to make the Skybolt business a complete political mess were some immoderate remarks on the American side. This gap was speedily filled by McNamara himself and Dean Acheson. In a speech at West Point on December 5 Acheson delivered his now-famous verdict on Britain: "Great Britain has lost an empire and not yet found a role." From Macmillan on down, the British reaction was splenetic.* As for McNamara, he observed at London

---

* Macmillan linked Acheson with Napoleon and Hitler as one of those who had guessed wrong on Britain.

airport just after arriving that "all five flight tests of Skybolt thus far have failed." [11]* The effect of this cold bath was to eliminate the admittedly small possibility that Skybolt might be taken over by Britain as an independent project. "The lady's reputation," Macmillan said a few days later, "has been compromised."

McNamara's meeting with Thorneycroft must have few if any precedents in Anglo-American relations. McNamara began with a detailed review of Skybolt's history, its soaring costs, its repeated failures, and so on. He "doubted the wisdom of continuing" to plan for Skybolt, but offered to discuss alternatives. One American who was present described this performance as a "brilliant exposition of a highly complex subject."

Thorneycroft, at another level, was also brilliant. While McNamara stressed the technicalities, Thorneycroft insisted on putting the matter squarely in the political context of the special relationship. "Skybolt," he said, "is the principal example of Anglo-American complementarity," and he warned that cancellation of the weapon would cut the ground away from those who had stood for close Anglo-American collaboration.[12] McNamara was forcibly reminded of the unspecified *contrepartie* of the Skybolt understanding—the basing rights at Holy Loch for American nuclear submarines. And then, Thorneycroft wondered aloud, was the United States hoping to destroy Britain's position as a nuclear power? Was that the real object of this crisis?

Thorneycroft's performance impressed the British much more than the Americans—and that was its purpose, really. A wise and experienced American official who was present said that Thorneycroft's statement, prepared in advance, was clearly

---

* Just before leaving Washington McNamara had read the airport statement to George Ball. Ball urged him not to use it, arguing that there was no point in foreclosing the possibility that Skybolt might be continued under a revised agreement. McNamara demurred, and indicated his intention to establish the point that the missile was just not practicable.

designed to convince the British military, many of whom were stamping angrily in their traces, that he and Macmillan would not abandon Skybolt without a fight. Macmillan had liquidated their own missile program; and now here they were about to be done out of the American alternative upon which Britain's position as a nuclear power was supposed to depend entirely in a few years' time. Inspired stories in the London press portrayed Thorneycroft as an heroic figure administering a much deserved dressing down to the Americans.

There was some desultory discussion of alternatives to Skybolt, none of which really interested the British. Then, almost *en passant*, Thorneycroft mentioned Polaris, and the Americans agreed to look into it. The point here is that Thorneycroft did not ask for Polaris and McNamara didn't offer it. But ever since their telephone conversation of November 9 Thorneycroft and his colleagues had been waiting for the Americans to offer Polaris (most of them had already written off Skybolt) and McNamara had been waiting for the British to ask him for something, most likely Polaris. For their own reasons, neither had wanted to take the initiative. For Thorneycroft, negotiations on Polaris would have revealed that Britain was abandoning Skybolt and provoked a nasty outcry from the RAF and others. For McNamara to propose it would have set off a tempest in the Skybolt lobby and resistance among those who wanted to see an end to Britain's independent nuclear role.* Macmillan himself had by now decided on Polaris, but for *his* political reasons did not want to be obliged to ask for it. Better to have Kennedy offer it; and that was the strategy. Until the scheduled meeting with Kennedy at Nassau, now just a

---

* Quite a number of Americans thought the financial implications of Polaris would discourage serious British interest, because getting Polaris would mean having to build American-type nuclear submarines, in addition to paying for a very expensive weapons system (probably about twice what Skybolt would have come to). They were wrong.

week away, Britain would officially stand by Skybolt. But first Macmillan would meet de Gaulle in the forest of Rambouillet.

During the missile crisis in October (which seems to have caused some huddling together of the lesser powers) several messages had flashed between Paris and London. Then, on November 18, Macmillan suggested to de Gaulle that it might be useful if they could meet before he saw Kennedy for the post-Cuba *tour d'horizon.* Obviously, Macmillan wished to smoke out de Gaulle on the British application to the EEC—and indeed to reach agreement on it. De Gaulle proposed a game shoot at the Château de Rambouillet on the morning of December 15, and on November 26 Macmillan agreed to this.

The French legislative elections had given de Gaulle and his party a parliamentary majority, an event without precedent in French Republican history. Now de Gaulle's hands were *entirely* free. But to do what? The missile crisis had left in its wake something he abhorred—the prospect of a Russo-American dialogue. For de Gaulle, who saw these things with greater speed and clarity than most people, a test-ban treaty and some limited degree of *détente* lay ahead. Moreover, the successful resolution of the missile crisis meant that Kennedy was now supreme among world leaders—the undisputed leader of the West, and more. Doubtless he would in time be prepared, in the absence of French support for American policies, to by-pass France. For de Gaulle, who was prone to putting himself in the place of American presidents, the outlook must have been dicey, though stimulating.

De Gaulle was among the most abusive of men, and it was in character for him to speak privately of Kennedy as a choir-boy or boy scout or to deride him, as he did to the late Sir Pierson Dixon, then British Ambassador in Paris, for not knowing how to use power. But it is known that this derision was calculated and masked a respect Kennedy had awakened in their 1961 meeting. The missile crisis aroused his genuine admiration.*

By mid-December Macmillan was in receipt of gloomy reports from the Foreign Office regarding de Gaulle's intentions, but he had no policy alternatives, being by now fully committed to taking Britain into Europe. There was to be no letup in the official optimism; Macmillan and de Gaulle, after all, could still sort it all out at Rambouillet. "How," asked *Le Monde*, "can one believe that the man who in June 1940 agreed with Churchill in proposing an indissoluble union with Great Britain could, at the hour of decision, exclude her from the European family?" André Fontaine was even more hortatory:

> The pressure that has been exerted for two years on the British to push them into the EEC exerts itself now on our country. France is invited to choose between participating in the creation of a Europe able to assert itself politically and even militarily, and the transformation of the states of the Continent into satellites of the United States that would have the freedom only of manifesting their ill humor.[13]

---

* De Gaulle's reaction to the missile crisis was entirely in character. Dean Acheson went to Paris on Monday, October 22, the day of Kennedy's historic statement, with a White House letter and the famous aerial photographs. De Gaulle read the letter and, even before examining the photographs, assured Acheson of France's support: "You may tell your President that France will support him. I think that under the circumstances President Kennedy had no other choice. This is his national prerogative and France understands." (Elie Abel, *The Missile Crisis* [Philadelphia: J. B. Lippincott, 1966], p. 112.)

De Gaulle, of course, was assuming that Khrushchev was bluffing, as he probably had been bluffing most of the time in Berlin. And de Gaulle believed that Kennedy's approach had the right combination of firmness and moderation. Thus, the United States would prevail, and the best course for France would be to support her. It was the kind of perception that de Gaulle could make in a flash. The Gaullists always made much of this spontaneous show of support for the United States.

The meeting began, curiously enough, with a dispute be-tween two of de Gaulle's aides, Burin des Roziers, who as Chief of Staff at the Élysée Palace was in charge of arrangements, and Ambassador de Courcel (his predecessor in the post). Courcel, like Macmillan, enjoyed shooting, and he was critical of the way Burin had positioned Macmillan for the planned pheasant shoot. Burin prevailed, and Macmillan in the end shot seventy-seven pheasants on a windy, rain-swept Saturday morning.

Then, before a blazing fire in a ground-floor room in the Château, next to the garden, the talks began. Macmillan was in good form, as he had been at Champs, even eloquent. But it was futile. De Gaulle's opposition to his guest's larger purpose became unmistakable, and the talks ended in a tense, even angry atmosphere. Britain had been rejected.

It began in restricted session, with only de Zulueta assisting Macmillan; on the French side there were Burin des Roziers and the interpreter, Andronikov. Curiously, Andronikov took no notes, which later suggested to the British that de Gaulle wanted to have the French record transcribed afterward in the Élysée Palace. The British record, transcribed and typed even before Macmillan and his party left Rambouillet, is regarded as the authentic version by various French officials, who conceded that the Élysée record is considerably less reliable.

The meeting opened with some discussion of the missile crisis and its implications. De Gaulle said he thought that the United States was morally at a low ebb, and was surprised at how bad American intelligence had been with regard to the missiles. He seemed to be trying to reduce the scope of the American achievement, while Macmillan defended Kennedy's conduct and leadership.

The Himalayan border conflict between India and China was touched on briefly. China was prevented by American and Russian nuclear power, de Gaulle said, from moving toward India or generally to the west and north. China would instead move toward Burma and Malaya, which would open up the Indian Ocean and Africa, lying beyond.

De Gaulle then noted that the real test for the West was Berlin; if the Russians annoyed the West in Berlin, the West should annoy them—at sea, in the air, and so on. He added, rather inconsistently but accurately, that the Cold War was not a success for Russia, who might now try making peace. There followed some discussion of Cuba, with de Gaulle saying that whether in Cuba or Berlin only the two great powers really mattered. Macmillan alertly replied that it was the disparity of power caused by Europe's fragmentation that permitted great-power supremacy.

They turned the conversation to the Brussels negotiations. Macmillan went over now well-trod ground. De Gaulle countered: British membership would change things in the EEC greatly; there was, of course, the agricultural issue, the real point being that French agricultural produce must be consumed. This was a very difficult problem, he repeated. He was very negative. Macmillan demurred. Britain was now prepared to have the consumer bear the cost of subsidizing agricultural produce. (He was saying, in effect, that his government was prepared to move away from the British system of agricultural support to the Common Market system; it was on this issue that the Brussels negotiations were bogged down, mainly because the British negotiators did not have sufficient latitude.)

The conversation reverted to world politics. Macmillan declared Britain's determination to maintain an independent nuclear deterrent. He would have to take up with Kennedy the question of Skybolt, or a satisfactory replacement for it. He was concerned, he said, not to reduce Britain's capacity to intervene east of Suez, but he did not know how Kennedy would react. (The latter comment indicated his awareness that some of Kennedy's advisers were opposed to pulling Britain's nuclear chestnuts out of the fire.)

De Gaulle then made an important series of remarks. He mentioned France's gaseous-diffusion plant at Pierrelatte, and noted that before his return to power the West Germans and Italians had been asked to share in the cost of building it and had naturally expected technical advantages in return —an expectation, he reminded Macmillan, he had squashed. De Gaulle then talked about the uncertainty that would follow Adenauer's departure in West Germany, and this led to general remarks about defense. Each country, he said, should defend itself. If by chance the Russians succeeded in crossing West Germany, France could defend herself (with the *force de dissuasion* was the implication). Adenauer, he continued, did not agree and believed that everyone should rally around West Germany; but France's position was different. De Gaulle would not oblige Norstad by giving NATO the four French divisions brought back from Algeria. Once you gave them up, he said, it would be hard to take them back, and they would be annihilated in Germany if fighting did break out. It would be wrong, de Gaulle added, to count on significant French involvement in NATO itself. France, he indicated, would be there less and less.

De Gaulle now turned to the subject of the fruitful Franco-British cooperation he envisaged on the Franco-British supersonic transport (the Concorde) and the Blue Streak missile. This was important. The French have since argued that, in mentioning Blue Streak, the defunct British ballistic missile, de Gaulle was offering Macmillan nuclear cooperation; more precisely, that he was proposing that Britain revive Blue Streak in collaboration with France instead of making new arrangements with the Americans at Nassau. Macmillan, they say, failed to reply, meaning that he was not really interested in a European policy, that the only arrangements that mattered to him and his government were those he could work out with Washington.

The British interpretation is that de Gaulle's reference to Blue Streak merely acknowledged that the missile represented Britain's contribution to an all-European rocket program.* Macmillan did not respond, first, because the remark was made quickly, almost *en passant,* and was vague; second, as a former British official well qualified in this regard says, because Macmillan was extremely irritated—de Gaulle was being negative about Britain's European bid and NATO as well. Whatever he might have been offering to Macmillan was purely bilateral. To the degree that he may have been serious, he was saying: you and I can collaborate on ballistic missiles, but it will be purely bilateral cooperation; Britain really has no place in Europe, and NATO no longer matters to France. Even if it had wanted to, no British government could have agreed to nuclear cooperation with a French government that denied Britain's European hopes and that apparently intended to end its own effective participation in NATO. Moreover, argue the British, why hadn't de Gaulle responded when, at Champs, Macmillan had at least twice proposed joint defense cooperation after Britain joined the EEC?

Toward the end of the session Macmillan put the historical argument. For centuries Britain's foreign policy had been aimed at maintaining an equilibrium in Europe. This, he said, would no longer be possible if Britain could not take part in Europe's political organization, in which France and West Germany were members but from which she was excluded.

For de Gaulle, this must have been an extraordinary mo-

---

* Britain and France, along with the other five members of the Western European Union, plus Australia, signed a convention in March 1962 establishing the European Launcher Development Organization (ELDO). It was a nonmilitary program with the objective of placing a European satellite in orbit. Blue Streak, although canceled in 1960 as a British weapons system, was still under development for nonmilitary experimental purposes, and it was to provide the first stage for the ELDO rocket. (The program has fared badly, and Britain may well withdraw.)

ment. Macmillan was making his, de Gaulle's, real argument. Inside a European community Britain would of course play her old game of balancing now this one, now that one; that was precisely what de Gaulle could not accept. He said nothing in reply.

The following morning, in the *réunion élargi*, the little group was joined by Lord Home and Sir Pierson Dixon on the British side, and Pompidou, Couve de Murville, and Courcel on the French. The meeting began with Macmillan repeating and summarizing Britain's position. De Gaulle recalled Churchill's famous admonition, that whenever Britain had to choose between the Continent and *le grand large* she would choose the latter. Macmillan responded that in 1940 Britain had needed American power, and moreover had stood alone for Europe. True, said de Gaulle, Britain was never so European as in 1940.

Then at last he came to the point. Britain's membership would change the EEC. The Scandinavian countries and then others would follow her. The French position within the Common Market would be reduced. The EEC itself would no longer be European but would be dissolved in an Atlantic trading system. As presently constituted, however, it suited French political requirements, especially vis-à-vis Germany. In conclusion, he doubted that Britain could meet EEC requirements, at least as France interpreted them.

Macmillan shot back. De Gaulle had just made a very serious statement: what he really meant was that there had been a fundamental objection to British entry from the beginning of the negotiations fourteen months earlier. Why hadn't he said so then? De Gaulle said it wasn't true. And Pompidou broke in, adding that it was just a matter of dates.

At this electric moment Lord Home, incredibly, turned the conversation to his favorite subject, Berlin. He alone spoke, and the gentlemen adjourned for lunch.

De Gaulle and Pompidou drew Ambassador Dixon aside, and de Gaulle said, presumably with a straight face, that he found these periodic meetings with Macmillan useful—one could even say they had revived the Entente Cordiale. Pompidou interjected, somewhat irrelevantly, that the whole point was that the French did not want to renegotiate the entire EEC agricultural policy in eight years. (The Common Market's transitional period was to end in eight years, in 1970.)

At lunch members of the British group questioned Couve de Murville on what de Gaulle had meant precisely in his negative concluding remarks. Couve replied that he didn't know what de Gaulle was talking about.

No recent high-level conference has had so many myths spun around it as this one. There is, for example, the story of a famous walk in the woods, when Macmillan and de Gaulle discussed Skybolt and nuclear defense; de Gaulle is supposed to have felt deceived; and a popular explanation is that Macmillan's French was not adequate to de Gaulle's subtle diplomatic style, and that, moreover, a high wind was blowing through the forest. In fact, there was no *promenade*, as there had been at other meetings. The weather was awful, and besides, Macmillan was in no mood to see de Gaulle privately, not at length certainly. He wanted witnesses. They did stroll briefly together at one point on the Château grounds, but Macmillan was alone with Ambassador Dixon on his only real walk in the woods; they wanted to talk privately and thought their rooms at the Château might be bugged.

Another, more specific, myth holds that Macmillan did not warn de Gaulle that he might reach agreement with Kennedy on a substitute for the Skybolt missile—a myth the Élysée nourished. A Quai d'Orsay spokesman said the Skybolt question had not been discussed, being of no concern to France, and de Gaulle told a group of French parliamentarians in early February that Macmillan "came to tell me we were right to build a nuclear force. 'We have ours,' he told me. 'It will be necessary to reach a point of uniting them in a European cadre independent of America.' There he left me to go to the Bahamas. Naturally, what happened [there] altered the tone of my press conference [when he vetoed the British application to the EEC]." [14] Here, de Gaulle was also encouraging another myth—that his decision to veto the British application was provoked by the Nassau conference. But the record of his conversation with Macmillan at Rambouillet establishes his prior unshakable resistance to British membership. Macmillan knew he was beaten when he left the Château.

De Gaulle's pleasure in settling what he clearly regarded as old scores with the British establishment would not have had a direct or controlling influence on his decision to block Britain, but the manner in which he sought to humiliate the British government certainly owes much to his wartime experience and the grudges acquired then that he will carry to the grave. To take just one example: Macmillan had a sentimental streak, sometimes aroused on large occasions when Britain's current needs were measured against her earlier glory. At one point during the Rambouillet meeting he wept openly. During a cabinet meeting in Paris the following Wednesday morning de Gaulle described it: "This poor man, to whom I had nothing to give, seemed so sad, so beaten that I wanted to put my hand on his shoulder and say to him, as in the Edith Piaf song, *'Ne pleurez pas, milord.'* " The anecdote, needless to say, was insinuated into the Paris newspapers. Another version, spread about in diplomatic circles, had it that de Gaulle actually told Macmillan that he reminded him of the old Piaf *chanson*. But it is inconceivable that de Gaulle actually said anything of the sort to the Prime Minister.

The British took nothing away from Rambouillet, except a joint statement, issued on French initiative, which referred the reader to the Champs communiqué, noting that the EEC negotiations "have been conducted and will be carried forward, in spite of the difficulties which have been encountered, in the spirit defined at the time of the Prime Minister's visit to the Château de Champs last June."[15] De Gaulle was only too glad to help Macmillan disguise the abject failure of the conference. He may not yet have decided exactly when he would formally put an end to the British hopes—probably he wanted first to see what emerged from the Nassau conference (Courcel had given him a realistically sober estimate of Britain's chances of redeeming the Skybolt fiasco)—to see if it might be possible (or desirable) to have it both ways: both exclude Britain from Europe and at the same time entice poor Macmillan, shorn of both Skybolt and his European hopes, into joining Britain's advanced-weapons technology—in warheads, guidance, and submarines—to France's more primitive program. Another, perhaps more central consideration was also pushing de Gaulle to mask his intentions. The author of *Le Fil de l'Épée* had lost none of his faith in the value of holding "in reserve some piece of secret knowledge which may at any moment intervene, and the more effectively from being in the nature of a surprise." The repudiation of the Anglo-Saxons' bold design would be applied with the greatest possible force. A genuine *coup de théâtre* was needed to blur Kennedy's Cuban achievement and to remind the world that France remained a pivotal force in the great events.

8

The Anglo-Saxons Routed

The meeting at Nassau on December 18–21, 1962, was everything a conference of the sort should not be. It was supposed to be one of those relaxed, informal U.S.–U.K. summit meetings (so highly valued by the British) that would allow Kennedy and Macmillan—in the affable mid-winter sunshine of the Bahamas—to exchange views on the missile crisis, the fighting along the China-India frontier, and the difficult Congo problem. But, dominated by the Skybolt affair, Nassau became an impromptu occasion for sorting out the vastly complex problems of nuclear sharing and related questions of NATO politics, without the benefit of the intensive joint staff work that would normally (and necessarily) precede such a meeting. Theodore Sorensen, who has written that the Americans viewed it as a "largely symbolic meeting," added: "The Nassau Pact . . . showed signs of hasty improvisation and high-level imprecision, of decisions taken by the President in Nassau before he was ready to take them in Washington, of excellent motivation and poor preparation." [1] In fact, Nassau was a mess, and most of the officials who were there privately conceded so later.

Preparation was, of course, excluded by lack of time. Mc-

Namara and Thorneycroft had met exactly a week earlier. In the intervening seven days Macmillan had had his last spin of the wheel at Rambouillet, and McNamara and Thorneycroft had been in Paris for the NATO Ministers meeting.

Even if the bureaucrats *had* been able to crank out some of the paper in seven days, they had had no instructions. Macmillan and Thorneycroft were concealing their recently awakened passion for Polaris with a virtuosity that would have done credit to de Gaulle himself; not even Ambassador Ormsby-Gore was instructed.

High-level comments on the American side served to deepen the British unhappiness, as well as to make things even more tense and confused, if that was possible. In a televised conversation with three journalists the day before Nassau Kennedy was very negative about Skybolt:

> We are talking about $2.5 billion to build a weapon to hang on to our B-52's, when we already have billions invested in Polaris and Minuteman. . . . We don't think we are going to get $2.5 billion worth of national security. . . .
>
> The United States has developed Skybolt. We put in $350 million. . . . If we [had] completed it, the British would have bought a hundred. And we would have bought one thousand. It would have cost us $2.5 billion.

He also restated his position on helping France:

> If the French decide they want to become a nuclear power themselves, that is their decision. The question is whether the United States should join in helping make France a nuclear power, then Italy, then West Germany, then Belgium. . . . Why duplicate what we have already done and are doing in Western Europe today, as long as our guarantees are good? *

---

* At the NATO Ministers meeting on December 13–15 McNamara pressed the Europeans to do more about reaching NATO's non-nuclear goals and showed little interest in the by now sensitive question of a nuclear role for the Continentals.

Kennedy was reflecting the dominant mood of his Administration; he and his colleagues felt they had proved something— established more clearly their right to lead—in the Cuba missile crisis. The irony is that on the following day Ormsby-Gore persuaded Kennedy to reconsider Skybolt. And just two days later the President was on the verge of offering de Gaulle as much nuclear aid as required to obtain France's continued and active involvement in the NATO Alliance system.

A favorite Gaullist myth about this fateful week in December is that Kennedy and Macmillan, even *before* the Rambouillet meeting, had agreed that Britain would acquire Polaris in place of the unfortunate Skybolt. To this day, high French officials continue to insist on this example of Macmillan's duplicity. But they know better; they were getting reasonably good information from their Embassy in London.

The fact is that Macmillan's entourage did not know until they had boarded the plane and opened their briefs that Polaris would be sought in place of Skybolt. In Washington some, but not much, interagency staff work had been done on various alternatives.

After boarding the plane for Nassau Kennedy changed into pajamas and prepared to go to work. He first summoned Ormsby-Gore, who was traveling on the White House plane and would remain with him throughout the trip. Kennedy was aware of the sentiment among a number of his own advisers that continued preferential treatment of the British would undermine his European policy, that now was the time to put U.S.–U.K. relations on the same footing as relations with other key European countries. But Ormsby-Gore took the line that the Europeans who might criticize further preferential treatment of Britain would attack even more strongly Kennedy's failure to extricate Macmillan from the Skybolt dilemma; they would be the first, he argued, to proclaim the betrayal of a European state and a vindication of de Gaulle's argument that the

United States sought only to dominate European countries, not to cooperate with them.

If Kennedy had not been impressed by this argument when his plane left Washington, he was when it landed in Nassau. Bundy and Ball had joined in the conversation for part of the trip, but with Ormsby-Gore present it was difficult for them to discuss the American position frankly with the President.

Ormsby-Gore was acting within his instructions, which meant somehow hanging on to Skybolt. He and Kennedy worked out an arrangement whereby the United States and Great Britain would jointly bear the further costs of developing Skybolt, even though the United States itself would not deploy the system. This might have settled the problem had not Macmillan and Thorneycroft already decided on Polaris. And by now quite a number of American officials were expecting to be asked for Polaris. Ormsby-Gore's achievement was not in obtaining a reprieve for Skybolt but in softening up Kennedy for a Macmillan *coup de théâtre* at Nassau. It is a measure of the degree to which events were telescoped that in another part of the White House plane, Assistant Secretary of State for European Affairs William R. Tyler was drafting a handwritten memorandum predicting that any agreement to replace Skybolt with Polaris would be used by de Gaulle as a pretext for vetoing Britain's EEC application.

On arriving at Nassau Kennedy was welcomed by Macmillan, who stressed the "vital part" played by their meetings (this was the sixteenth) in the special relationship. But the hospitable Caribbean sunshine did nothing to alter the mood of the British delegation, which was bitter and tense. Henry Brandon, a veteran British correspondent, found a "resentment and suspicion of American intentions such as I have never experienced in all the Anglo-American conferences I have covered over the past twenty years." [2]

Still, the appearances of affability were maintained. "The

official parties drove off to their villas at the Lyford Cay Club, an exclusive establishment of the kind that seem to flourish in British colonies where American influence leaves only the Union Jack and the constabulary uniforms to suggest that they are not some offshore extension of Miami Beach. The two heads of government are occupying quarters within walking distance, and they will meet briefly later and then dine together." [3] As planned, the talks began with a relaxed survey of U.S.–U.K. policy toward India, the Congo, test-ban negotiations, and NATO's non-nuclear forces. But that evening Macmillan apparently disclosed to Kennedy for the first time his ambition to acquire Polaris.[4] The balance of the conference was absorbed by convulsive efforts to put together a nuclear package that would satisfy everyone. It is not an easy moment to reconstruct; probably no two participants would agree on a single version of what actually happened. Settling one part of the problem abruptly obliged the parties to deal with another part of it— and on a crash basis.

First there was Skybolt. Kennedy proposed the 50-50 arrangement that he and Ormsby-Gore had worked out, but Macmillan said no; the "lady's reputation had been compromised." Another air-to-ground missile, Hound Dog, was offered, but it, too, was declined. Macmillan wanted Polaris.

Kennedy was concerned. By now he had reports from his various advisers and ambassadors in Europe that another bilateral nuclear arrangement would give France a pretext for blocking Britain's European bid.* He showed Macmillan some of the telegrams and described the concern of his advisers.

Kennedy's people apparently did not understand the EEC negotiations, Macmillan observed. All that remained to be settled was the question of British agriculture; the nuclear issue

---

* These messages were relayed to Nassau from Washington. There had not been time to solicit embassy views before the conference.

and the Brussels negotiations were not connected. Technically, Macmillan was right, although disingenuous. De Gaulle, after all, had just told him that Britain's presence in the EEC was unacceptable to France; thus, nothing that happened at Nassau could worsen matters. But Macmillan did not even intimate that the meeting with de Gaulle had gone badly. And, according to Sorensen, the American Embassy in Paris had recently reported that the French were resigned to British entry.[5]

George Ball and other Americans were opposing a Polaris deal on the grounds that Macmillan didn't really want the missile—not, at least, over the long term—so much as he wanted a device that would carry his government and party past one more election. And, in fact, at one point Macmillan dramatized his domestic difficulties in a typically eloquent and wide-range statement. He returned to the Great War of 1914–1918 and the depletion of his generation; he evoked Britain alone in 1940, and the pivotal role of British-based scientists in the Manhattan Project; even if forsaken by America, Britain would soldier on alone, continuing to bear her international responsibilities. He warned Kennedy that a failure at Nassau might mean the collapse of his government and its replacement with a less pro-American, possibly neutralist, one. Was Kennedy ready to accept the responsibility for that? He continued on for some time in this vein, apparently profoundly moved. Finally Kennedy led him away for a walk. They swiftly reached agreement on Polaris. At that point it occurred to Kennedy that he had better obtain something on *his* side, and aides set off to write the Nassau communiqué, a document whose meaning was sufficiently imprecise to require weeks, if not months, of postconference negotiations by special teams to unravel.

Kennedy was not ready to accept the responsibility for bringing down Macmillan, whose judgment of the British political scene he felt bound to accept. "A fondness developed between them which went beyond the necessities of the alliance.

. . . Told after the Nassau agreement . . . that he was 'soft' on Macmillan, Kennedy replied: 'If you were in that kind of trouble, you would want a friend.' " [6] Yet Kennedy was guided by more than admiration and friendship for Macmillan, Alec Douglas-Home, and Ormsby-Gore. At bottom, his gesture was inspired by the special relationship itself, whatever its disrepair. Some of his advisers wanted to liquidate the relationship, to see Britain subsumed in a European grouping that would eventually speak with one voice. But Kennedy, as we have seen, was suspicious of large designs, apparently even those he had sponsored himself. He was much less concerned with the conceptual view of the large questions than with the operational problems themselves. And in any case, he was unwilling to cast aside an interlocutor he knew and understood—Britain—for a nonexistent united Europe.

According to the British, Kennedy was also guided by his concern that if he left Nassau empty-handed Macmillan would turn to de Gaulle; more precisely, that a Franco-British nuclear arrangement would begin to replace the special Anglo-American ties. The threat of this, they say, was implicit in Macmillan's otherwise nostalgic peroration. But the Americans do not agree. One of them has said: "He never threatened us with France." This is further evidence of, if nothing else, the communication gap between the two sides. Macmillan was concealing the bad news from Rambouillet, while his hint that he had a French card to play was apparently too subtle to be grasped by the Americans.

Like most political chiefs (de Gaulle included), Kennedy tended to focus on a problem as it became operational. Almost certainly, he did not know what he would do when he arrived in Nassau. Although the "problem" with Britain had been "operational" for some time, it had not, for all the reasons already noted, come into sharp Presidential focus. At Nassau Kennedy focused—and decided. But in politics, improvisation means trouble. Disposing hastily of one issue usually means that other problems which might otherwise remain on the shelf abruptly become operational, too. The Nassau conference offers a perfect example of how high the cost of improvisation can be. By making Polaris available to Britain, Kennedy was obliged to get something in return, if only to satisfy strong bureaucratic pressures—perhaps a commitment from Macmillan that the British Polaris submarines would be put at the disposal of NATO, so as to "fuzz" their purely national character. And helping Britain again, not to mention debating NATO's nuclear prospects, meant that the old question of helping de Gaulle would once again have to be faced. In brief, Kennedy, who had intended nothing more than a *tour d'horizon* with his friend from No. 10, found himself beset by issues which, he must have thought, either had been resolved (helping France) or should never have reached so advanced a stage (NATO nuclear planning). One of his senior advisers who was at Nassau says: "The nuclear question was not a first order of business until the Skybolt thing flared into a crisis." What he means is that Kennedy never intended to force the pace of the NATO partners' nuclear aspirations: if they wanted a larger voice in nuclear strategy or some sort of joint access to the control of NATO nuclear weapons, let them ask for it. Kennedy preferred the status quo, and he had little appetite for the various schemes and placebos designed to relieve Europe's nuclear frustrations.

One such scheme would have amounted to a European nuclear force, developed slowly as Western Europe moved toward unity. In a speech in Copenhagen in September, Bundy had fluttered Europeans by saying: "It would be . . . wrong to suppose that the reluctance which we feel with respect to individual, ineffective, and unintegrated forces would be extended automatically to a European force, genuinely unified and multilateral, and effectively integrated with our own necessarily predominant strength." [7] Such language committed the White

House to very little, since that sort of European unity seemed a
distant prospect, even in the palmy summer of 1962. Another
approach was contained in the celebrated multilateral nuclear
force (MLF), which had been threading its way through the
Washington labyrinth since the late days of the Eisenhower
Administration—a mixed-manned fleet of surface ships (or
submarines—the mode changed back and forth for a time)
armed with Polaris missiles, jointly owned and operated by
various NATO members, each of which would have had a veto
over the use of the nuclear weapons.

The MLF was less theoretical than some of the other
schemes, if only because it had a fair amount of bureaucratic
support in Washington. It also had a modest White House en-
dorsement, hedged with the condition that the Europeans
would have to show substantial interest in the proposition.
Again, Kennedy was unwilling to force this sort of thing on
them and he was never fully persuaded that they would take it,
since the proposal carried with it an American veto over the use
of the weapons and thus didn't alter the status quo very much.
But the MLF was useful to Kennedy and would remain so.
Whenever he was asked in a press conference about Europe's
nuclear responsibilities Kennedy could point to the MLF as
something the United States would be willing to join in, provided the European allies wanted it enough to pay a fair share
of the cost.

Now, at Nassau, Kennedy found himself pressing the multilateral idea on Macmillan, who seemed to prefer something
short of a jointly owned and operated (mixed-manned) force
—something that was instead "multinational," which meant
nationally owned and controlled unclear weapons put at the
disposal of NATO. This would change nothing, really—not
even appearances—and was irreverently described at the
time as a means of taking one's clothes out of one closet and
putting them into another.

Fitting these conflicting views of the two delegations into a single communiqué, mainly the responsibility of Bundy and Ormsby-Gore, was a prodigious piece of instant diplomacy. Time was short, and the issues were as confused as they were complicated. Kennedy and Macmillan had at best a shaky grasp of the meaning of some of the key terminology. They sat alone in a small cabin at the end of a pier, with advisers running to and fro getting agreement on the many highly technical points, the implications of which were often unclear to everyone. Macmillan, it seems, never really understood that the MLF would require mixed manning (in any case, the term "mixed-manned" appeared in neither the communiqué nor the private memoranda of understanding exchanged between Kennedy and Macmillan). And the issue of multilateral versus multinational forces was resolved by putting both in the communiqué, with the parties agreeing to a multinational element in NATO, while further agreeing to use their "best endeavors" to develop a multilateral nuclear force. It couldn't have been more confusing, especially since the critical passage failed to state whether Britain's Polaris submarines would be in the multinational or multilateral elements. The British, committed to nothing beyond "best endeavors," left Nassau confident that the mixed-manned notion would not trouble them for long. In agreeing to assign their Polaris fleet to NATO they had drawn from the Americans the right to recapture it whenever "supreme national interests [were] at stake" (clearly the only time a government would contemplate using nuclear weapons).

With Anglo-American difficulties seemingly out of the way, Kennedy and Macmillan now had to face the question of de Gaulle, if only because France was in a position to dissolve or gratify Britain's Common Market hopes. Macmillan had no choice but to appeal the verdict of Rambouillet. Kennedy, while he knew nothing about Rambouillet, could see that Britain was in trouble all along the line. He arrived at Nassau determined not to aid France's nuclear-weapons program. He left convinced that if nothing else could purchase de Gaulle's cooperation, it would have to be tried. He was encouraged in this view by Bundy and Assistant Secretary of State Tyler. Neither had any illusions that de Gaulle's cooperation could be "bought," but they felt that, whatever the price, a big effort had to be made to normalize relations with France.

Largely unnoticed in the general confusion was a letter Kennedy had received from Khrushchev while at Nassau reopening the question of a nuclear-test-ban treaty. It was easily Moscow's most forthcoming message on the subject to that date. Kennedy's advisers were too absorbed by their labors to give the letter close attention, but the President was aroused by it; one person, as close to his thinking at the time as anyone, has said that Kennedy quickly began to view the Nassau issues in a world context. In the conciliatory tone of Khrushchev's letter Kennedy scented the possibility of limited *détente* and a more stable relationship between the great powers. By giving France nuclear aid, he might obtain de Gaulle's cooperation for a test-ban treaty as well as a less obstructionist Atlantic policy, while Khrushchev might then get China's signature on the treaty, too.

In offering substantial aid to de Gaulle Kennedy was not yet running a serious risk of committing himself. The chances were at least 50-50 that de Gaulle would say no. And even if he said yes, there was always the hurdle of the Joint Atomic Energy Committee. Did Kennedy, then, really want de Gaulle to accept? Apparently yes. Bundy says the offer to France was a "Sunday try" to bring de Gaulle into the fold. And, according to one account, somebody "important on the American side . . . commented: 'Thank God for Skybolt. It has opened the way to getting the French back into NATO.' " [8]

Macmillan was if anything even more determined to corral de Gaulle. As we have seen, he had long been urging some sort of de facto tridirectorate on Kennedy, and now the moment had arrived. Better to have France's relations with the Americans on a more or less equal footing with Britain's than to have de Gaulle as a chronic adversary. Indeed, helping de Gaulle to achieve what he had originally seemed to want was not a heavy price to pay for gaining entry into the Common Market. Together, France and Britain could control Europe's political (and nuclear) development and maintain a check on West German energies, a foreign policy that would be applauded by the Conservative party and in due course by the British electorate.

Some weeks earlier Washington had agreed to sell France the Skipjack nuclear-submarine technology, in the form of either a completed hull or the nuclear component. Hard-line State Department objections—the West Germans would be upset, the MLF undermined—were beaten down by the Pentagon's dubious argument that the agreement would create a certain French dependence on Washington. In fact, the acquisition of Skipjack would have had the effect of saving France two to four years in acquiring an operational nuclear-submarine capability. But the Skipjack offer was overtaken by Nassau. Even before the communiqué was issued Kennedy and Macmillan notified de Gaulle that France would be eligible for the arrangements already agreed on for Great Britain. In other words France could have the Polaris weapons system provided that she, like Britain, would put her nuclear submarines under NATO command (with the same right of reversion if the national interest so dictated). But France, unlike Britain, had neither the thermonuclear warheads for the missiles nor the submarine technology, as de Gaulle's Minister of Information was quickly instructed to point out. How, then, could the Polaris deal interest de Gaulle, especially since he had not even been invited to take part in the discussions? Much more would be needed. And both Kennedy and Macmillan were determined to avoid an immediate turndown by de Gaulle, and the prospect of protracted negotiations did not bother them. Even if they failed in the end they might take Britain past the shoals of the Brussels negotiations and into the Common Market. That was how Kennedy saw it.

Ambassador Charles Bohlen, assigned to the Paris Embassy during the missile crisis, arrived in Nassau on the last day of the conference and returned with Kennedy to Palm Beach that evening. He received instructions to open negotiations with de Gaulle as soon as possible—instructions closely coordinated with those received by his British colleague, Sir Pierson Dixon. Both were to see de Gaulle and make it clear that his problem was understood in Washington and London; that France would obviously require more than the Polaris itself, but the full scope of nuclear assistance would be subject to negotiation and to de Gaulle's willingness to put the weapons at NATO's disposal in a nominal sense. It is essential to understand what this would have meant. Like Britain, France would have retained full operational control of her American-supplied missiles but would have allowed them to be "targeted" in accordance with the NATO threat list. This would have amounted to their "assignment," in a loose sense, to NATO. Neither mixed manning nor any other dilution of French national control was envisaged—not, at least, as Dixon and Bohlen presented the issue to de Gaulle.

They saw him, respectively, on January 3 and 5. Dixon went further than Bohlen, giving de Gaulle to understand that whatever France would require in addition to Polaris would be made available. (This would have meant, besides submarine technology, thermonuclear warheads or the necessary design information, or possibly both.) He exhorted de Gaulle to accept and even mentioned the possibility of a tridirectorate. Although Bohlen was more guarded, it can be assumed that he stretched his instructions to the limit, conveying the impression that negotiations could lead to an arrangement going well beyond the mere sale of the unarmed Polaris missile system.

No great feat of imagination is required to see the advantages—and single disadvantage—for de Gaulle in this proposition. Militarily, he could move swiftly toward achieving a small but secure subsurface and fully modern nuclear force. Alone, France was at the very least a decade away from such a capability and running the risk that her nuclear weapons would be obsolete as they became operational. And the arrangement within de Gaulle's grasp would mean an enormous saving in French resources. Politically—and, for de Gaulle, the political consequences were, as always, controlling—the offer meant recognition of France as the West's third and last nuclear power. Political and military parity with Britain would be achieved. French supremacy vis-à-vis her West German neighbor—the real purpose of the *force de dissuasion*—would be guaranteed. How could one exaggerate the importance of all this? Several French officials and high civil servants were aroused by what seemed a very long step toward the *directoire à trois* presumably so close to de Gaulle's heart. They hoped he would negotiate to the hilt and accept.

But the single disadvantage remained, and it is most unlikely that de Gaulle was tempted for even a moment by what the Anglo-Saxons seemed to be offering. Parity with Britain had never interested him. What he wanted was French supremacy in Western Europe. Accepting the Nassau arrangement would have obliged him to admit Britain into Europe, and the meaning of that was plain. France would not be the sole nuclear power in the European community, and French political influence would be that much less.

A notion treasured by some in France which has found remarkable acceptance in Britain and America, too, is that Nassau provoked de Gaulle into vetoing the British application to EEC. Britain, the argument goes, after striking a European pose, again chose preferential arrangements with Washington; as an afterthought the Anglo-Saxons offered de Gaulle a piece of the action which they had worked out between themselves and which suited French requirements not at all. This was worse than an insult; it showed no understanding of de Gaulle and his dedication to a Europe progressively free of American influence. The only truth in all this is that the Nassau conference probably hastened the veto and made it easier for de Gaulle to administer. Even before Nassau—before Rambouillet—de Gaulle was completing preparations for a big step toward his "European"—that is to say, French-led—Europe.

In the early autumn of 1962 de Gaulle and Adenauer had agreed to solemnize with a treaty, or executive agreement, the closer Franco-German relations they had brought about. It would commit the two governments to consulting "before any decision on all important questions of foreign policy . . . with a view to reaching as far as possible parallel positions." For the old Chancellor, the accord would signify Franco-German reconciliation, his crowning achievement; for de Gaulle, less sentimental, it was to be the centerpiece of his European policy. For two years he would struggle to move toward his version of "Europe," with Bonn in tow. In vetoing Britain, de Gaulle knew he would need at least the tacit compliance of Adenauer, who would inevitably be strongly pressed by Washington, by London, and by many of his own people to defend the British application. With the treaty ceremonies scheduled for January, de Gaulle must have considered the risk of an Adenauer defection at best marginal. He could always rely on the understanding between them that in constructing Europe, de Gaulle's France had won the role of architect. And he could rely as well on Adenauer's profound dislike of the Kennedy

Administration, not to mention his long-standing distrust of the British.*

Although prepared to do anything to block Britain, de Gaulle probably would have preferred to stretch out the EEC negotiations to see what might happen. Perhaps Macmillan might feel hard-pressed and lonely enough to come to a military agreement with de Gaulle, while accepting something less than full membership in the Common Market—status as an associated trading partner, perhaps. De Gaulle knew that one day the British would take part in the European Community, but first he wanted them shorn of their special ties with America and their special arrangements east of Suez, and, frankly, he wanted them as weak as possible. "I will have them stripped naked," he began to tell people in the winter of 1962–1963.

Now, however, Macmillan not only had acquired Polaris, he wanted to strike up, with Kennedy, a nuclear partnership with de Gaulle. To make matters even more pressing, the British, having foolishly allowed the Brussels negotiations to bog down on the issue of protecting their farmers (and the Tory MPs who represented the farmers), were bestirring themselves to make the last necessary concessions. The moment to strike was at hand.

The immediate tactical position of the three players—de Gaulle, Kennedy, and Macmillan—is worth considering. Kennedy's was much the most complicated; he was confused and disturbed and pulled in different directions. Although strongly pressed to patch up the "special relationship" and to make

---

* Not long before his death Adenauer told an interviewer, "The British . . . have no particular urge to work. After they were thrown out of northern France, they turned to trading and colonizing and acquired an easy way of life—different from the hard work that is the style on the Continent. They are still at it." (Cited by George W. Ball in *The Discipline of Power* [Boston: Atlantic–Little Brown, 1968], p. 78.)

a workable arrangement with de Gaulle, he had always been determined to move slowly, if at all, on the NATO nuclear question. Yet now he found himself on the verge of offering de Gaulle unspecified but very substantial nuclear aid. Most members of the Joint Atomic Energy Committee would strongly oppose this, and their resistance would be fortified by Admiral Rickover. Yet even if Kennedy had wished to consult Rickover and the Joint Committee, there had not been time to do so.

Everything about Nassau aroused the President's suspicions. It seemed a catch-all jerry-built affair. Kennedy told anyone who cared to know that he didn't entirely understand what he and Macmillan had done, or were undertaking to do.* His anxiety was apparent in the defensive tone he took in a background news conference at Palm Beach ten days after the meeting:

> [I am] aware, probably, that we are going to incur at intervals people's displeasure. . . . I think too often in the past we have defined our leadership as an attempt to be rather well regarded in all these countries. The fact is you can't possibly carry out any policy without causing major frictions. I think what we have to do is be ready to accept a good deal more expressions of newspaper and governmental opposition to the United States in order to get something done than we have perhaps been willing to do in the past. I don't expect that the United States will be more beloved, but I would hope that we could get more done.[9]

Le Monde headlined its story on the Palm Beach "backgrounder": "President Kennedy Has Decided to Direct the

---

* Some weeks after returning from Nassau Kennedy asked Richard Neustadt, who served as a private White House consultant, to prepare a comprehensive report on the entire Skybolt affair, more exactly, to explain how the White House had gotten itself so far out on this treacherous limb. Neustadt's report was completed and read by the President just a week before the latter's death.

Western Alliance Without Bothering Himself Too Much with Possible Objections of His Allies." [10] The irony is that the agreements made at Nassau committed the United States to closer forms of cooperation with its chief NATO allies. For sheer confusion and contradiction, the moment was rare.

For de Gaulle, it was the age-old game which he had played so often, demanding as it always did the immaculate secrecy of solitude, signs both positive and negative to throw the other players off balance, and a swift but brutal stroke—the solution of "explosive liberating force"—that, whatever the shock or dismay it caused, or perhaps because of it, achieved an effect of lasting importance. Sorensen wrote, "The angry initial reaction in the United States and Great Britain [to de Gaulle's press conference] was due in part to surprise—not at de Gaulle's attitudes, which were old, but at his tactics, his willingness to act so abruptly, brazenly and brutally, and with so little notice to his allies, when he might have blocked all the same efforts more subtly and gradually." [11] The Gaullist method was not yet understood.

De Gaulle listened respectfully to the urgings of Dixon and the more guarded Bohlen. He told the former he would be "very prudent," and both Ambassadors received the impression of a man looking hard at a proposition and certainly not ruling out negotiations. Bohlen told reporters that he anticipated lengthy negotiations.

Another, very different sort of event played its part in lulling the Anglo-Saxons. Early in December the French government had agreed to send the Mona Lisa to Washington for exhibition at the National Gallery of Art; there would be "no exhibit of the masterpiece other than the three-week display in Washington." André Malraux was charged with accompanying the painting, which arrived in the United States in early January. Malraux then told Kennedy, presumably on Élysée instructions, that President de Gaulle envisaged long negotiations and, by one account, a possible meeting with the American President.[12] In effect de Gaulle was encouraging Kennedy's own view of things. The President had said at Palm Beach, "I would say it will take a good many weeks, possibly months, to work this out. It isn't something that the French or anyone else can give an answer to of yes or no."

More negatively, however, de Gaulle's Information Minister, Alain Peyrefitte, was instructed to say after a cabinet meeting on January 2: "Contrary to Great Britain, France has undertaken [her nuclear program] with her own resources, and she intends to pursue it by her own means." [13]

Ambassador Alphand was now instructed to see Kennedy and find out whether the Polaris offer might include the warhead and submarine technology. On December 29 Alphand went to Palm Beach and talked to Kennedy at length on a yacht belonging to the President's friends, the Charles Wrightsmans. In response to the key question Kennedy said rather vaguely that if the French wished to take up his offer of Polaris and explore the matter further, that would be perfectly normal and acceptable. This bit of evasion was intended to demonstrate flexibility. Alphand failed to detect it and thought Kennedy was being unresponsive; but—and the point bears repeating— Kennedy had not intended to be negative. At this moment he was unprepared to carry matters very far himself, as he had not yet taken soundings with the Joint Atomic Energy Committee or its terrible-tempered cicerone, Admiral Rickover. It was Bohlen in Paris, and not the President, who was supposed to stimulate negotiations.

The purpose of Alphand's journey to Palm Beach is subject to two interpretations, both of which probably have some truth. First, it was a logical and customary way for the French President, having seen Dixon and Bohlen, to get a French reading on the issue at hand. Still, de Gaulle did not normally rely on his ambassadors for such insights. The second possibility is that dispatching Alphand to obtain assurances from Kennedy was comparable to de Gaulle's purpose in floating the tridirectorate in 1958, the idea being to get another unsatisfactory reply. With no time to secure his Congressional or bureaucratic bases Kennedy could not have given Alphand concrete assurances on December 29, any more than Eisenhower could have said yes to the tridirectorate. A closely involved American diplomat known for his dispassionate and balanced judgment says, "It was a mistake for the French to have asked for assurances if they were interested in negotiating, as it would have been dynamite for Kennedy, what with the Joint Committee, etc."

Washington was aware of the danger in Alphand's mission, for the Ambassador was known to be badly informed. Like many other French ambassadors, Alphand was in a sense cut off from much of the normal flow of information. Many French diplomats tended to report what they thought the Élysée Palace wanted, or expected, to hear. Thus, exchanges with responsible officials were limited by the latter's concern about what would be made of the conversations. Such embassies, operating in a kind of vacuum, become a focus, not for privileged information and insight but for the discontented and disgrutled of the host country's bureaucrats (and sometimes political opposition).

De Gaulle had scheduled a press conference for January 14, and it was not expected that he would deal—at least, not categorically—either with the Nassau proposals or the Brussels negotiations on Britain's entry into the EEC. On January 11 London and Washington were further lulled by reports of a luncheon conversation in Paris between Edward Heath, then directing Britain's Common Market application, and Couve de Murville, during which Couve had said: "If you can negotiate your way into the Common Market on economic grounds, no power on earth can keep you out." *

These comforting words aroused the suspicion that perhaps Couve de Murville was not informed of the General's intentions. Although de Gaulle admittedly took nobody into his confidence until the last minute, Couve de Murville and Pompidou must have been aware by January 11 of what would happen on January 14. Pompidou, speaking to journalists at a reception on January 11, said that the real difficulties in the Brussels negotiations remained to be overcome; the talks between Heath and Couve de Murville did not indicate that any substantial progress had been made in reconciling differences over how to fit United Kingdom agriculture into the EEC system. France was not trying to bar Britain from the EEC, he said, but the French government sometimes felt that Britain looked at the EEC as a free-trade zone rather than as a group of countries with common economic rules.[14]

Macmillan's position was the least complicated. Unlike Kennedy, he was not troubled by doubt as to the wisest course to follow; unlike de Gaulle, he was not playing some Byzantine game. It had been a season of political reverses for Macmillan. Even the Nassau conference, considered within his government as a great personal triumph, had been soured by a curiously negative press and public response, which saw only that Britain was committed to replacing Skybolt with a much more expensive weapons system (one that would require building submarines as well) which would only increase her dependence on America even as she was preparing to move out from the "special relationship" and into Europe. Having carried the Tory party to the brink of Europe, Macmillan and Heath were struggling to give the Brussels negotiations the additional

---

* It was felt in some well-informed circles that Couve de Murville also favored negotiations on the Nassau offer and may even have urged this course on de Gaulle.

momentum to achieve a breakthrough, and, they hoped, Nassau would serve that great purpose, if no other.

Some would fault Macmillan for having underrated de Gaulle's hostility to British membership in the EEC. But he believed, reasonably though mistakenly, that de Gaulle's objections were linked to specific issues—defense, agriculture, and so on—which could be dealt with as such. Most of his colleagues tended to agree with him. Macmillan further believed that the important business with France would have to be worked out between de Gaulle and himself; this, too, was reasonable, as de Gaulle seldom entrusted major matters to other people. By the time of the Rambouillet conference, it was too late to mount another policy. Contingency planning for policy in the event of a veto would only have reduced the momentum Macmillan needed.

There remains the apparent refusal of Macmillan and Heath to face fully the gloomy sentence delivered at Rambouillet. Yet this, too, is in a way understandable. It was perhaps impossible for any politician to have fully accepted such an anathema. Macmillan and his colleagues—Heath especially—were so absorbed by the negotiations as to be psychologically unprepared to accept that these had been condemned to failure from the beginning. Only a rare sort of British or American politician could have had such terrible perception. Few, if any, understood then that de Gaulle's approach to statecraft was radically different from their own. For Americans and British, negotiations are not supposed to fail but to lead somewhere—to a definite conclusion, a compromise, the broad lines of which are usually predictable in advance. What Macmillan did not understand—what Harold Wilson, who might have benefited from Macmillan's experience, did not understand—was that de Gaulle was not a man who negotiated. He declaimed, he dictated, he sometimes made sweeping concessions in the grand manner (viz., Algeria); above all, he said no in the grand manner. In early 1967, at the time of the second British application, one heard people in London who should have known better saying: "He wouldn't veto again. He couldn't." But he did, again in a press conference, without even allowing negotiations to begin.

Macmillan, who had so much admired de Gaulle, was the most harshly punished by him, since the British position vis-à-vis de Gaulle was weaker than any other. In the Gaullist view, Britain was *demandeur*, a self-anointed victim. Britain *was*, of course, *demandeur* but still had much to offer de Gaulle. And Macmillan *had* offered at Champs to meet him at least halfway. He still would have at Rambouillet. But de Gaulle had much earlier decided to set sail alone, with only Adenauer to make the necessary weight. For Macmillan, it was a cruel and unmerited turn of fortune. His shattering defeat at de Gaulle's hands has tended to dim his quality and accomplishments. He was the ablest British politician of his day—by a clear margin —and among the most farsighted. In accepting the reality of the EEC (whatever the early efforts of his government to dilute or derail it) and worrying always that it might develop politically without Britain, he was well ahead of the greater part of his party and of all but a tiny handful of the Labour party. Just maneuvering the decision to join the EEC through the Conservative party was a major achievement. Perhaps it blurred his perceptions of the external difficulties, but the evolution of the Tory party away from the "special relationship" and toward Europe was largely his work. The Labour party has since experienced a similar evolution, but it took much longer and was less the work of leadership than of circumstances.

To the list of dramatis personae one must not forget to include Konrad Adenauer. Although the Nassau conference had been applauded nowhere, the most hostile reaction to it had aroused in Bonn. Adenauer had first waxed indignant on behalf of his confederate, de Gaulle, against whom the feckless

Anglo-Saxons seemed to be ganging up; then, as reports began arriving, his government became angry and concerned, if not alarmed, about West German interests. A major step affecting Western defense had been taken and West Germany had not been consulted. Although the scope of the Anglo-American offer to France was not known to the West Germans, or for that matter to the American Embassy in Bonn, Adenauer's government was not slow in finding traces of the detestable tri-directorate.

Four days before de Gaulle's press conference Under Secretary Ball arrived in Paris en route to Bonn to pacify Adenauer. Shortly after arriving he saw Couve de Murville and indicated to him that the MLF was now a serious matter in Washington and would be seriously put forward. (Remarks he made at the airport in Washington had added up to the same thing.) Dixon and Bohlen, earlier, had not linked the Nassau offer to the MLF, and Sorensen's account of the Nassau crisis says de Gaulle was to be given the necessary assistance "if the French aligned their force with NATO under something like the Nassau formula";[15] nobody could say precisely what the Nassau formula was, but it may be assumed that nothing very substantial, certainly no mixed manning, had been demanded of de Gaulle. In the eyes of some Americans and British, Ball's stress on the MLF dulled France's interest in the Nassau offer and thus helped de Gaulle to decide against accepting. This is doubtful. Almost certainly de Gaulle had decided much earlier that accepting the Nassau offer could not be fitted into his great enterprise of building a Continental European bloc with Adenauer. By January 10, when Ball arrived, de Gaulle was doubtless already preparing those portions of his press conference dealing with Britain and Nassau (the section on Britain runs to several pages, and de Gaulle was known to write and memorize the passages several days in advance). The day before, André Fontaine had written in *Le Monde:* "After a profound study of the Bahamas agreement, our leaders would conclude that Britain has accepted, in fact, complete integration of her national defense system in the American system." [16]

The term "press conference" did little justice to the semi-annual pilgrimage of the Paris press corps, government ministers, and assorted notables of the city to the Élysée Palace. It was, rather, a piece of theater, a happening, an event of sometimes capital importance—a ritual with all the panoply and pomp of a royal ceremony, but few royal heads of state performed so brilliantly or to such effect as this plebiscitary monarch.

At the stroke of 3, the great figure would appear through parted brocade curtains. The assemblage, standing for his entrance, would resume its seat. Questions would be accepted and grouped, while the hands clasped and unclasped, not from nervousness but anticipation. Every phrase of the responses had been memorized, and the questions were an essential but tedious bit of prologue, solemnly acknowledged. Now and then, after one passage had been declaimed in language of immaculate purity, a journalist would be asked to repeat his question, not because it had been forgotten—it was irrelevant anyway—but simply to release the audience for a moment the better to recapture it fully. At least twice questions were answered that were never asked. Especially sharp thrust were greeted by applause, or by applause and laughter both, if that was the intended effect.

At 4:20 p.m., on January 14, 1963, another bravura performance was over, and the Anglo-Saxons routed. Europe was denied to England. Macmillan's and Kennedy's modest hopes of snaring de Gaulle with the lure of nuclear aid and a NATO tridirectorate were dead. Only Franco-German cooperation had found a positive note.

On the same day—at nearly the same moment—Kennedy

was delivering his State of the Union address, in which he expressed hope for the Nassau agreement in words that would sound ironic only seconds later:

> Last month Prime Minister Macmillan and I laid plans for a new stage in our long cooperative effort, one which aims to assist in the wider task of framing a common nuclear defense for the whole alliance. . . .
>
> We remain too near the Nassau decisions, and too far from their full realization, to know their place in history. But I believe that, for the first time, the door is open for the nuclear defense of the Alliance to become a source of confidence, instead of a cause of contention.

"They won't wear it," some cried out in Britain, meaning that the other members of the EEC would not stand by and allow de Gaulle whimsically to liquidate the now fourteen-month-old negotiations for Britain's entry. But they were wrong. Apart from West Germany, the others could do nothing except protest bitterly against France for the record and complain privately, with some justice, about Britain playing into de Gaulle's hands by not having speedily settled the agricultural issue.

At official levels the Anglo-American reaction was muted. No. 10 Downing Street moved to cancel a trip to Paris that Princess Margaret had planned for January, while President Kennedy quietly withdrew the Skipjack submarine offer. Also, at the unveiling of the Mona Lisa, he scrapped a graceful prepared statement for an overdrawn and tasteless bit of lampoonery in which he referred to France as "the leading artistic power in the world." Malraux, trying to keep up appearances, had earlier replied to a question on whether the painting would be sent to any other country by saying: "Only one country in the world saved France twice in this century." [17]

Just hours after de Gaulle's exalted moment the focus shifted abruptly to Bonn, where the Franco-German treaty preparations were under way. Jean Monnet urged Adenauer not to sign unless de Gaulle lifted his veto. Forces within the West German government, led by Foreign Minister Gerhard Schroeder, were pressuring the Chancellor to use his leverage with de Gaulle to help Britain. Washington added a passionate voice (Kennedy himself intervened). But it was no use.

In this case, de Gaulle was really *demandeur,* although obscuring the fact. A special bilateral tie with Bonn had been his idea. The language had been drafted in the Quai d'Orsay and modified somewhat by the Germans. Having failed to move Italy and the Benelux countries toward his version of political Europe, de Gaulle was bent on moving in the same direction *à deux.*

With considerable pomp and ceremony, dimmed only slightly by the gloomily disapproving Schroeder, the treaty was signed on January 22. Just eight days earlier, the day of de Gaulle's press conference, Adenauer had told George Ball that Germany would join the MLF and contribute a major share of the cost. Now, during the ceremonies at the Élysée, he confided this decision to de Gaulle. There was much that Adenauer didn't understand. For de Gaulle, this would rob the treaty they were signing of its real content, for then as always he saw the MLF as an anti-French device designed to neutralize the effect on West Germany of his own *force de dissuasion.* And he was partly right.

De Gaulle acknowledged Adenauer's confidence by saying that since France was building her own nuclear force the MLF was of no interest to him, although he could understand that West Germany might want to consider the matter. And that was to remain the French attitude just as long as the MLF seemed more abstract than real. Actually, West German participation in such a project, if it should ever show signs of life, was inadmissible to de Gaulle; in time, that would be made clear.

In Washington, where much cocktail and dinner-party conversation was dominated by the clever people who could explain the difference between multilateral and multinational forces, a curious asymmetry was emerging. Various elements of the State Department and the foreign-policy Establishment were determined that the dismay and bitterness aroused by de Gaulle's veto of Britain should be used to promote the fortunes of the MLF. Some of them—perhaps not many—were seized with anxiety that the Franco-German treaty might prefigure an inner European coalition with a nuclear component—possibly some variant of the original Strauss–Chaban-Delmas agreement. (The anxiety was misplaced; it never was and never would be any part of de Gaulle's purpose to allow German access to nuclear weapons.) The MLF had a subtler and rather more plausible purpose of blurring the distinction between Europe's nuclear haves and have-nots. Put differently, de Gaulle would have difficulty in using his nuclear advantage to exact political concessions from a West German government participating in a MLF.

Yet Kennedy remained leery. He never permitted the bureaucrats to press for the MLF on Capitol Hill. He authorized ambassadors to explore the MLF with other governments, but he would never commit the White House—that is, his envoys were not instructed in the normal sense of the term and the other government was never fully clear on the degree of the White House commitment.

Kennedy's reservations were strengthened by his growing preoccupation with arms control. Although some officials argued in favor of the MLF on arms-control grounds—it might lower the possibility of some nations taking the nuclear path —the Russians were certain to see it, or would choose to see it, as a device by which West Germans would one day control nuclear weapons.

What is certain is that after the French veto of Britain,

Kennedy gradually became more relaxed about Alliance politics. *Détente* seemed a more tempting and perhaps even more
reasonable long-run goal than improved Atlantic arrangements.
Although Khrushchev was an enemy, there was some identity
of interest between Washington and Moscow, however limited.
Between the White House and the Élysée Palace there was
really none. And communications were down.

The events of January were decisive in de Gaulle's history
with the Anglo-Saxons. In a way the preceding four years,
from his tridirectorate proposal on, had been preparation for
that moment—for the rupture—which alone in de Gaulle's
eyes would guarantee "free hands."

An anti-American and anti-British propaganda campaign
was launched at the same time, pointing up the break.* It was
inaugurated by a brief television program called "The Anglo-
Saxons," which followed scenes of de Gaulle and Adenauer
embracing after signing the Franco-German treaty. As described in one report, the film "sought to show in about ten
minutes the special relations between the United States and
Britain since the time of the *Mayflower*. . . . The fact that
uncomplimentary remarks about bad taste in the United States
were also part of the program increased the irritation of many
Frenchmen." [18] In *Les Échos*, a Paris business daily, the publisher, Emile Servan-Schreiber, said the show reminded him of
the attacks on Britain and the United States made during the
war in the Nazi-controlled French-language press.[19]

Some days later Ambassadors Ormsby-Gore and Alphand
made a joint television appearance in Washington, during
which Ormsby-Gore, quite on his own initiative, remarked that
de Gaulle envisaged an alliance with Russia and cited passages
from de Gaulle's memoirs to sustain his argument. This was

---

* The campaign endured. It was waged with particular force on television,
and once provoked a well-justified official objection from former Ambassador
Charles Bohlen.

picked up by Gaullist newspapers in Paris, one of which accused Britain of unleasing psychological warfare. But the White House wasn't listening. Kennedy, still buoyed by Cuba, was becoming more and more absorbed by other matters and less sensitive to the great scold of the Élysée Palace.

The year 1963 was for the most part a bad year for de Gaulle. It started off with a gratifying bang but from then on went badly until the death of Kennedy, a great stroke of political luck for de Gaulle. Obviously, de Gaulle took no personal satisfaction in Kennedy's passing. Nobody who understands de Gaulle would accept any such suggestion. He had admired Kennedy and was conscious of Kennedy's interest in him; he considered Kennedy a player, an opponent, of high caliber. Still, in cold political terms, with Kennedy's death the Élysée Palace, not the White House, now sheltered the world's most prestigious and alluring political figure. Indeed, in the space of a few months, all of the West's ranking political chiefs except de Gaulle departed the political scene, leaving behind lesser figures. The death of Pope John removed yet another leader with a strong grip on the popular imagination.

It was a transitional moment, with the old leadership moving to the sidelines, the Cold War ice jam loosening. For de Gaulle, the months that followed the signing of the treaty with West Germany brought nothing but disappointment. The treaty had provoked the Americans to tighten their links with—their hold on, in his view—Bonn. As the end of the Adenauer era came into view, Germany found herself being gradually pushed toward an impossible choice between Washington and Paris. United States–West German defense arrangements became so close as to amount to a special bilateral pact within NATO. McNamara was virtually functioning as a superminister of the West German government, influencing budgetary decisions and so on. And in ratifying the treaty, the Bundestag had attached a preamble which provided that the agreement did not affect the rights and obligations flowing from other multilateral treaties and specifically called attention to the goals of NATO and EEC. The Americans had had more than a little to do with the language of this preamble, as de Gaulle must have known. De Gaulle was seldom optimistic, and now his doubts about the treaty became visible. The preamble really meant that the treaty was stillborn.

Two days before the first semiannual Franco-German summit meeting (July 4–5, 1963), as provided for in the treaty, de Gaulle received a number of French deputies and senators at a dinner. To some who spoke in skeptical terms about the treaty, he said, *"Les traités, voyez-vous, sont comme les jeunes filles et comme les roses: ça dure ce que ça dure. Si le traité franco-allemand n'était pas appliqué, ce ne serait pas la première fois dans l'histoire."* And then he added the celebrated lines of Victor Hugo: *"Hélas, que j'en ai vu mourir de jeunes filles."*

Two days later, in Bonn, he was welcomed by the world's best-known fancier of roses, the old Chancellor, who mentioned having just read that roses and young girls pale quickly. But, he said, "the roses I planted at Rhoendorf [his residence] have passed the winter brilliantly." And he compared Franco-German friendship to a rose that will always have buds and blossoms.

De Gaulle in reply invoked Ronsard's rose: *"une rose ne dure que l'espace d'un matin."* But, he added, a *rose garden* lasts a long time if one wishes it to, and the treaty should then be compared less to a rose than to a rose garden.[20]

Both in word and deed, de Gaulle continued to harass the Anglo-Saxons. At the spring NATO Ministerial meeting the new McNamara strategy of "flexible response" was finally accepted by the other governments but vetoed by the French representative on the Military Committee. This was probably applauded silently by most of the other European members, few (if any) of whom felt comfortable about the new strategy. But for the Americans it didn't really affect matters. Rhetoric aside, the doctrine of controlled response had somewhat less to do with NATO than with the Pentagon; it was one of a number of devices to concentrate control of nuclear weapons in the office of the Secretary of Defense.

Kennedy was embarked on the ceremonial European tour of his Presidency at about this time. The moment was not propitious for a visit to Europe and he had nearly called off the trip. Macmillan, enfeebled by his winter reversals, was embroiled in the Profumo affair; he was to leave office in three months; Adenauer would follow some weeks later; in Italy Pope John was dying. But Kennedy went ahead with his plans, whatever the risks, in order to reach European public opinion "in the wake of de Gaulle's charges against the United States." [21] And the glowing success was dimmed not in the least by de Gaulle's gesture, taken three days before Kennedy's departure, in withdrawing French naval forces from the NATO North Atlantic fleet.* Kennedy was greeted particularly warmly in West Germany, where he strongly endorsed the so-called Atlantic Partnership (by then known as the "grand design"). Europeans were immeasurably heartened by these words:

> The future of the West lies in Atlantic partnership—a system of cooperation, interdependence, and harmony whose peoples can jointly meet their burdens and opportunities throughout the world. Some say this is only a dream, but I do not agree. . . .
> And that is why we look forward to a united Europe in an Atlantic partnership—an entity of interdependent parts, sharing equally both burdens and decisions, and linked together in the task of defense as well as the arts of peace.

---

* He had withdrawn most of France's naval forces from NATO when he quit NATO's Mediterranean fleet in 1959; leaving behind the others may have been an oversight.

This is no fantasy. It will be achieved by concrete steps to solve the problems that face us all: military, economic, and political.

With Kennedy's return from Europe began the amenities leading up to the signing of a limited nuclear-test-ban treaty. This accord with Moscow signified the changing world political environment made possible by the Americans' successful crisis management of the previous October. Only France and China abstained. Although de Gaulle's rejection of the treaty was predictable and consistent, Kennedy and Macmillan first made another "Sunday try" to corral him. The Nassau proposition was, in effect, resubmitted: in return for signing the test-ban treaty, de Gaulle was given to understand (in letters from Kennedy and Macmillan) that unspecified but substantial nuclear help would be provided. A senior member of the Kennedy Administration says the offer to de Gaulle was open-ended. "In effect, we asked him what sort of nuclear cooperation he would require in order to sign." Typically, the British letter was more explicit (Macmillan's bitterness apparently did not interfere with policy) and made clear what the American letter really meant—that the French weapons program would not be handicapped by adherence to the test-ban treaty, since her nuclear allies would provide data and techniques that could otherwise be obtained only by protracted testing in the atmosphere (prohibited by the treaty) or underground (where de Gaulle was not equipped to operate).*

This final effort to gain French adherence to the test-ban agreement offers a view of Kennedy's persistent unwillingness to abandon the unattainable—a workable relationship with de Gaulle. Other objections aside, de Gaulle clearly could not accept a treaty that seemed to signal the start of a great-power

---

* For France, a limited test-ban agreement meant a complete ban, as France had not yet begun to miniaturize her nuclear weapons.

dialogue. And if he *had* accepted, Kennedy might conceivably have lost the treaty in the Senate, where hostility to de Gaulle was still on the rise.

De Gaulle brusquely rejected this second—and last—Anglo-American effort to give France a preferential position vis-à-vis the West Germans and other Continental allies. Typically, London and Washington got their answer in his semiannual press conference (of July 29):

> The United States . . . sees tempting prospects opening up before it. Thus, for example, all the separate negotiations between the Anglo-Saxons and the Soviets—which, starting with the limited agreement on nuclear testing, seem likely to be extended to other questions, notably European ones—until now in the absence of the Europeans, which clearly goes against the views of France.
>
> Q.: If by chance the United States and Great Britain were to propose supplying France with all she needed for her nuclear armament . . . would you agree to placing your signature at the bottom of this agreement, thus establishing France as the fourth nuclear power? [The questioning journalist was remarkably well informed, or making a good guess. The Anglo-American offer was a well-kept secret.]
>
> A.: You know that France's signature is not given to a series of hypotheses, none of which until now has even begun to be implemented.

The July 29 press conference marked the end of Anglo-American efforts to do important business with de Gaulle. If Kennedy never fully abandoned hope of normalizing relations, he was largely disabused. In October 1963 he asked Couve de Murville, visiting at the White House, to specify the changes France wanted in NATO, toward which de Gaulle was so hostile. Couve de Murville replied that the question was premature and advised the President to forget it. Clearly, he didn't know exactly what was in the General's mind (although he had suspected or known for a long time that eventually de Gaulle would leave the NATO organization and possibly the Alliance itself). Just before he died, in an interview with the French journalist Jean Daniel, then of *l'Express*, Kennedy observed wryly that de Gaulle "requires a certain amount of tension in his relations with Washington"; he was, "decidedly, the strangest great man of our time." [22]

Yet Kennedy, typically, was negotiating for a working-weekend visit by de Gaulle to Hyannis Port. De Gaulle, after all, was the one European leader with both a point of view and political weight. Kennedy had always hoped to hear a European point of view. He was not a traditional diplomatist seeking to gain position or leverage on his opposite numbers. He had never tried to impose his views on the Europeans. Rather he sought always to work something out. He hoped the Europeans would settle on a European solution to joint problems and then take it up with him. (This partly explains his ambiguous position on the MLF; he let it proceed internally—within the bureaucracy—but was reluctant to press it on Western Europe.) Kennedy sought an interlocutor in Europe, and in West Germany specifically. He got neither. Obviously, de Gaulle could have had the European role in return for very little; but he would never come even a small part of the way, a disappointment that Kennedy accepted philosophically and without bitterness. Equally, he had hoped to find some West German —a minister or even an ambassador—with whom he could deal realistically on the Berlin problem. Schroeder might well have been this person, but he became Foreign Minister too late to alter the pattern of the Kennedy-Adenauer relationship, never good, or even to influence the Chancellor's thinking on most matters. The Foreign Ministry often had one policy, Adenauer another.

This is one way of saying that Kennedy never really had a European policy. His grand design was clearly unacceptable

to de Gaulle; for this and other reasons, Kennedy the prag-
matist never fully committed himself to it. On the other hand,
the European unity movement (on which the grand design relied) was both desirable and entirely consistent with American
foreign policy since the Marshall Plan. Moreover, de Gaulle's
unshakable hostility became steadily clearer; although he
was the sole figure who could lay a strong claim to leadership
in Europe, he would deploy his strength only to advance a
largely irrelevant claim to greatness. Kennedy doubtless understood all or most of this toward the end; and if he was reluctant
to animate a strong policy it was because he saw all the pitfalls.
He agonized, but never decided. He gave Atlantic politics a
great deal of thought and attention, but his wary and pragmatic
attitude inhibited boldness. Some who were closely involved
believe that, had he lived, he might have deployed his great
prestige in Europe in a struggle designed in the end to diminish the influence and prestige of the colossal anachronism
who was ruling France. It is doubtful that Kennedy ever entertained such a romantic view of the future. Like de Gaulle, he
took things as they came and did with them what he could.
Unlike de Gaulle, there was nothing he wanted to tear down;
his purpose rather was to rationalize and improve the existing
system within the limits set by politics.

In a rash moment Kennedy told a journalist, "Charles de
Gaulle will be remembered for one thing only, his refusal to
take that [the test-ban] treaty." [23] This, of course, was nonsense. De Gaulle will be remembered longer and better for a
number of other decisions—among the most notable being his
rejection of the Nassau proposal. By accepting just a little
water in his wine, he could have achieved the uppermost goal
of postwar French foreign policy—assurance of political supremacy vis-à-vis Germany. But he was determined to pursue
a will-o'-the-wisp. Eventually, he hoped, the Soviet Union would
play the game—would recognize de Gaulle as its interlocutor

in the West. The Americans would go home, and a new European security system would emerge as a kind of Franco-Russian condominium designed to contain Germany. It was hopeless in 1963 and was no less so in the following years. But, to repeat de Gaulle's words, "Leaders of men . . . are remembered less for the usefulness of what they have achieved than for the sweep of their endeavors. Though sometimes reason may condemn them, feeling clothes them in an aura of glory."

De Gaulle never faltered in striving to give substance to his vision of France's role, and to infuse his countrymen with the same lofty sense of their destiny. Thus, he rejected the "twin-pillar" rhetoric of Kennedy and the others with the supreme aversion he had for any enterprise that might limit France's freedom of movement instead of extending it. At any time until the latter part of 1963 or thereabouts, de Gaulle could have been president of a United States of Europe. After that, it was too late.

9

Contact with Moscow

The morning after John Kennedy's death in Dallas, de Gaulle remarked to the British Ambassador, "At heart, he was a European." [1]—the highest of tributes to the star-crossed young colleague and rival, who had wanted few things more than good relations with de Gaulle's France.

President Lyndon Johnson, like his predecessor, was eager to reach a workable understanding with de Gaulle, and arranged to meet with him privately at the State Department after Kennedy's funeral. He pressed de Gaulle to come to Washington early in 1964 (Kennedy had reached an agreement in principle for a working-weekend visit to Hyannis Port). Johnson might have known that de Gaulle's cautious, if not cryptic response, with its reference to diplomatic channels, was equivocal. But the result, perhaps inevitably, was a misunderstanding, and the new President told a group of governors whom he saw immediately afterward that a meeting was on.

If for Johnson it was an awkward beginning, de Gaulle was surely not displeased. He had nothing really to discuss with the Americans. Indeed, he knew that relations with Washington were likely not to improve but to worsen, and he may have hoped to provoke an unguarded reaction in the White House, which would help him shift the blame for any deterioration to the American side. Private reports that Johnson's weakness was vanity inspired de Gaulle to make unflattering remarks about him, assuming (rightly enough) that these would find their way to the White House. Johnson never took the bait, and this was a continuing source of annoyance to the General.

What de Gaulle knew and Johnson did not was that France was preparing to extend the conflict with the Americans to the roomy terrain of East Asia. On January 27, 1964, the French government extended diplomatic recognition to Communist China, a gesture which, as with most of de Gaulle's actions, was designed to serve multiple purposes. As de Gaulle saw it, China, the political and cultural pivot of Asia, was to Asia as France was to Western Europe, and he envisaged a cultural and commercial purpose for France's presence there—based on this perception of China's primacy in Asia and on France's long-standing relations with her. (The French have traditionally been influential in Shanghai and in the province of Yunan, having built the railroad connecting Kunming and Haiphong, the port city of North Vietnam.) And then China, a vast country with global political attributes, was virtually devoid of Anglo-Saxon influence; the United States was altogether absent, and the British were barely present, with a small office headed by a chargé d'affaires, all but ignored by the Chinese. A French Embassy, however, would restore some measure of French influence—chiefly because France sympathized with China's aversion to the heavy American presence in Southeast Asia and was ready to prove it. Also, besides vexing the Americans, an exchange of embassies with Peking would remind Khrushchev, who still refused to take de Gaulle seriously, that it was also in France's power to stir the troubled waters of world Communism. This was as important a part of de Gaulle's purpose as any other. With Washington and Moscow having achieved a test-ban agreement and possibly moving toward a great-power understanding, it was elementary and quite in character for de Gaulle to edge toward China and stir up trouble for both the Russians and Americans in Southeast Asia.

Still, Washington appeared to be taking a more philosophical view of the General. The *New York Times'* diplomatic correspondent observed:

> Today the General is no longer viewed here as a 10-foot-tall creator of obstacles, but rather as a peculiarly willful obstructionist. His notions of self-interest strike Washington as annoying and misguided where a year ago they seemed wholly defeating and malevolent. President Johnson is setting the tone, and his equanimity is probably more conducive to composure than the simultaneous campaign of the Department of State to curb all forms of Francophobia.

The reporter went on to note Johnson's feeling that he had gotten de Gaulle's agreement for a state visit to Washington, and the French government's efforts to shift the meeting to French soil in the Caribbean. France was also stirring up trouble for the United States in other, awkward places, as for example, Peace Corps units in French-speaking countries in Africa. But whatever the difficulties, the article concluded, Johnson "doesn't want to fuss with the General or fuss about the General." [2]

As it happened, this was Johnson's attitude toward de Gaulle throughout his tenure in the White House. Whatever the provocation, he almost never replied to it, and if so with composure. This was the course urged on him by McGeorge Bundy and Charles Bohlen, although both believe it was a decision he made on his own. From the beginning, Johnson was less impressed by de Gaulle than either of his predecessors. Unlike Eisenhower, he was not burdened with sentimental wartime associations, and his regard for de Gaulle's towering presence in the world was predictably less than Kennedy's; and then, of course, he was the beneficiary of their luckless French experiences.

Although not entirely unexpected, France's recognition of China was something of a surprise. By design or accident, Pompidou had thrown doubt on the likelihood of French recognition in early January by declaring that it "was not for tomorrow." [3] But concern grew during the month, and the American government at one point sent a note to the Élysée trying to discourage the move.[4]

For the old-fashioned nationalist of Maurrasian bent—the self that inspired much of de Gaulle's purpose—diplomatic recognition of China was essential to the truly global diplomacy for which France was now preparing. If less mighty than the superpowers, France would play them off against each other while aligning herself with the declared goals of the Third World (where de Gaulle's prestige, thanks largely to the Algerian settlement, was immense). Add to this the radiant force of French culture, and the vision of Maurras in 1910 became the temptation of de Gaulle in 1964. As Maurras said:

> Circumstances are propitious for the interposition of a state like our own. This fortunate constitution of ours . . . would open the way to the best, most active, and most fruitful policy of influence; for our king, as absolute master of his army, navy, and diplomatic corps, would enjoy the necessary independence to watch for the inevitable excesses of arrogant policy abroad which the Germans, the Russians, the British, and the Americans could not avoid making.
>
> We would need neither to seek friends nor to invite them; the secondary states would be driven in our direction by the force of circumstances; we would see them flock to us. It is up to us, then, to be wise enough and show ourselves vigorous enough to inspire confidence, to appear as effective protectors and not as tyrants. This league of lesser peoples could entrust us with its

military command, and the policy which the kings of France always followed—of blocking the creation of any world-wide monarchy or the excessive growth of this or that coalition—would again triumphantly shine forth from Paris. As in times past, by reason of the numerical inferiority which sometimes hampered us without putting us at a real disadvantage, we may not take up as much space on the map as the biggest powers; we shall, however, enjoy moral authority, based on a very much better kind of strength. More skillfully than Prussia or Piedmont before the unifications of Germany and Italy, we shall multiply our assets by an adroit use of friends, protégés, and newly liberated peoples trained and strengthened by our help. This policy of generosity will bring other rewards besides its beauty, for our chivalry will elevate us to empire.

And if we are tempted to believe we are isolated, let us remember all the people in the world who still speak French or Latin: vast Canada, and those boundless opportunities which Central and South America open before us! This is not the stuff to resist a bold French approach. The French spirit has innumerable objects to choose from.[5]

And now de Gaulle in his news conference of January 31, 1964, replying to a question on how Latin America fitted in his policy of cooperation with developing countries (a question very possibly planted and, curiously enough, following a request for de Gaulle to give a judgment on the Fifth Republic's constitution after five years of experience), said:

[The] undertaking goes beyond the African context and actually constitutes a world-wide policy. By this means, France may turn toward other nations on other continents which are more or less broadly developing, which attract us instinctively and naturally, and which, wanting for their own development the kind of support given in our spirit and in our way, may want to associate us directly with their progress and, reciprocally, take part in all that concerns France.

It is of this, for instance, that we spoke with Lester Pearson,

Prime Minister of Canada, during the friendly and fruitful visit
he recently paid us. It is of this that we intend to speak, in the
near future, with Lopez Mateos, President of Mexico, and later,
no doubt, with the governments of the South American states on
the occasion of the journeys I hope to have the honor of making
there. It is of this that we shall speak to our friend Prince
Sihanouk, the Cambodian Head of State, then to His Majesty the
King of Laos, and to his Prime Minister Prince Souvanna
Phouma, when we receive them in Paris. . . .

No doubt the effort which we Frenchmen are capable of making materially . . . is limited by our resources, which are not
vast. But our own [domestic] progress affords us means that are
increasing from year to year. Moreover, the problem often consists in bringing our friends the yeast of technical and cultural
progress, and this requires human capacities and cordial understanding even more than money. Lastly, we may believe that
tomorrow's Europe, organized as we propose, would in solidarity
with us play a larger part in this enterprise on which the fate of
mankind depends. Everything is related. What we are trying to
do to create a Europe that will be itself falls in with what we
are doing for the peoples rising within our civilization. Yes,
cooperation is, henceforth, a great ambition of France.

In short, the Third Force must secure the backing of the Third
World; and equally, France's limited capability, explicitly acknowledged, to play a large role in the progress of the developing nations would expand once Europe was organized under
French leadership.

De Gaulle's affinity for the sensibilities of the new nations
was an attitude of uncertain vintage and depth. In the postwar
years he had often opposed efforts to loosen France's grip on
Indochina. In 1946, for example, two faithful Gaullists were
sent to Indochina, one, General Leclerc, to command the
ground forces, the other, Admiral Thierry d'Argenlieu, as High
Commissioner. Leclerc was impressed by the determination of
the Vietnamese to be independent, and he advocated giving

their freedom to them within the framework of some mutually acceptable agreement; he did not doubt that an agreement could be reached. Thierry d'Argenlieu, on the other hand, sought to re-establish French sovereignty and refused to deal with Ho Chi Minh. A year later Léon Blum, then Prime Minister, wanted to replace Thierry d'Argenlieu with Leclerc, but Leclerc refused under pressure from de Gaulle.[6] * Paul Ramadier, Blum's successor, also tried and was also refused, again presumably for the same reason.

The advent of Lyndon Johnson coincided with a more wideranging and aggressive French diplomacy, of which the focal points were Southeast Asia and Germany. The Élysée now took aim at the American involvement in France's old colonial dependencies of Laos and Vietnam, and would put even greater pressure on the Washington-Bonn link. In early February de Gaulle granted an interview to C. L. Sulzberger, as always a means of reaching the world beyond the Élysée Palace. This is how General de Gaulle saw the year developing, wrote Sulzberger on February 3, 1964: The United States would be irritated for some months about his Chinese and Southeast Asia policies; and de Gaulle saw no possibility of meeting Johnson at any time or place that year. The United States would be tied down in Vietnam, and de Gaulle would

> therefore seek to move forward in Europe and Latin America at U.S. expense while [the United States] concentrates on the East. . . .
>
> He feels Russia is terrified by the prospect of any unified Germany, neutralized or not, because of Russian national, not Communist ideological reasons. . . . And the French believe that, regardless of the Bonn-Washington flirtation, West Germany will remain part and parcel of that European formation France aspires to lead. . . . De Gaulle therefore reckons accord-

---

* Leclerc, a distinguished soldier and patriot, was closer to de Gaulle than most of his other colleagues either before or since.

ingly: France must keep Britain out of "Europe." But "Europe" is moving toward economic unification.

Paris, Sulzberger concluded, was working for an independent West European bloc at the expense of American interests.[7]

De Gaulle rarely offered so sharp a preview of his immediate expectations—as often as not a peek behind the curtain was a snare, a means of putting people off the track—but this was a reliable and prescient account of much that lay ahead. Not that anybody paid much attention. French public relations was busily softening and blurring the General's line. He and Couve de Murville appeared, respectively, on the covers of *Newsweek* and *Time* in early February. Pompidou, speaking before the American Club of Paris on February 24, remarked (quite wrongly) that agreement between France and the United States was total on fundamental issues and that divergencies were only on the surface; Ambassador Alphand conveyed the same message on the same day to the Economic Club of Detroit. On March 5 *Le Figaro* urged a de Gaulle-Johnson meeting. And the French press was again taking up the cherished theme that if de Gaulle had chosen to be a *cavalier seul,* it was because Washington did not know how to make common policy with him.

Other newspaper stories began to appear noting de Gaulle's belief that he could, with Peking's help, neutralize Laos, Cambodia, and Vietnam. The source of tension between Paris and Washington was at this point not so much Vietnam as Laos. President Kennedy's decision, taken not long after his arrival in office, against trying to impose an anti-Communist solution in Laos led to the negotiated settlement concluded in Geneva in July 1962, which provided for a neutral Laotian regime led by Prince Souvanna Phouma, a sensitive, well-intentioned man endowed with a French education, a French wife, and a strong French bias fully reciprocated at the time in Paris. On the Western side, the agreement had been worked out by the United States, Britain, and France. The latter two had always taken essentially the same view of the Laotian problem: whatever differences they had were obscured by their joint aversion to the American notion of trying to impose a right-wing solution in a place where it just couldn't work. All the Americans who participated in the negotiations praised the French performance during the period leading up to the 1962 agreement.*

The trouble started after the settlement, which required close supervision and seemed, at best, a means of institutionalizing the political confusion of the picturesque little non-country. No one thought the agreement would be respected indefinitely, certainly not by the Communist Pathet Lao, supported by Hanoi and easily the most potent political force in Laos. Thus the Americans urged France to maintain and even enlarge the military assistance group she was authorized by the Geneva agreements of 1954 to assign to Laos. The French balked. They had, after all, just ended the Algerian war, and de Gaulle was eager to begin identifying France with the nationalistic currents running through so much of the Third World. And then, the idea of playing the American game in a former French colony—indeed, in an area where Roosevelt once hoped to remove the French presence—was certain to have little appeal. Many French diplomats also objected because they feared that elements of the French army remained wedded to the bad old political objectives. And there were some Frenchmen—Gaullists especially but not exclusively—who suspected that the United States was determined to supplant them in Laos, where French influence had been supreme. (French is the

---

* It was Ambassador Pierre Falaize who dealt most closely with Souvanna Phouma in behalf of the common Western position. But he worked closely with his British colleague and with the new American ambassador, Winthrop Brown (who had arrived in the final months of the Eisenhower Administration).

language of all the schools except one, built with American aid, where the teachers instruct in Lao; and the politicians usually write in French and then have their speeches translated into Lao.) Even the United States' request for a stronger French military presence was even interpreted by some as an effort to diminish France by saddling her with military obligations (this ignored the situation in Vietnam, where Kennedy had already started an American military build-up). France's military presence, so the argument ran, would serve to stabilize a situation from which only the United States could profit. The Pathet Lao played on this French concern.

In the autumn of 1962 military forces loyal to Souvanna Phouma, i.e., the government, had asked France for military assistance of a "nonhardware" variety—blankets, uniforms, medicine, and so on. The blankets and warm clothing would be used in the Plaine des Jarres, the theater for much of the serious fighting in Laos and often cold at night. Paris said no, and Souvanna Phouma turned to Washington, as he has been obliged to do ever since. Months later, in early 1963, the Pathet Lao attacked the pro-government forces in the Plaine and slowly drove them to a more southern base which they defended until April 1964, when they were forced to retire.

In November 1963 Pierre Falaize was replaced as Ambassador in Vientiane, and relations between the American and British Embassies and that of France declined sharply. Falaize had taken what might be called a conventional Foreign Ministry view, but his successor (doubtless with different instructions) adopted a more Gaullist line, and seemed mistrustful not only of his Anglo-American colleagues but apparently of the 1962 settlement as well. A tendency developed on the French side to set Souvanna Phouma in conflict with the Americans; at least, this is how the Americans saw it. In any case, Souvanna Phouma, long the Paris favorite, began to slip from French esteem.

The change of ambassadors coincided, perhaps only by chance, with de Gaulle's abrupt assumption of the direction of France's Southeast Asian policy. Like other political chiefs, de Gaulle did not take a strong position on a given issue until it became—for him—an operational matter: Southeast Asia had become just that. Thus, in the autumn of 1963 one Paris embassy was already forecasting a hard anti-American French line in Asia and de Gaulle's recognition of China, if only as a reaction to the test-ban treaty and the possible start of a Russo-American dialogue.

In April 1964 Souvanna Phouma was overthrown by two generals and then reinstated as a result of international efforts in which everyone except China cooperated. (The French, however, launched a whispering campaign designed to show that the Americans were really behind the affair; while quite untrue, the canard had superficial plausibility, given Washington's earlier penchant for unhorsing Souvanna Phouma.) At the same time Couve de Murville, in an interview with the Associated Press, was surprisingly indulgent.

> I think it's completely ridiculous to say that what we are doing or saying with regard to Southeast Asia has anything to do with anti-Americanism. I feel that in this part of the world, as in others, I can say it. Our interests and our goals are the same. One must know whether these countries remain or are becoming free and whether they aren't falling under the domination of the Communists. . . .
>
> Vietnam is currently a very delicate problem, an affair in which the United States, our friend, is deeply engaged and for which it is assuming the largest part, not the only part, of the effort to be made. I believe therefore that we should discuss it prudently, and certainly not in public.[8]

Couve de Murville's comments were misleading; de Gaulle's attitude was hardening all along the line. At the end of May Robert Anderson went secretly to Paris as Johnson's personal emissary as part of an effort to arrive at some sort of modus vivendi. He managed to secure an agreement that George Ball would see de Gaulle the following week.*

Ball arrived just after Couve de Murville had addressed the National Assembly where he was now calling for the negotiated neutralization of Vietnam and Laos; the French were suggesting, according to a *New York Times* dispatch, that de Gaulle would go further along this line when he saw Ball and would propose a three-stage solution. In the first stage, South Vietnam would be neutralized; the fourteen powers that had guaranteed the neutrality of Laos would agree to guarantee South Vietnam's. A "third-force" government would be formed that was neither pro-American nor pro-Communist. In the second stage, North Vietnam would be neutralized (how this would be done was never made clear). And in the third stage, the two halves would be reunified under international auspices.[9]

De Gaulle's position, as expressed to Ball on June 5, was that China was not an expansionist power. The United States, he noted, was deploying military forces far in excess of anything France had ever put into Indochina; she might succeed militarily, but never politically. The country was "rotten," he argued; when South Vietnam's President Diem was alive one had at least had a government to deal with. (Nevertheless, calculated French indiscretions had provoked a rupture between Diem's regime and France.) Ball's difficulty was that he agreed with part of this argument, though by no means all of it. For example, he tried to suggest that another large international conference would not accomplish much, since it was doubtful that

---

* Ball was a curious choice of envoys, given his consistent opposition to the American military build-up in Vietnam. When Kennedy had faced the question whether to raise the number of American military personnel there to 16,500 Ball had told him that such an increase would generate pressure for still greater increases and that in three years he would have 300,000 people in Vietnam. Kennedy had disagreed sharply.

even an effective cease-fire could be arranged. (De Gaulle's more optimistic assessment of the prospects for such a conference did not, by the way, reflect the reports he was receiving from his own civil servants.) Ball's visit failed to narrow the differences between Washington and Paris. Still, most of the press, including some of the most astute writers on newspapers like *Le Monde* and *The New York Times,* suggested that the flurry of talks had restored contact, that the climate was improving to the point that one could expect a Johnson-de Gaulle meeting after the American elections in the fall. The depth of the rift was still not clearly seen outside the governments.

In his next press conference, on July 24, de Gaulle elected to probe what he now regarded as American vulnerability in Vietnam and Laos. Washington "considers itself as being invested throughout the world with the burden of defense against Communism," he remarked. "It can be added, without any intention of being derogatory, that their conviction of fulfilling some sort of vocation, the aversion they had to any colonial work which was not theirs, and finally the natural desire in such a powerful people to ensure themselves of new positions, determined the Americans to take our place in Indochina."

He continued in this vein and proposed a renewal of the fourteen-nation Geneva Conference for the purpose of neutralizing Southeast Asia. Finally, he declared that "the powers that directly or indirectly bear a responsibility in what was or is the fate of Indochina, which are France, China, the Soviet Union, and America, be effectively resolved to be involved there no longer." This was scarcely serious, since de Gaulle, who was the first to describe Western Europe as a French sphere of interest, or magnetic field, was known to believe that China's political influence must inevitably radiate through much of East Asia.

Later in the summer the worsening situation in Laos seemed sufficiently critical to the French government to warrant calling a meeting in Paris of the princes representing the traditional three factions. The affair went badly, mainly because Souvanna Phouma was subjected to a good deal of French pressure to align himself more closely to the Pathet Lao and even make concessions to them. An article in the Paris *Herald Tribune* under the headline "Paris Reported to Toe Peking's Line on Laos," with the subhead, "Alarming Even the Russians," suggested that the Soviet Union was as unhappy as France's allies by her conduct during the conference:

> "We just don't understand what the French are up to," said a high Russian diplomat here. "Listening to them you'd think you were hearing the Chinese."
>
> The French claim they are merely providing a neutral place for the three princes to meet. But sources close to the conference report that the French have applied unrelenting pressure on neutralist Premier Souvanna Phouma to accept Pathet Lao demands.
>
> They have closeted Prince Souvanna Phouma with anyone who could conceivably convince him, from President Charles de Gaulle down to relatively obscure diplomats who knew him years ago. They brought in Pierre Falaize, now Ambassador to Lebanon and former envoy to Laos, to back up the entreaties of Pierre Millet, the present Ambassador in Vientiane.
>
> But Prince Souvanna Phouma has held firm to his demand that the strategic Plaine des Jarres, now dominated by the Pathet Lao, be neutralized before he will go to a new fourteen-nation Geneva conference on Laos. . . .
>
> Some conference sources are convinced that in the French pressure on Prince Souvanna is an implied threat to withdraw their support of him as Premier and to back Prince Souphannouvong, the Pathet Lao chief. The Russians here have repeatedly told Prince Souvanna that they firmly back him. They say they have had no contact with the pro-Communist delegation.

The article concluded by ascribing to diplomatic sources the view that the Pathet Lao did not really want another Geneva conference but was "only interested in talking while they consolidate the large gains they made on the Plaine des Jarres since April, when the cease-fire worked out at the original fourteen-nation Geneva Conference in 1962 broke down." [10]

The meeting of the three princes in Paris offered a rare glimpse of the ironies and complexities of world politics. De Gaulle, unable to convene a fourteen-nation conference on Vietnam, chose to try to arrange a similar conference for the problems of Laos, hoping thereby to acquire some initiative in Southeast Asia and harass the Americans at the same time. But the Americans were no more prepared to accept a large conference on Laos than they had been on Vietnam. The Soviet Union, on the other hand, could not gracefully oppose such a conference but was nonetheless content with the status quo in Laos and irritated by de Gaulle's tactics. With his recognition of China and other gestures, de Gaulle, in Russian eyes, was undercutting their anti-Mao propaganda and mischievously placing France and China in a kind of tacit alignment against the "two hegemonies." (Although Prince Souphannouvong was partly a Soviet creation, he had, inevitably, become Hanoi's man; the hard core of Laotian Communism is controlled by North Vietnamese; some of the leaders are in fact partly Vietnamese. Moscow has little to gain from a Communist regime in Laos. Souvanna Phouma, however dependent on the Americans he may have become, was a moderate influence who often voted with Moscow in the UN and supported Soviet claims to be an Asian power so as to participate in the Afro-Asian conference that never took place.)

In any case, Paris and Washington were now as far apart in Southeast Asia as in Europe. For de Gaulle, a major American presence was as unacceptable in French-speaking Asia as in Western Europe. And he had everything to gain and nothing to lose in moving away from Souvanna Phouma toward Souphannouvong. Since the former now relied on the Americans, the latter had become the more neutral of the two, according to this

view, which held that the real leftists were not Souphannouvong's group (the Neo Lao Hak Sat), which calls itself a party
but is really a front organization, but the more extreme and
uncontrollable elements of Laotian Communism. The French
favor the schematic design in Asia, and the Americans, rightly
or wrongly, tend to dismiss it as largely irrelevant.

In adjusting his Laos policy de Gaulle was playing neither to
Moscow nor to Peking, but in a sense to both. On the one hand,
he was splitting off from Washington and staking out independent ground. On the other, he was aligning himself with the
reality of tomorrow, if not today. For de Gaulle, Laos was and
must remain within the French cultural orbit, but was histori-
cally and inevitably within the Vietnamese sphere of influence.
(And Hanoi, certain one day to rule all Vietnam, fell within the
Chinese sphere of influence, although de Gaulle did not regard
Vietnam as a potential satellite of China, given its independent
history and character and its strong overlay of French culture.)
De Gaulle would doubtless have been content to see the Laotians ruled from Hanoi one day, provided they continued to
speak French.

Since France's role in Southeast Asia depended, in de
Gaulle's view, on the elimination of any significant American
presence, whether political, military, or cultural, France must
align herself with the anti-American forces of the area, be they
Vietnamese or Chinese. France could share influence with a
Communist country—as with Russia and China in Cambodia
or with Hanoi in Laos—but never with the United States. In
every case, France would play the secondary role, complement-
ing and perhaps influencing the role of the more directly involved Communist power.

It is difficult to measure the impact of this policy in Southeast Asia. Although the notion that French and Chinese projects are complementary there fits awkwardly with reality,
in the long run France probably will have a place, doubtless

modest but important, in Laos, Cambodia, and Vietnam. France can supply numerous volunteer teachers and technicians and they would probably be welcome, provided French activities do not exceed the limits set by Hanoi and Peking. It seems less likely that the North Vietnamese will tolerate indefinitely the unique role of the French language in Laos. (In Vietnam, English has become a widespread second language in the South, and even in the North some English is taught.) With the passage of time France may well divide the modest outsider's role with various countries of the region—Japan and Australia—which also have something to offer the peoples of the old French Indochina.

As for his China policy, de Gaulle seemed to believe that since France (unlike the United States) did not oppose China's quest for pre-eminence in Asia, Peking would welcome her secondary cultural and commercial presence, the more so since France's goals were modest and French policy ready to complement Chinese efforts to reduce American influence in Asia. This has proved wrong. The French Embassy in Peking is as isolated as any other; the Ambassador has as much difficulty in arranging appointments at the Foreign Ministry as any of his colleagues. The Chinese trade more with West Germany, which has no embassy in Peking, than with France. In short, China's traditional xenophobia and special aversion to Western societies appears to make no distinction in favor of France.*

The skirmishes between Paris and Washington in Southeast Asia distracted little attention from the main—and open —clash between the two capitals on nuclear and German policy. This was still a time when some in Washington, especially in the Pentagon, were taking the line that as the French

---

* Perhaps de Gaulle recognized the limits of his China policy. Toward the end of his Presidency there were signs of rising French interest in Japan, a country he once tended to view with condescension.

learned more about nuclear weapons and their effects they would become more responsive to American strategic thinking. This was not the case. De Gaulle made a short radio-television address in April (1964) in which for the first time he referred to the United States as an "uncertain" ally. France needed a nuclear force; in the absence of such a force she had to rely "upon a foreign protectorate, and for that matter, an uncertain one." [11] For their part, individual Gaullists, including some in the government, continued to complain that Washington had never responded to the tridirectorate memorandum of September 1958. (One prominent American official discovered that some of them actually believed this, at least until May 1964 when the State Department gave James Reston the gist, but not the text, of de Gaulle's proposal together with Eisenhower's reply, portions of which Reston quoted. One of his articles noted that de Gaulle had just withdrawn all naval officers from NATO command; Johnson, according to Reston, said, "It's too bad, but I'm not going to fuss at him." [12] And a concluding piece documented both Eisenhower's and Kennedy's efforts to meet de Gaulle a good part of the way, only to be rebuffed or ignored.)

The twentieth anniversary of the Normandy landing of June 6, 1944, was approaching. Nobody expected de Gaulle to attend the ceremonies, but the surprise was general when it was announced that Premier Pompidou would not be going either but would accompany de Gaulle instead to August 15 ceremonies commemorating the French landings on the southern coast.*

Of more importance, Johnson committed himself, or so it seemed, to the project for a Multilateral Force. Until then, de Gaulle's government had ignored the MLF, always assuming it had more "theater" than reality. Kennedy's ambiguous at-

---

* According to the Paris *Herald Tribune* of May 30–31 the United States Embassy had earlier been told that Pompidou would attend the Normandy ceremonies.

titude toward it deepened existing doubts, in both Washington
and Europe, that it would ever go much beyond the conversa-
tional stage. But a Presidential commitment, never likely under
Kennedy, put the MLF in a new light; it was now United
States policy to organize a NATO mixed-manned force, to obtain a charter with as many signatories as possible in the
months ahead. The MLF advocates, with the wind at their
stern, hoped to have a treaty by the end of 1964. Given the
basic purpose of the project—to offer West Germany some
sense of participation in nuclear strategy and control—it was
certain to arouse the implacable and majestic resistance of de
Gaulle.

It is not surprising that de Gaulle's next semiannual meeting with his German colleagues, as provided for by the
Franco-German treaty, was a complete failure. Chancellor Ludwig Erhard had just returned from Washington in June, where
a communiqué had noted the contribution to be made by the
MLF and referred to the unanimity of the two governments in
supporting the struggle against aggression in South Vietnam.
This support for American policies in Southeast Asia now "astonished" de Gaulle, who expressed regret that Bonn was not
following his example in recognizing China.[18] More important,
de Gaulle tried to discourage Erhard's interest in the MLF by
emphasizing the European character of France's *force de dissuasion*. He even suggested rather vaguely the possibility of a
West German contribution to it, but the discussion bogged
down quickly when it became clear that nothing beyond a
financial contribution—neither technology nor co-participation
—could be envisaged.*

De Gaulle's aversion to Bonn's romance with Washington
was sharply pointed up in his July 24 press conference.

---

* This incident has since been denied on both sides. Nevertheless, it did
occur and was known in Bonn diplomatic circles.

One cannot say that Germany and France have yet agreed to make a policy together, and one cannot dispute that this results from the fact that so far Bonn has not believed that this policy should be European and independent. If this state of affairs were to last, there would be the long-run risk of doubts among the French people, of misgivings among the German people, and, among their four partners of the Rome Treaty, an increased tendency to leave things as they are, while waiting, perhaps, to be split up. . . . [France] is now strong enough and sure enough of herself to be able to be patient, except for major external changes which would jeopardize everything and therefore lead her to change her direction.

These were strong and menacing words, calling into question the Franco-German treaty, the European Community, and France's place in the Western system. Bonn and Washington replied at once (the latter less sharply than the former). *Le Monde* noted that Johnson, by answering de Gaulle within 24 hours, was breaking with his own tradition; it also called attention to the absence of rancor and generally moderate tone of his remarks, which said that the United States was not trying to dominate any European country, or trying to force anyone to choose between Paris and Washington.[14]

In fact, Washington and Paris did appear to be locked in a test of strength for Bonn's loyalty. De Gaulle had menaced the West German government. Washington, in turn, was trying to head off the possibility (never great) of a French-led West European bloc, and was pushing hard for the MLF. McNamara, largely on his own initiative, had launched a program of meetings with the West German Defense Minister and military chiefs of staff. (Whether the State Department had even approved what amounted to bilateral military arrangements within NATO is far from clear. Except for those who favored the MLF, State Department officials were either being shunted aside from German affairs, or opting out, or both.) Yet curiously enough, the MLF, if not directly opposed in the Pentagon, had little real support there—except from the Navy, which swiftly developed a vested interest in the idea of the sea-based force. It was a confused and contradictory situation—not so unusual for Washington—but a perfect setting for de Gaulle's special talents. (By an odd coincidence this was also the moment when Washington was delivering the KC-135 jet tankers purchased by France two and a half years earlier, upon which de Gaulle's nuclear bombers were fully dependent.)

The months from October 1964 to February 1965, if less spectacular than the comparable months of 1962–1963, were no less pivotal. The drama was less public—certainly less spectacular—but as rich in consequence. Both were transitional moments in that each served as a prelude to yet another dramatic and largely unexpected downward turn in relations between France and her Anglo-Saxon allies. The events of the autumn and winter of 1962–1963 allowed de Gaulle to play the solitary horseman of the Western bloc; the parallel period two years later allowed him to desert his European role for the larger world stage. His "European" Europe was not yet built, but no matter. Relations with China had been "normalized." The Third World policy was under way, solemnized by a 26-day trip to ten Latin American countries and by the break with America in Asia. The Cold War for all practical purposes seemed to be over. The United States had won, but refused to draw the consequences and was committing itself to a vast enterprise of clouded prospect in Vietnam. The time had come for de Gaulle to prove to Moscow that France was a serious and uncommitted power with a global vocation.

Khrushchev still continued to refuse to take de Gaulle seriously.*

---

* Earlier, "[He compared] de Gaulle's influence over Adenauer . . . to the

In more dispassionate and durable parts of the Soviet government de Gaulle had been a debatable figure for perhaps as long as a year. Everything suggested he had real nuisance value. But his China policy showed that, if ignored, he could also be a nuisance to Moscow. Moreover, Europe's stability and Germany's non-nuclear status were largely guaranteed by the heavy American presence in Western Europe; by setting off polycentric currents in the Western system, de Gaulle might generate parallel impulses in Eastern Europe or rekindle the German dynamic—or possibly do both. It was one thing to rail against the prevailing security system, as Moscow has always done, but quite another to contemplate the possibly appalling consequences of its collapse. Seen from Moscow, de Gaulle might be an agent of disorder in Central and Eastern Europe. And then, his South American odyssey showed that he meant what he said about fishing in the troubled waters of the Third World. He told the Uruguayan government, "World peace should not turn on the struggle between two great giants; there is need for a new movement, a new position." And he forecast an intermingling of the members of blocs of nations as a result of "acquired affinities, practical reasons, and even, let's use the word, similar political views." [15]

None of this, however, was of the same level of importance or interest as de Gaulle's hardening attitude toward Bonn. For in Moscow as in Washington, the problem of Germany brings together the major foreign-policy considerations.

De Gaulle did not defeat the MLF, but he helped by intimidating Erhard and his entourage. And Erhard's reservations, as much as anything else, finally turned Johnson away from the idea.

De Gaulle's assault against the MLF was a complex affair,

Russian peasant who caught a bear barehanded but could neither bring it back nor make the bear let loose of him." (Theodore C. Sorensen, *Kennedy* [New York: Harper & Row, 1965], p. 554.)

also involving the Common Market. The issue in the latter case was how to reach agreement on a common price for grain, the most stubborn obstacle in the path to the common agricultural market, which for France was the chief attraction of the whole EEC enterprise. As an exercise in the measured use of political strength, this was one of de Gaulle's truly impressive performances, and it offers a nice glimpse of the Gaullist method. The object of all the pressure was the West German government. Erhard wanted the MLF but shrank from France's cherished grain price, which would mean lowering West Germany's high prices and thus court trouble with the farmers (to say nothing of the large subsidy needed to make up the difference between the lower single price and the old high price). All this with general elections in the year ahead.

De Gaulle's first priority was defeat of the MLF, but the initial stress was put on the grain-price issue. On October 21, following a cabinet meeting, Minister of Information Peyrefitte issued an ultimatum which said in effect that unless the agricultural market was organized along the agreed lines, "France would cease to play an active part in the EEC." [16] A week later Couve de Murville, addressing the National Assembly, said France had "to act in full recognition of the risk of a break-up which the conduct of certain partners forces us to regard as a possibility." This speech also linked for the first time the MLF to the Franco-German troubles. Two days later Pompidou put the matter in a still harsher light. In two straightforward sentences he offered Bonn a choice between swallowing the grain price and rejecting the MLF, or seeing the dissolution of both the Common Market *and* the Franco-German treaty: "The agricultural common market must take shape, for without it the industrial common market will simply collapse. . . . If the multilateral force were to lead to the creation of a German-American military alliance, we would not consider this as being fully consistent with the relations we have with the Federal Republic which are based on the Franco-German Treaty." [17]

Erhard, then, had to accept the common grain price or take responsibility for the collapse of the Common Market, and he had to change his mind on the MLF. In fact, de Gaulle was using the grain-price issue to compel Bonn to reject or at least slow down on the MLF. He would probably have let Erhard wriggle off the grain-price hook, at least until after the German elections in September, provided the MLF was discarded. As things turned out he had it both ways.

French interest in killing the MLF was equaled only in Moscow, where it was officially viewed as the device by which the West Germans might in the long run gain independent control of nuclear weapons. And the high point of the MLF drama coincided with the fall of Khrushchev.

In a sense the decks were cleared. Soviet press comments on the sinister axis that had been born with the Franco-German treaty in January 1963 were largely shut off after Khrushchev's fall and the launching of a tougher French diplomacy. In December de Gaulle, who exactly three years earlier had refused to acquiesce in talks with the Russians on Berlin, blocked a four-power declaration on Germany during the semiannual NATO Ministerial meeting. He had come full circle. And while provoking Bonn, he must have further intrigued the new Soviet leaders. Moscow had always taxed de Gaulle, rightly enough, with saying one thing to him and another to the Germans. The events of the winter changed that.

In mid-December an interesting Russian turned up in Paris en route home to Moscow from a trip to the United States. He was an international commentator for *Pravda,* and known to have strong connections on the Central Committee. In Paris he talked to a number of notables—he dined, for example, with a prominent Gaullist newspaper publisher—and seemed interested in the MLF and de Gaulle's intentions in the event the project drew the breath of life. One of his interlocutors kept a record of their conversation.

The Russian began by saying the Americans had decided to give the Germans a nuclear role. The Soviet Union could not accept this. It was not a question of war, but such a gesture would increase West Germany's capacity for political blackmail; the situation was dangerous. In Washington he had gotten the impression (based on conversations with a White House figure, among others, he said) that the United States intended to rely chiefly on West Germany and Japan, in its view the most stable powers in Europe and Asia. Would de Gaulle break the Franco-German treaty if the MLF were created? he asked. Would he withdraw from NATO?

His French interlocutor pointed up the obvious difficulty for de Gaulle in breaking altogether with Bonn and the other West Europeans and in operating alone. The Russian replied by raising the Rapacki Plan, which called for the neutralization and demilitarization of territory on either side of the Iron Curtain. Would France support such a revised security system? It would make the MLF unnecessary. Wouldn't this be a way out of the impasse? Should not France and the Soviet Union discuss such an approach? After all, there was nothing prejudicial in proposing *détente* measures; the path had been opened by the Americans. De Gaulle could find all the alibis he needed; the Russians were ready to help him in many ways. "But I must know what he wants. Otherwise we are wasting our time."

The Russian was asked whether he was thinking of doing something before or after an MLF was created. Before, was the reply; nothing would be gained by acting after; it would be too late.

De Gaulle's New Year's Eve address to the nation signaled that he was poised to move European politics into a new phase. He was due to meet Erhard at Rambouillet on January 19, but he preceded the meeting with a flurry of diplomatic activity in Eastern Europe.

Poor Erhard thought he had purchased concessions from de Gaulle that could be exploited in his forthcoming elections. He arrived with a plan for European political unity that seemed to differ little from de Gaulle's thinking. But de Gaulle was not interested, not so long as Germany remained moored to America. Shelving the MLF, it turned out, was not enough; it had to be *buried* and, with it, the United States' anomalous role in West German affairs. In effect de Gaulle was putting before Erhard the impossible choice—Paris or Washington. West Germany needs both. In any case, Erhard didn't understand. He thought the conference had gone well. De Gaulle had scheduled a news conference for two weeks later; "Think of me on February 4," said Erhard. "It will be my birthday." [18] De Gaulle promised to note it, but he had chosen this date (also the twentieth anniversary of the opening of the Yalta Conference) as the occasion for a statement no part of which would gratify *any* of the high hopes Erhard naively carried away from Rambouillet.

All of General de Gaulle's seventeen press conferences were studiously momentous, with some, as the saying goes, more momentous than others. The press conference of February 4, 1965, belongs to the latter category, formalizing as it did the dramatic shift that was under way in French foreign policy. First and foremost, de Gaulle said, discussion of the question of divided Germany should be confined to European states. Then he linked German reunification to the defense question; for Bonn to opt for a revived MLF or some variant of it, he said, would amount to renouncing the possibility of an eventual reunification agreement with Russia and Eastern Europe. And then an old Gaullist vision, after three years of obscurity, was abruptly reborn: "Europe, the mother of civilization, must establish herself from the Atlantic to the Urals. . . ."

The implications were too sweeping for instant comprehension. *Le Monde* asked: "Has de Gaulle given Germans a choice between the United States and reunification?" Among other things, he affected to be doing just that. The press conference also meant that the Franco-German scaffolding upon which de Gaulle had for years tried to erect his French-led West European bloc was to be scrapped, at least for a time. The Common Market itself was undergoing a serious Gaullist review. The United States, vulnerable now in Southeast Asia and burdened with the failed MLF, was to be harassed wherever exposed. February 4, 1965, was also the chosen hour for an assault on the gold-dollar exchange system—the basis of the world monetary structure—and a call for a return to the gold standard. France had been arguing for reform of the monetary system, but not for its upheaval, as de Gaulle was now proposing. But here, too, de Gaulle was formalizing policy. A few weeks earlier his government had launched a gold-purchase program designed to reduce drastically French dollar balances and hence increase the pressure on American finances, already vulnerable on balance-of-payments grounds and with the war in Vietnam dimming prospects for improvement.

It was all vintage de Gaulle. An exuberant piece of theater proclaimed France's long-awaited, independent, full-blown global diplomacy—the *grande politique extérieure* that would re-establish her in the first rank. With characteristic flair and presumption de Gaulle was using circumstances to give credibility, if not substance, to an exalted vision. The break with Washington and London for practical purposes was complete. Contact with Moscow had at last been made.

10

De Gaulle between the Blocs

Just a few weeks before the press conference of February 4, 1965, de Gaulle had granted C. L. Sulzberger another of his privileged glimpses behind the curtain. In this case, de Gaulle was certainly signaling Moscow. The interview, which took place on December 27, coincided with the collapse of the MLF and France's hardening line on Germany.

The following points emerge from Sulzberger's account of de Gaulle's intentions: (a) France would remain within the North Atlantic Alliance but would withdraw from NATO in 1969; de Gaulle "wants to conserve the Alliance while dissolving its organizational structure." (b) De Gaulle was preparing slowly and gradually for some kind of eventual European political and military collaboration in which France would have a clearly dominant role. (c) He thought German reunification was out of the question for years to come. Partition was unfortunate, but it would be explosively dangerous to try to end it. (d) His opposition to United States policy in South Vietnam was clearly expressed.[1]

All of this was clearly intended to persuade the new Soviet leadership that de Gaulle could be their *interlocuteur valable* on the things that mattered most. His China policy showed that he meant business and could be troublesome. His assault on the MLF, a project as disturbing to Moscow as it was dear to many in Washington, showed that the conflict with the Americans was no superficial affair and could be turned to Soviet advantage. In short, de Gaulle could be useful to the new Soviet regime if cultivated, a problem if ignored.

Three days after the February press conference the United States bombed North Vietnam for the first time. Soviet Prime Minister Alexei Kosygin was visiting Hanoi at this precise moment, and this added drama to an event heavy enough in disturbing implications. Some sovietologists believe that Kosygin was humiliated. They feel he was trying to persuade the Communist bloc that Johnson had more to lose than to gain by extending the war and would doubtless try to move toward a Laos-style settlement.

In any case, Moscow elected to be highly offended by the incident, and Kosygin returned from Hanoi determined to play it up *fortissimo*. For a sympathetic ear, he didn't have far to look, and he promptly sent de Gaulle a letter containing a message to be passed along to the Americans. It said that no solution of the Vietnam war was possible without a cessation of the bombing. Whatever else the letter said, this was taken by the Élysée to mean that escalation of the war excluded the possibility of closer relations between the United States and the new Soviet leadership. So much the better from de Gaulle's point of view; he relied heavily on that letter.

The blossoming *rapprochement* with Moscow gave de Gaulle still greater freedom of movement; the role of an endlessly moving figure in the eternal ballet was now his. What did it matter if the performance merely pointed up the central theme without advancing it? Theater for theater's sake was the means of bringing his unruly and politically wayward people face to face with the splendor of their heritage. Tactically, the other performers must be alternately cajoled and menaced. Thus, the

West Germans were reminded of the unspecified advantages flowing from the Treaty of Paris concluded by de Gaulle and Adenauer, and warned that a Russo-American agreement could only be taken over the heads of the Europeans and to the special cost of the German people. The Russians were shown that only de Gaulle could weaken NATO and the Alliance, and perhaps even goad the Americans into making unilateral troop reductions in Europe; at the same time they were cajoled about their German policy—if Bonn and Washington stayed close, said de Gaulle, it was because the West Germans had no place else to turn. "Help me with the Germans," he asked in effect. "Don't change the substance of your Germany policy, but alter appearances. Ease up and help me quicken the pace of Bonn's new *Ost-Politik,* her search for more relaxed and normal relations with Eastern Europe." De Gaulle, of course, intended France to be the beneficiary of all this. If and as the Germans grew less fearful of Moscow, they would depend more on de Gaulle for his intercession there and elsewhere in Eastern Europe, where he would run interference for them. History was unlikely to repeat itself, he thought, and there was no likelihood of another Rapallo or that, having made the introductions, he would, in the words of an old French proverb, finish by working for the King of Prussia.

In this constant maneuvering for advantage the Common Market and NATO were pieces on the board. De Gaulle deplored both, although each was—and continued to be—useful to him. The year 1965 would be dominated by his sallies against both institutions, each fitted to his election timetable and subsequent visit to Moscow.

Reducing the scope of the Common Market was a project that de Gaulle had contemplated for years. As early as 1960 he had sent down word through his government that severe limits should be put on the Commissions of the three European Communities (EEC, Euratom, and the Coal and Steel Community).

But France's authority within the EEC lagged well behind de Gaulle's magisterial fiats at that time, and not even Adenauer was prepared to support him. Five years later the key to the problem of refitting the Common Market to the Gaullist design was still Bonn. With West German support de Gaulle could impose his will on Italy and Benelux; they would either have to go along with him or share the blame for breaking up the Common Market. But now Bonn was again to be menaced. To block de Gaulle or to abet the pretensions of Community-minded "Europeans" would, the French argued, risk the dismemberment of the EEC. De Gaulle had twice threatened the Community with extinction: one could not doubt his sincerity.

With his five partners tamed, the task of throttling down NATO would be greatly simplified. Whether at the European or Atlantic level, the detestable principle of integration would be plunged into irreversible decline. Most important, to reduce the Common Market and American influence in Europe would give Moscow a lot to think about. The great role of arbiter on the German question might hang in the balance.

The grain-price agreement of December 1964, so important to France, had created a kind of euphoria in Common Market circles, which in turn induced the EEC Commission in Brussels to place before the six governments a set of proposals that would take the Community farther along the path of integration than any of the governments was then prepared to go. De Gaulle made an issue of this imprudent, though not illogical, gesture and in June 1965 provoked a crisis in the form of a six-month boycott of the Common Market and related institutions. His partners were given the choice of either permitting him to empty the EEC of its supranational characteristics or accepting its liquidation.

The most important—and least expected—element in the response of the Five, the other EEC members, was a strong position taken by West Germany. Led by Foreign Minister Schroeder, Bonn saw that reduction of the Common Market was only a part of de Gaulle's larger purpose—to break down resistance to his bid for leadership of Europe, with France, not America, eventually guaranteeing its security. The West Germans saw that this would mean a revised European security system, organized around a spurious Franco-Russian condominium, and they were firmly opposed to it.

In this they were strongly and skillfully supported, especially by the Dutch, who took the hardest line, and the Italians, who played a key role in reconciling the often divergent views of the other members.

Still, the surprise was general when de Gaulle's attempted *coup de main* at least partially failed. In calling his bluff the Five probably surprised themselves as much as anyone else. De Gaulle found himself obliged at the end of six months to return to Brussels on terms he could have had at any time before or after the start of the crisis.

De Gaulle's aversion to NATO was well known. Some French commentators—even some diplomats—had always taken the line that he objected less to the organization than to its Anglo-Saxon control, that his purpose was to reform, not destroy, the organization.* In fact, de Gaulle never considered reforming the admittedly American-dominated organization. Now, in April 1965, he made a short, but even for him defiant, radio and television address keyed to the sensitive anti-American chord.

However large may be the glass offered to us, we prefer to drink from our own, while touching glasses round about. Cer-

---

* During a parliamentary debate in October 1965 Couve de Murville seemed to substantiate this belief: "Now, in 1965, we say that before 1969 reforms will be necessary. This doesn't seem to me a particularly revolutionary statement, seven years after having declared our dissatisfaction. In the remaining four years it is essential to arrive at a result. . . . All we ask is a reasonable discussion of the affair." (*Journal officiel*, October 20, 1965.)

tainly, this independence . . . has not failed to surprise, even
to scandalize, various circles for which France's vassalage was
the habit and the rule. . . . The fact that we have reassumed
our faculty of judgment and action in regard to all problems
sometimes seems to displease a state which may believe that, by
virtue of its power, it is invested with supreme and universal
responsibility. . . . The reappearance of a nation whose hands
are free, as we have again become, obviously modifies the world
interplay which, since Yalta, seemed to be limited to two partners. But since this division of the world between two great
powers, and therefore into two camps, clearly does not benefit
the liberty, equality, and fraternity of peoples, a different order,
a different equilibrium, is necessary for peace. Who can maintain this better than we—provided that we remain ourselves.

This renewed assertion of independence coincided with a
visit to Paris of Soviet Foreign Minister Gromyko—an event
that titillated Paris, flustered Bonn, and helped even the dim-
mest onlookers to capture the point of what de Gaulle was saying. At about the same time, Sergei Vinogradov, the popular
Soviet Ambassador in Paris, was leaving for another assignment. At the farewell dinner for him de Gaulle thoroughly
aroused the West Germans by citing again the traditional
friendship between France and Russia. This, among other
things, moved even Adenauer, now retired, to warn of "Franco-
Soviet encirclement" and to write to his great comrade and fel-
low European expressing concern about the drift of events.

June 18 was an important day in de Gaulle's campaign to
weaken the Common Market and NATO. On that date the effort
of Gaston Defferre to form a center-left federation, based
mainly on the Socialist party and a large Catholic center party,
collapsed; Defferre's defeat at the hands of the party chiefs
seemed to mean that de Gaulle would enter the December presidential lists untroubled by serious opposition. Just as victory in
the legislative elections in November 1962 had cleared the way

for him to turn down Britain's application to the EEC, so now did de Gaulle feel free to take on the Common Market and NATO.

Twelve days later, on June 30, the great Common Market psychodrama began with a sudden French boycott of the Brussels institutions, despite private assurances to the West Germans that a crisis would be avoided. The early days of the boycott also coincided with first signs that the long-awaited NATO drama had reached the planning stages. De Gaulle's penchant for feinting other parties out of position and hiding his intentions was never more vividly displayed. At no point in the months leading to the NATO crisis did he break faith with the precept that "first and foremost, there can be no prestige without mystery, for familiarity breeds contempt," that the game is "to give nothing away, to hold in reserve some piece of secret knowledge which may, at any moment, intervene, and the more effectively from being in the nature of a surprise. The latent faith of the masses will do the rest." [2]

Throughout the summer of 1965 diplomats were told to expect a NATO crisis in the early months of 1966. De Gaulle told George Ball in August that within a year all NATO military units based in France would be under French command. And in September, at his semiannual news conference, as usual devoted mainly to foreign policy and in this case to the Common Market crisis and East-West politics, a clear warning on NATO emerged:

> Above all, it is a question of keeping ourselves free of any vassalage. . . . So long as the solidarity of the Western peoples appears to us necessary for the eventual defense of Europe, our country will remain the ally of her allies; but, upon the expiration of earlier commitments—that is, in 1969 by the latest —the subordination known as "integration" which is provided for by NATO and which hands our fate over to foreign authority shall cease, as far as we are concerned.

A spring NATO crisis was the continued forecast in the autumn of 1965. Then, France's presidential elections in December, in which de Gaulle was forced into an embarrassing second-round run-off, were followed by a lull. The Common Market crisis was settled in January, but suspense about de Gaulle's NATO intentions was rising. The Quai d'Orsay was acting with neither precise instructions nor information at this point. On January 31, Hervé Alphand, the Secretary-General of the Foreign Ministry and formerly Ambassador in Washington, gave a luncheon for a small group of American newspapermen at the Hotel Crillon. He wanted mainly to talk about Vietnam, but also advised the journalists, almost certainly on instructions from the Élysée which had nothing to do with de Gaulle's still unrevealed intentions, not to expect a NATO crisis. And on February 10 a Western ambassador was taken aside by de Gaulle at the annual dinner for the diplomatic corps and told that France intended to do nothing of a dramatic nature about NATO; the ambassador immediately found himself the target of discreet inquiries from French Foreign Ministry figures eager to learn what their leader was saying. On February 21 de Gaulle referred to NATO in another press conference as an "American protectorate" and made reasonably clear his eventual intention to leave it; but he was studiously vague about the timing:

> Without going back on her adherence to the Atlantic Alliance, France will, between now and the final date set for her obligations, which is April 4, 1969, continue to modify successively the measures in current practice, insofar as they concern her. What she did yesterday in this respect in several domains, she will do tomorrow in others, of course while taking the necessary measures so that these changes take place gradually and so that her allies are not suddenly, because of her, inconvenienced.

The notion that de Gaulle had decided against immediate action on NATO took hold easily. His regime had endured a good deal of drama. The six-month boycott of the Common Market had been a mistake; the presidential elections had been awkward. Finally, the scandal of the government's apparent involvement with the abduction and murder of the Moroccan political leader Mehdi Ben Barka erupted right after the election and deeply embarrassed the regime. (De Gaulle had even felt obliged to mention the affair in his press conference, where he called it "vulgar and second-rate.")

Most of the best-informed people in Paris, whether diplomats or journalists, whether French or foreign, were deceived. De Gaulle never had abandoned his plan for a spring NATO crisis; it was one of the reasons he had ended the boycott of the Common Market. Even for him, two crises *sous le bras* at the same time would have been hard to manage. Moreover, he was intending to visit the Soviet Union in early June (22 years after his famous encounter with Stalin), and to launch a NATO crisis *after* that was out of the question, since it would then appear to be a direct consequence of the visit.

For quite a long time—years, in fact—the Americans had persistently urged de Gaulle to offer suggestions on NATO reform. Early in January de Gaulle summoned NATO's Secretary-General Manlio Brosio and told him France would *not* put forward proposals aimed at making NATO a more desirable instrument from France's point of view. Such proposals, de Gaulle assured Brosio, would not receive proper consideration, for the Americans, after all, were fighting a war in Vietnam and would be unable to focus seriously on NATO reform.

Just after the February press conference, de Gaulle surprised his government—at least the Prime Minister and Foreign Minister and, who knows, perhaps one or two others—by telling them that at the earliest possible moment he would end French participation not just in NATO, but possibly in the Atlantic Alliance as well. His disconcerted ministers were instructed to have memoranda prepared dealing with the implications and modalities of extricating France not just from NATO but from the Alliance itself. This posed an awkward problem. Publicly and privately, de Gaulle had given assurances on every side that, whatever happened with NATO, France would remain a part of the Alliance. His tolerance of alliances between sovereign states (as opposed to his aversion to integrated structures) was well established. Now he seemed on the verge of removing the distinction between alliance with the other Western powers under the North Atlantic Treaty and participation in the military-command structure. Much more important, to quit everything—to dissolve his last link with the Western Alliance—could prejudice France's position in Germany as one of the victorious powers; French legal rights on such issues as access to Berlin, a voice in that city's affairs, and the right to deploy military units in West Germany flow primarily from the original occupation arrangements and a set of agreements reached by the occupying powers in 1954.

These rights and France's role in Germany had been and remained vital to her foreign policy. Theoretically they would not be affected by withdrawal from the Atlantic Alliance, but in practice they probably would be. After all, if de Gaulle could justify denunciation of the treaty on the grounds that circumstances had changed, so then could the others ignore his privileged place in German affairs on the grounds that he had unilaterally transformed the conditions on which this position was based. He would, in effect, have opted for a fully neutral position between the blocs.

Moreover, complete withdrawal from the Alliance would do France no good vis-à-vis the Soviet Union. De Gaulle's usefulness to the Russians would decline with the decline in his nuisance value, obviously greater inside the Alliance, where he could continue to block, alter, or otherwise influence allied policies.

Such was the reasoning of the hastily prepared memoranda from the Quai d'Orsay. The memoranda offered various methods—some mild, others strong—of dealing with the "NATO problem": for example, a simple requirement that all NATO units on French soil be placed under French command, and then, more drastic, France's withdrawal from NATO and cancellation of the bilateral agreements under which the United States and Canada stationed troops on French soil. De Gaulle chose the latter option.

Had he *really* been tempted to withdraw from the Atlantic Alliance at this stage, or did he merely wish to see what the internal reaction would be to the notion? Probably nobody— no member of his entourage or government—could answer this question. In any case, at the chosen moment in late February the Ministry of Foreign Affairs was apprised of the matter and given ten days or so to prepare the necessary papers. De Gaulle himself wrote four explanatory messages in his own hand to President Johnson, Chancellor Erhard, Prime Minister Wilson, and President Giuseppe Saragat, leaders of the biggest member states. To show that France recognized which of these was most affected by the action, Couve de Murville delivered the letter for Johnson to Ambassador Bohlen two days before presenting the other messages to the other Ambassadors. The letters were each about two pages in length, and though similar in content, they were not identical. The letter to Johnson did not mention de Gaulle's concern about France being dragged into a war in Southeast Asia, but the letter to Wilson did. And the letter to Johnson, unlike the others, restated France's intention to remain a part of the Alliance until 1969, provided that circumstances did not change:

France . . . plans as of now to remain when the time comes a party to the treaty. . . . This means that unless in the three coming years events change the basic facts directing East-West relations, she would in 1969 and beyond be determined as today to fight on the side of her allies in the event that one of them should be the object of unprovoked aggression.

Here again, de Gaulle was acknowledging the pre-eminent American role in NATO. To the others, he merely offered assurances of his intention to remain within the Alliance; to the Americans, he came close to the truth of the matter—he would stay in only so long as it suited him, and he was leaving himself an "out." The letter to Erhard alluded to the Treaty of Paris and Franco-German solidarity, but referred to 1869 instead of 1969, a lapse which in German diplomatic circles inspired the comment that the General believed himself to be on the eve of the Franco-Prussian War of 1870.

Why did he do it, why at this time? was the question asked by numerous surprised observers in the days that followed. André Fontaine tried to answer the question when he reported that in his last cabinet meeting de Gaulle had told his ministers that "it had been necessary for him to exploit the moment that he was still in power in order to do what had to be done, given that he couldn't be certain that those who came after him could or would want to do it." [3] This partly explained the motivation. But the precise timing of the move was not instantly appreciated in the world beyond the Élysée Palace, and was related to the Russian trip and also to the legislative elections scheduled for March 1967. As noted, de Gaulle obviously couldn't risk withdrawing from NATO right after returning from Moscow. On the other hand, he wanted to do it far in advance of the next elections, which, if they went well for the Gaullists, would tend to legitimize his Atlantic, as well as other, policies. As so often before, he was maneuvering French society behind his foreign policy, instead of relating its immediate needs and interests to his government's program.

For the allied capitals, de Gaulle's withdrawal from NATO

had many implications, all of them disturbing. Politics aside, France was the geographic and logistical heart of NATO, as well as headquarters. The gaping hole left in the middle of Western defenses raised all kinds of questions: Would, for example, French air space be available in the event of crisis or conflict?

In Eastern Europe the reaction was more complicated. Obviously, the Soviet Union took satisfaction in seeing NATO weakened. Still, French withdrawal in the end would mean a larger and more influential role for West Germany and perhaps a tightening of the Washington-Bonn axis. Although the pluses doubtless outweighed the minuses from the Soviet point of view, de Gaulle, again, was rocking the system upon which Europe's stability was based. His thrusts had to be seen as two-edged. His assertion of independence from America would touch sympathetic chords in some parts of Eastern Europe and arouse concern in others. Fontaine described a conversation with an East European diplomat: " 'France's decision,' he said in effect, 'disappoints us. We were hoping she would manage a reform of NATO which would have allowed us to obtain some redistribution of roles within the Warsaw Pact. In showing there is no middle ground between integration and withdrawal, she risks perpetuating the situation which currently exists in our pact, where all the commands are held by the Soviets and where there is no question that any of us could withdraw as long as the German problem is unsettled.' " [4]

His June trip to Moscow was for de Gaulle the beginning of a period of almost constant movement, literally as well as figuratively; it ended with the disaster that befell him and his government in May 1968. Besides Russia, he would visit French Somaliland, Cambodia, Rome (for the tenth anniversary of the Rome Treaty), Canada, Poland, and Rumania. And he went twice to Bonn for the meetings called for by the Franco-German

Treaty. His dealings with the United States and Britain in this period were minimal, negative, and notable chiefly for a second rejection of Britain's effort to join the Common Market and a constant, often violent harassment of the United States. It was an eventful two years, even for de Gaulle, and in exhausting the dramatic content of every event he quite simply went too far; "he exaggerated," as the French would succinctly put it. By and large, they approved the broad lines of de Gaulle's foreign policy as they understood it, while tending to deplore the brutality with which it was so often applied. But at some point, perhaps in the late summer of 1967, a line was crossed. After that the unending drama of de Gaulle's foreign adventures seemed a trifle absurd, hence distasteful and even embarrassing. It was as if a geological formation, the support for his regime, shifted. It settled back in place, but, as events would show, less securely.

None of this is to suggest that the calamity of May 1968 that brought France to the edge of revolution was inspired by a reaction against the General's magnificent obsession; but this was among the many elements that weakened support for the regime and left it vulnerable to the powerful, if inarticulate, contagion of protest. At all levels of French society one heard throughout that incredible period bitter complaints against the regime's quest for a prestige that could only be earned abroad and that seemed to exclude a commitment to the great task of improving French life and adapting the French system.

The voyage to Russia, for both sides, was largely ceremonial. Franco-Russian *rapprochement* was celebrated; de Gaulle was given a tour across the vastness of Russia, one purpose of which was to show him that the country did not divide at the Urals. He had assured a few key figures among the moderate opposition that he would exercise "prudence" in Russia. The Soviets, for their part, who had not developed—and haven't to this day—a "French policy," cultivated de Gaulle and permitted him—at least up to a point—to affect the role he wanted. His nuisance value was recognized, but difficult to appraise in terms of its long-run utility to a conservative Soviet government preoccupied with both internal pressures and "polycentric" currents in the Communist bloc.

De Gaulle cut a grand figure in the Soviet Union and titillated the traveling press corps with his repeated references to "Russia"—carefully confining his use of the term "Soviet Union" to references to the state and his official hosts—and St. Petersburg instead of Leningrad, and so on. Less noticed but more important was the agreement he concluded for Franco-Russian scientific and technical cooperation, which led to the formation of a joint commission on the ministerial level and several working groups. Among other things, this agreement allowed France to launch satellites and space vehicles with Soviet rockets from Soviet installations. And it cleared the path for a scientific-technical relationship as close as the two governments chose to make it. The other agreement of consequence was that Kosygin would pay a reciprocal visit to Paris toward the end of 1966.

At the University of Moscow de Gaulle did disconcert the press corps momentarily with a reference to the "new alliance of Russia and France." His entourage minimized the remark, reminding the reporters that it was a nonofficial occasion, and recommended that they be guided by the statement at the end of the conference, which said nothing about an alliance and merely proposed that the movement toward *détente* continue toward *entente*.

De Gaulle's speech at a Kremlin banquet in his honor was unremarkable, and faithful to the thematic element of his policy:

Without disregarding in any way the essential role that the United States must play in the pacification and transformation of the world, it is the restoration of Europe as a productive whole, instead of its being paralyzed by a sterile division, that

is the primary condition for France. . . . An *entente* between
hitherto antagonistic states is, to the French, above all a European problem. . . . Until the time when all of Europe reaches
the point of finding together the ways and means leading it to
these essential goals, everything, in our view, commits France
and the Soviet Union to do so between themselves right now.

While de Gaulle was in Moscow it was announced or, better,
leaked that he would go to Cambodia at the end of August, with
interim stops in French Somaliland and Ethiopia. This next
trip started badly. De Gaulle was greeted in French Somaliland
by independence-minded Africans brandishing anti-French
posters, which mightily displeased him; hints that the CIA had
conspired to embarrass him began to circulate. But the visit to
Cambodia was another celebration, the high point of which was
the French President's speech in Pnom Penh Stadium, de
Gaulle's strongest anti-American statement to date. France's
colonial past was effaced in harsh new distinctions between her
present enlightened attitude and American culpability:

> Following the Geneva Agreements of 1954, Cambodia chose,
> with courage and lucidity, the policy of neutrality which fol-
> lowed from these agreements and which, as France's responsibil-
> ity was no longer being exercised, alone would spare Indochina
> from becoming a field of confrontation for rival combinations
> and ideologies and an attraction for American intervention. . . .
> France has taken a stand. It is on the basis of her condemnation
> of the present events. It is taken on her determination not to be
> automatically implicated, wherever and whatever may happen,
> in the eventual extension of the drama and, in any event, to keep
> her hands free. . . . If it is unthinkable that the American war
> apparatus will be annihilated on the spot, there is, on the other
> hand, no chance that the peoples of Asia will subject themselves
> to the law of the foreigner who comes from the other shores of
> the Pacific, whatever his intentions, however powerful his
> weapons.

The decibel level was going up, and the imperturbable White House line on de Gaulle was hardening. Two attitudes now colored Washington's view of the General. One attitude was frankly bitter, the other tended to shrug him off as not a serious figure.

The bitterness was understandable. Washington had never publicly criticized France's policies in Algeria, yet for the United States merely to abstain on an occasional resolution in the UN General Assembly criticizing those policies was sufficient to set off a shrill French reaction, above all from the Gaullists. Even those officials in Washington who opposed or feared the deepening involvement in Vietnam resented de Gaulle's cynical exploitation of the American predicament. In any event, rightly or wrongly, he was to be treated less and less as a statesman who could affect the main currents of American foreign policy. He had done what he could to weaken NATO, his ability to block initiatives was now understood. But Washington was losing interest in schemes for uniting Europe and for solving the nuclear-sharing riddle. Just keeping the lid on while coping with an expanding war in Vietnam was the problem. Third World nationalism, not the endless quarrels of the divided Europeans, was now the concern in Washington. The focus had shifted to where the action was, or seemed to be.

Still, de Gaulle scented blood. His semiannual press conference of October 28 was the occasion for another blast at American hegemony, while the Vietnam war was characterized as "the bombing of a small people by a very large one." * Still harsher comment on Vietnam was contained in his brief and traditional New Year's Eve broadcast:

> France, which has regained her independence and is giving
> herself the means for it, is thus going to continue to direct her

* He devoted a great deal of attention to French Somaliland at this time, suggesting that if the territory opted for full independence, it could count on no support of any kind from France. Clearly, his experience during his visit there rankled.

action toward continental *rapprochement* . . . all this with
the goal of helping our continent to reassemble all its states,
step by step, from one end to the other, so that it becomes the
European Europe. But, while Europe thus takes the road to
peace, war rages in Southeast Asia—unjust war, since it results
from the armed intervention of the United States on the territory
of Vietnam, detestable war, since it leads a great nation to ravage
a small one.

Just a few weeks earlier Kosygin had paid his reciprocal visit
to France, but nothing much came of this largely ceremonial
occasion, for reasons concisely expressed by André Fontaine in
an article some months later:

> The most commonly accepted explanation [for the lack of con-
> crete political results] is linked to the German problem. Moscow
> asks of France that it recognize East Germany, and the General
> refuses. Coming from a man who has said privately a hundred
> times that one should "start with the facts" (which is the point
> of view of the Soviets), and who, if our information is correct,
> said to Mr. Kosygin when he came to Paris last winter that he
> was "neither very enthusiastic nor very much in a hurry" for
> German reunification, this refusal is probably not enough to
> account for the visible persistence, in matters of European secu-
> rity, of almost total deadlock in Franco-Soviet relations.
>
> The real reason, to our way of thinking, is to be found in
> another direction. The Fifth Republic and the Soviet Union are
> both trying to create a "new alliance," but they are not directed
> against the same opponent: for the Élysée it is the United States;
> for the Kremlin, it is Germany. . . . When the head of state
> speaks of "Europe from the Atlantic to the Urals," he expresses
> the core of his most constant thought, namely that Europe should
> belong to the Europeans, which, in his eyes, is what the Russians,
> Communists or otherwise, are and the Americans clearly are not.
> Such a Europe can only result from the cooperation of its mem-
> bers, particularly of its three main ones—France, Russia, and
> Germany. The first one having succeeded, thanks to him, in

effecting a reconciliation with the two others, it now remains for her to reconcile them with each other. Once this has been done, the Americans would no longer have any reason to stay on this side of the ocean. According to him the Vietnam war, equally unpopular on both sides of the Rhine, offers an opportunity to achieve this, the implication being of course that France and the Soviet Union would constitute the two main "pillars" of this new "balance." [5]

This article captured the essence of de Gaulle's enterprise, all too rare a journalistic event. The great purpose—to stabilize a Europe secured in the West by France and in the East by Soviet Russia—was, of course, far beyond France's limited capabilities, as the Russians appreciated perhaps more acutely than anyone. Only the United States could secure Western Europe and guarantee West Germany's non-nuclear status, absolutely central to Soviet policy.

Legislative elections were to be held in March 1967. On February 9, the eve of a three-week campaign, de Gaulle addressed the country—a gesture of doubtful propriety, since he was hardly a neutral figure and was taking advantage of his above-the-battle position to make a partisan speech:

> Before the official opening of the competition that will decide the country's vote, I must say what is at stake. . . . Since history, the Constitution, and the mandate of the people confer on me the mission of guaranteeing the nation's destiny, the obligation of maintaining the continuity of the state, and the duty of ensuring the regular functioning of the powers of the Republic . . . I have the duty of pointing out to you what, in this respect, is of vital importance for France. . . .
>
> It would in any case . . . be most equitable and desirable that [a Gaullist] majority win. But in the present circumstances, it is absolutely necessary. For the three partisan groups which seek to replace the majority and in so doing to impose their policy on the Republic could only, were they to succeed, whether

singly or by two or even all three combining, lead to utter ruin. Juxtaposed in order to destroy, they would, indeed, just as was once the case, be incapable of constructing.

As in all his consultations with the people, de Gaulle was defining the choice as being between himself and chaos. The invincibly paternalistic attitude reflected in the first of these quoted paragraphs, together with the low opinion of his countrymen's political capacities implied in the second, had more than a little to do with the near disaster a year later. He concluded by charging his opponents with wanting to "sacrifice" French independence "in opposite directions: some to obedience to Russia, others to American hegemony." Thus, the Soviet menace could be banished from the realm of diplomacy but remained close to the center of Gaullist politics; but that was something Moscow understood, and tolerated.

The elections were a disappointment, although the Gaullists and their allies retained a slight majority in the Assembly. In any case, de Gaulle felt free to return to the game of international politics. Britain was again rapping on the door of the Common Market; Harold Wilson would soon be crossing the Channel to talk to de Gaulle for the second time; and de Gaulle himself was planning to attend a summit meeting in Rome of the six member states of the EEC to commemorate the tenth anniversary of the treaty establishing the Communities. A press conference was in order. On May 16 he discussed the development of the Common Market largely in terms of uncongenial American actions and purposes, supported in every case, according to him, by Britain. Then he turned to the question of Britain's renewed interest in joining Europe and, with evident pleasure and some misrepresentation, sprayed it with cold water. The purpose was to discourage the British from bidding again, but it was too late for that. Wilson had decided to apply and would see it through. (His conversion to "Europe" had a good deal more to do with domestic British politics than to a sudden perception that the long-run cure for Britain's ebbing political fortunes and sluggish economy was the EEC. In short, he chose to play the European card as a home-front diversion. Still, whatever the original motivation, he became a full-fledged and determined convert.)

Wilson and others on the Labour party front bench had boasted that they could get on with de Gaulle and had even suggested that de Gaulle had an honest grievance against Macmillan. A few weeks after de Gaulle's rejection of Britain in January 1963 Wilson had told Ambassador de Courcel that the General had been right to veto Macmillan's Common Market bid. He said he had read de Gaulle's veto statement twice and wouldn't change a comma.

The two leaders first met in late January 1965 when de Gaulle went to London for Churchill's funeral and Wilson paid him a courtesy call at the French Embassy. It was an occasion that Wilson must, or should, look back on with some embarrassment, for he now reminded de Gaulle that three weeks after the famous French veto he had told the French Ambassador that France had made the right decision, that Britain had not been ready then and was still not ready to join the Common Market. He emphasized Britain's need for cheap food and his own reluctance to impose on the British economy the strains that membership in the Common Market would create. He could not say that Britain would not join one day (Wilson, like so many political chiefs, keeps all doors ajar), but he suggested that for the moment the two countries concentrate on bilateral technical cooperation.

Exactly two years later, in late January 1967, Wilson, now a convert making the rounds of the capitals of the Six, and trying to advance his own Common Market initiative, visited de Gaulle. He was received cordially but noncommittally. In June he went again, even though de Gaulle's May press conference had been very negative. The conversations were somewhat

vague, and nothing of consequence emerged. Wilson was forthcoming on some points, evasive on others. He told de Gaulle
flatly that he was not going to buy the Poseidon missile—the
successor to the Polaris, with which British nuclear submarines
are equipped and which, unlike the Poseidon, might not be able
to penetrate antiballistic defenses. (This revelation had already
been made, if more ambiguously, in the House of Commons a
few days earlier.) Wilson presumably intended to show de
Gaulle that he was not wedded to the American military establishment, but he gave no clue as to whether Britain was preparing to opt out of the nuclear club eventually, or might be
seeking another nuclear partner. In short, nothing Wilson said
suggested that he would play the defense card, as Macmillan
had done at Champs, in pressing his European hopes. This was
just as well, as he would have gotten no further than Macmillan
had. De Gaulle ignored his remark about Poseidon, just as he
had ignored Macmillan's comments at Champs.

Wilson's predicament was in any case abruptly shunted to
the back pages by the Six Day War in the Middle East, a development to which de Gaulle reacted in a way that shocked ad-
mirers and at least temporarily alienated important political
supporters. Prior to the outbreak of hostilities he issued a
warning to Israeli Foreign Minister Abba Eban not to strike
first. He received Eban, then en route to Washington, on May
24, the very day he proposed a review of the Middle East situation by the four powers with special responsibilities in the
area—Britain, France, the United States, and the Soviet
Union. This was an effort to become the arbiter among the
great powers, then bitterly split over Vietnam. And de Gaulle
was also assuming that the Russians would readily accept a
proposal legitimizing their Middle East involvement. Somewhat disconcertingly, Washington and London approved the
idea, but Moscow said no. De Gaulle's mood worsened. On

June 2 he issued a brief statement which sought to discourage hostilities by warning that "the state that would be the first . . . to take up arms will not have [France's] approval or, even less, her support."

All this was hardly unreasonable; taking a neutral position while the great powers, for one reason or another, found themselves in a proxy confrontation might have been useful. Certainly, de Gaulle's stand found favor with a majority in France, if not perhaps in Paris. As chief supplier of arms to Israel, yet with a fund of credit and good will on the Arab side, France could be a constructive influence.

But the following days showed that France's policy in the Middle East crisis was to be a function of de Gaulle's quarrel with the United States. France might be Israel's sole source of advanced-weapons systems, such as jet aircraft, but de Gaulle was determined to prevent a political victory for the Anglo-Saxons and their protégé, Israel, at the expense of the Soviet Union and its putative protégés, Egypt and Syria. The anti-American chord was played in a somewhat different key. The Élysée line now suggested that American power had reached a point where it menaced the world-power balance. There were not two superpowers, just one, and France, to correct the imbalance, would rally to the Soviet Union. After first discouraging UN intervention in the Middle East de Gaulle supported Moscow in calling for an emergency meeting of the General Assembly.

On June 16 Kosygin arrived in Paris, en route to the UN meeting in New York; he was profoundly disturbed by the effect of the Six Day War on great-power politics. De Gaulle believed that Moscow and Washington were now so far apart as to rule out the possibility of a meeting between Kosygin and Johnson (he was still relying on Kosygin's letter), but most French diplomats close to the affair assumed that Kosygin was going to New York chiefly to see Johnson, if a meeting could be properly worked out. The purpose of the Paris stopover was to obtain de Gaulle's support for the Soviet position.

Two days later Wilson arrived in Paris in his second futile try to catch the brass ring. He and Mrs. Wilson were received in grand style as the first official guests of the recently restored Grand Trianon at Versailles. The Prime Minister and de Gaulle talked at length about the disturbing world situation, as well as the Common Market.

Wilson departed on the 20th, and the next day de Gaulle stunned everyone, including all or most of the members of his own government (and presumably Wilson), by issuing what has been described as "a violent text, probably the most radical one written by the chief executive of an industrial state for the past several years." [6] He blamed the war in the Middle East, China's hostility, and other difficulties on American intervention in Vietnam. The scope of this indictment went well beyond the propaganda issuing from Moscow and the Arab countries. Couve de Murville was in New York, and it is generally believed in Paris diplomatic circles that he had no advance warning of the statement. Hervé Alphand was informed only fifteen minutes before it was given to the press. [7]

This statement, together with France's support in the UN for Yugoslavia's resolution demanding Israel's unconditional withdrawal from occupied territories, set off what was probably the first major current of unease within the French administration and even within the government. France was voting with the Soviet bloc and against her allies, who were supporting the more moderate—and successful—Latin American resolution.

Disaster bred disaster. Kosygin did see Johnson, at Glassboro. France's support for the Communist-bloc-supported resolution failed to make a difference, and, worse, only four of the French-speaking African countries voted with her.

In Bonn, at a meeting of French and German government

ministers three weeks later, de Gaulle defined the fundamental
issue as the "enormous power of the United States. . . . By
virtue of this fact there are two alternatives. One can accept
things as they are: this is the easiest course, and means that one
must be a part of a whole dominated by American power. And
there is the other alternative, that of safeguarding our national
personality." [8]

A few days later de Gaulle's rejection of "things as they are"
attained a vertiginous peak in Montreal, with his *"Vive le
Québec libre"* exhortation. It was another, and equally rare,
act of verbal violence.

For de Gaulle more than for most politicians, language was a
weapon. From the start he used it to extend his limited power to
influence events. But if he employed language with a flair beyond the reach of most men, he let it carry him to the wilder
bounds of provocation. Language was the medium for de
Gaulle's violence. His stand on the Six Day War had cost him
support in French political and intellectual circles, but he
hadn't lost the country. The Quebec indiscretion, while less important, cost him support at all levels. Many Frenchmen felt
humiliated by what seemed a clear piece of folly. Provin-
cial newspapers wondered anxiously whether France would
have to take on the financial burden of a free Quebec. As if all
this were not enough, Frenchmen returned home from their
August vacations to find that public-transportation rates had by
administrative decree been virtually doubled in their absence,
and worker contributions to the social-security program
slightly increased. Neither parliament nor public opinion had
been consulted.

By now the unease with de Gaulle's Middle East policy and
subsequent activities had developed into a ground swell of criticism. De Gaulle sought to justify his actions in a broadcast to
the nation on August 10; those who doubted the wisdom and
desirability of his daring initiatives were compared to Goethe's

Mephistopheles: "I am the spirit who denies everything," with France in the role of the "unfortunate Dr. Faust [who] falls into one misfortune after another, right up to the final damnation." Typically, he set up a straw man, defining the elements of discontent as "the votaries of Atlantic obedience."

This characteristically defiant statement both dismayed and embarrassed numerous Gaullists and sympathizers. And de Gaulle's official spokesmen, who had tried to give the *"Vive le Québec libre"* an innocent interpretation, were routed by his reference to the "unanimous and indescribable desire for emancipation that the French of Canada have shown the President of the French Republic." They should have been more prudent. As early as 1960 de Gaulle had declaimed, "French Canadians, take your destiny into your own hands!" But the world had paid little attention then.

The undercurrent of unrest now found expression in political action. Valéry Giscard d'Estaing, the Benjamin of center-right French politics,* seized the events of the summer to dissent from de Gaulle's style, if not his policies, which Giscard was then obliged to support. (Even with the support of Giscard's bloc of forty-odd deputies, the Pompidou government had a majority in the National Assembly of only nine, which meant that if he defected Giscard would saddle himself with the responsibility of bringing down the government and risking new elections). His declaration that "the agony is the fear that the solitary exercise of power . . . will not prepare France for her future" was a sensational move.[9] It was followed by more and more open discussion of *après-Gaullism.* A Gaullist minister with an independent political base, Edgar Faure, spoke of it in a magazine interview, and a former secretary-general of de

---

* His party of Independent Republicans was part of the Gaullist coalition in the National Assembly, but not part of the Gaullist political formation itself.

Gaulle's political party said that Giscard had merely said aloud what everyone was thinking.

De Gaulle paid no attention. A trip to Poland in early September kept the ball in the air. Traditional Franco-Polish friendship was celebrated. The Poles' enthusiasm for France and things French—ubiquitous, exuberant, and touching—failed to hide the absence of political gains. Speaking before the Sejm (Poland's parliament), de Gaulle called for Franco-Polish efforts to build a new European order from the Atlantic to the Urals; a more conciliatory Polish policy on West Germany, to which France, he noted, was reconciled; and Franco-Polish efforts beyond Europe in such places as the Middle East and even Vietnam. Wladyslaw Gomulka's reply was remarkably blunt. Poland's prewar alliance with France had been disastrous for both countries, he reminded de Gaulle, and Poland's links with the Soviet Union and other socialist countries, including East Germany, were now her principal guarantee of security.[10]

De Gaulle also pledged France's support for the Oder-Neisse line as Poland's western frontier. This was expected, and the West German government had been notified that this well-known position would be stated. But neither the Germans nor anyone else was prepared to hear him describe the Silesian city of Zabrze, still called Hindenburg by the Germans, as "the most Polish of all Polish cities." [11] This gratuitous remark earned de Gaulle nothing but a rebuke from the West German government and press. A Polish journalist from a newspaper in Kraków wrote:

> The issue of this border . . . was undoubtedly exploited by the President of France during his Polish visit . . . and if it failed to produce the anticipated enthusiasm, it was because both official Warsaw circles and the public at large were perfectly aware of the fact that a guarantee of the Oder-Neisse border

given by France is not necessarily an event of major importance.[12]

In France reactions to the Polish trip were cryptic. Even the normally pro-Gaullist newspapers seemed reluctant to swallow the official claims that the journey had been an important success. The popular mood, or much of it, was expressed by some normally sympathetic cartoonists who now took the line that the President of France was traveling too much. Still, if the French were losing their taste for the drama, de Gaulle had lost none of his.

11

Decline and Departure

De Gaulle had ruled for nearly ten years. He was 77. He had spent three score years and ten preparing himself for a vigorous and aggressive old age. The weight of time and unique burdens had dulled neither his remarkable faculties nor his attitudes. The turmoil and drama, so much of it contrived, were doubtless therapeutic—the effect of all those years held in check by the stimulation of combat. The doubt and discontent bred by his majestic disregard for other views and even for some objective realities had not reached serious proportions, and at times seemed nonexistent. Indeed, just a few days before the implausible drama of May 1968 a national opinion poll announced that fifty-seven per cent of the French people were satisfied with de Gaulle. His hands were still free.

During the crucial secret negotiations preceding the devaluation of the British pound in November 1967 France was the only major country to refuse to pledge that it would not devalue its own currency. Devaluation by France would have wiped out the effects of British devaluation and could also have set off a chain reaction putting the dollar under unbearable pressure. Leaks from the French government to the press were timed to do the greatest possible damage. *Le Monde*'s financial correspondent was able to report that months earlier France had withdrawn from the eight-nation gold pool, thereby obliging the United States to pick up an additional nine per cent of this stabilizing activity. He also reported that Britain had required $2,000,000,000 in short-term loans since the summer—a disclosure which, as *The Times* (London) pointed out, "showed everybody that there was indeed a crisis on for sterling." [1] Hints from Paris that the pound might face still further devaluation helped to quicken the surge toward gold. America's prestigious former Under Secretary of the Treasury, Robert V. Roosa, called these French tactics "mischief making." [2]

French pressure against the dollar expressed a genuine European bias.* As in the case of other earlier transatlantic disputes, the Gaullist position expressed a European impatience with the long American shadow. And just as Continentals doubted American nuclear guarantees, so was there doubt whether Washington really wanted to eliminate its balance-of-payments problem or whether, rather, it would use American investment in Europe as a form of economic colonialism.

Still, while de Gaulle's case against the dollar touched a responsive European chord, his remedies—a return to the gold standard or doubling the price of gold—had no appeal for other European governments or for most central bankers.

The gold crisis coincided with de Gaulle's sixteenth press conference, held on November 27, 1967. The preoccupation with foreign issues was virtually complete; the subjects were world trade and finance, the Middle East, Quebec, Poland, Britain's Common Market application, and Constitutional questions. The tone of this press conference richly confirmed the opinion of one ambassador in Paris that de Gaulle's line would

---

* De Gaulle's impatience with sterling's troubles was partly a function of his opposition to the dollar: a decline of the pound puts the dollar under more direct and heavier pressure. Also, sterling's tendency to wobble was a useful issue to throw up against Britain's Common Market hopes.

harden because age was hardening his prejudices even if it wasn't blurring his style. His position on the Middle East problem was prefaced by remarks that not only betrayed his irritation with Israel but carried the risk of injecting an anti-Semitic note into the affair. Many, he said, had wondered whether the Jews, having

> remained what they had been down through the ages—that is, an élite people, self-confident and dominating—once they gathered on the site of their former grandeur might come to change the very touching hopes they had had for nineteen centuries into a fervent and conquering ambition. But despite the tide, sometimes mounting, sometimes receding, of ill will which they provoked, more exactly which they caused in certain countries and at certain times, a considerable capital of interest and even sympathy formed in their favor, especially . . . in Christendom.*

Quebec was treated at great length. The present status of French Canada was put in historical perspective, and then, abruptly, de Gaulle's preoccupation with the function of the French language in fulfilling France's destiny was injected:

---

* This paragraph inevitably led to the charge that de Gaulle was anti-Semitic. Here and there, the influence of Maurras and Barrès was noted. But it is not a sustainable charge. Nothing in de Gaulle's record suggests that he was influenced by so base an attitude. His antagonistic comments about Israel should rather be seen first as a typically Gaullist calculation that the moment to expand French influence in the Arab world was presenting itself; anger against the normally Gaullist French Jews who had denounced and perhaps undermined his Middle East policy; and, finally, irritation with Israel for having struck first in June 1967 after he had told her not to.

France's Grand Rabbi, who had a private talk with de Gaulle in early 1968, later described him as having been surprised by the emotion created by his statement on the Jewish people. According to de Gaulle it was misinterpreted. In his view it was a justified eulogy of the worth of the Jews.

The Élysée had embargoed delivery of French military equipment to all the Six Day War combatants. This denied to Israel, among other things, 50 Mirage-V jet fighters, for which two-thirds of the purchase price had already been paid. Just after his press conference de Gaulle lifted the embargo in Iraq's favor, and there ensued a complex negotiation (later to fail) involving the sale of the same airplanes to Iraq and French efforts to acquire exclusive rights to a large unexploited Iraqi oil field.

[The Québecois] consider the mother country no longer as a very dear memory, but as the nation whose blood, heart, and spirit are the same as their own and whose new strength is particularly suited to contribute to their progress; conversely, their success could provide considerable support for France: progress, cultural expansion, and influence. Thus, in particular, the fact that the French language will win or lose the battle in Canada will weigh heavily in the struggle waged on its behalf from one end of the world to the other.

Quebec's arrival at "the rank of a sovereign state, master of its national existence," was proclaimed, and then:

To be sure, this State of Quebec will have to settle with the rest of Canada, freely and on an equal footing, the conditions of their cooperation in order to control and exploit a very difficult nature over great expanses and also to cope with the encroachment of the United States.

He concluded on a typically aggressive note by quoting Paul Valéry's complaint that "too many French people have very vague and hastily conceived ideas about Canada" and Valéry's suggestion that "we could all too easily criticize our educational system." "What," de Gaulle then asked, "would he have said of our press, had he lived long enough to read all that so very many of our newspapers published . . . on the occasion of the visit General de Gaulle made to the French people of Canada?"

De Gaulle's comments on Great Britain amounted not only to a second veto of her bid to enter Europe but yet another threat to the Common Market itself. Wilson's application was the "fifth act of a play during which Britain's very diverse attitudes with regard to the Common Market come one after another without seeming to be alike." Moreover, France was willing to consider some alternative to the EEC—a free trade area, say, that would include Britain and others now outside the Common Market.

But . . . it would first be necessary to abolish the Community and to disperse its institutions . . . Everything depends, therefore, not on negotiations—which for the Six would be sounding the knell of their Community—but, rather, on the determination and action of the great British people, which would make it one of the pillars of European Europe.

De Gaulle was, or seemed to be, riding high. The outcry against his press conference—his most boisterous ever—and actions during the gold crisis bothered him not in the least. On the contrary, he was getting a reaction from the Anglo-Saxons. Untroubled by doubt, unquestioned by anyone in his government or entourage, unchallenged politically, he observed at the end of the press conference:

Everyone knows that if ever the President's faltering in his duties were to open the breach to these assailants [his political adversaries], the resulting political and social chaos, the economic, financial and monetary deterioration, and the international decline would inevitably place France in the hands of one or the other of the two main foreign powers.

As the year 1968 arrived, de Gaulle sounded positively euphoric. In his New Year's Eve message to the French people (in which the people of French Canada were included), he issued a prophecy that would not survive a gray and rainy Paris spring:

In the political area, our institutions will be at work. Therefore, one does not see how France could be paralyzed by crises like those from which we suffered so much in the past. On the contrary, as the ardor of renovation grows and as its promoters, above all the young, do their task, there is reason to hope that, in step with this, our Republic will find more and more active and extensive assistance. In any case, in the midst of so many countries shaken by so many jolts, ours will continue to set the example of efficiency in the conduct of its affairs.

The same lofty tone dominated his toast at a farewell luncheon given at the Élysée Palace for Ambassador Bohlen on January 30.

De Gaulle was now turning his attention to an old passion—his nuclear strike force. He had never really taken any more seriously than anyone else the meager capabilities of the early generations of the *force nucléaire stratégique* (FNS), only the first of which was operational. But the moment had arrived to design the later generation—the fourth—which would eventually give France a big-power strategic capability. The first step in preparing the public and the parliament was General Charles Ailleret's article calling for a defense policy directed against all points on the compass (*tous azimuts*). French policy, he said, must take account of all possible hazards. No distinction was made between the United States and the Soviet Union. Either one of the great powers might attack France in order to use her territory and resources in a struggle against the other, or one might launch a pre-emptive strike against France to deny these resources to the other. The need for long-range ballistic weapons was emphasized, and reference was made to the possibility of spatial nuclear forces as well.[3]

De Gaulle was generally understood to have inspired this article, which he endorsed some days later in a talk at the École Militaire. But what it precisely intended to convey was a source of much speculation. Did it mean, for example, that de Gaulle was planning to withdraw from the Atlantic Alliance? Somebody (doubtless General Ailleret) called in a journalist and clarified the message by extending the main points. It was not a question of abandoning alliances, still less of *défense solitaire*. If the Russian menace should reappear, one could have an Atlantic Alliance, or if the danger came again from the Germans, an alliance with Russia would be in order.

Little doubt was left that France was poised for a quantum

jump to the outer reaches of strategic weaponry. Minister of Defense Pierre Messmer stated that the government was about to choose its mix of strategic forces for 1980, the development of which would begin in 1970: "It is a great political decision and it is also a military choice, for our strategic forces could fulfill this mission either with ground-to-ground missiles with a range of 8–10 thousand kilometers, or with nuclear submarines armed with MRBMs, or with a combination of the two." [4]

A remarkable trinity of options was under review for decision by the summer. They amounted to choosing between a dramatic expansion of France's nascent nuclear-submarine program—a jump from five boats to ten or twelve (the stated goal was four); a replacement of the submarines as they became obsolete with a large force of ICBMs—which would require immense strides from French technology, surpassing even the solution of difficulties in the submarine-launched missile technology; or a mixed force of submarines and ICBMs. Technological problems aside, for France to build and deploy any of these forces before the weapons themselves became obsolete could only have been achieved by foregoing a great deal of social progress and adaptation.

The *tous-azimuts* doctrine set off a new wave of unease, not so much in the press and among the opposition political circles but within the government itself and among senior civil servants in key ministries. No more than a few seconds of informed reflection was needed to measure the impact of any one of these options on the inflation-prone French economy and the somewhat overvalued franc. Pompidou, then Prime Minister and preoccupied by domestic issues, was unhappy and told one Gaullist deputy (later a member of the government) that Ailleret's article was "inopportune." Debré, then Finance Minister, was believed to share this sentiment. Not that it mattered. Nobody, including the Prime Minister, could moderate defense policy or any other policy set by de Gaulle. And de Gaulle had decided that a military program with the main purpose of establishing the distinction between France and Germany was to become the earnest of France's inviolability and global vocation. It had all been anticipated by his speech at the École Militaire in November 1959. (See page 64.) Nothing Ailleret had said went beyond those few spare phrases uttered nearly ten years earlier.

What, meanwhile, was de Gaulle going to do about the Atlantic Alliance? Typically, opinion even among the best-informed French government officials was divided. Almost certainly, de Gaulle himself was not sure what he would do. A plausible guess is that much depended on Vietnam. If the Americans ended the war and opened the way to a dialogue with Moscow, de Gaulle would be tempted to withdraw from the Alliance on grounds that America was preparing to settle broad issues over the heads of its European allies. If, on the other hand, the war continued to weaken the American position in Europe and elsewhere, he doubtless would have been happy to continue using his place within the Alliance to harass the Americans and maintain leverage with the West Germans.

Apart from his erasing of Harold Wilson's European hopes, de Gaulle's thrusts against the Anglo-Saxons had been mostly verbal for some time. But the two gold crises in the winter of 1967–1968 offered occasions, and he made the most of them. It may well be true that the French government did nothing fundamental, or underhanded, to enlarge the financial crisis —France had much earlier run down the reserves of dollars that de Gaulle had been converting into gold—but his harassing maneuvers were troublesome enough. And by now a large part of American and British public opinion was outraged or bewildered, or both. In a sense, though, it was a last hurrah. Never again would his *ex cathedra* ultimatums, threats, and judgments have quite the resonance they had had before.

In January 1848 France seemed serene, peaceful, and prosperous. The violent demonstrations that had occurred at the start of Louis Philippe's reign were scarcely remembered. The present regime was endorsed by a tame Assembly, and the peasant class, whatever its suffering, was told by Guizot, *"Enrichissez-vous par le travail."* Lamartine declared, *"La France s'ennuie!"*

Pierre Viansson-Ponté, political editor of *Le Monde*, echoed Lamartine on March 25, 1968: *"La France s'ennuie."* He, too, was to be borne out some weeks later; 1968, like 1848, was a time of upheaval.

Quite clearly, preoccupation with foreign policy is an indulgence that in the end must create strains, since society is normally concerned less with foreign than with domestic affairs. De Gaulle had given France stability, for which the French were—and to some extent still are—grateful. And he had reawakened French self-respect. World War II and the disappointments, failures, and setbacks of the postwar period were to some degree effaced by de Gaulle's will to efface them. His claim to legitimacy was not denied; on the contrary, much was owed him, and the debt was honored in elections and numerous referenda.

Still, society is capricious, and French society, according to de Gaulle and other experts, is more capricious and unpredictable than most others. De Gaulle flattered himself as having stabilized France, only to discover on the tenth anniversary of his return to power that the stability was a façade concealing traditional elements of instability, reinforced by pressures built up over a decade in which the Gaullist regime had done little to reform the most archaic parts of the system.

France in early May was calm, relatively prosperous, and growing used to the absence of strife and conflict. But the French, as André Maurois has observed, do not live on happi-

ness. It now appears that de Gaulle's regime never fully re-
covered from the shock of his failure to carry the country
on the first round of the 1965 presidential elections. Even
more serious was his reduced majority in the legislative elections fourteen months later. It was not so much a question of
discontent with his policies; the broad lines of his foreign policy were generally approved. But much of the younger population was rejecting the style and the obsession with external
accomplishments. To seek *rapprochement* with Russia while
taking one's distances from America and NATO was acceptable, but undermined by de Gaulle himself—by the exaggera-
tion, by the pervasive glitter and eighteenth-century manner, by
a style inspired by reverence for country and distrust—not in-
difference, but distrust—of any alternative to himself. Other
figures, other regimes, had discredited themselves, if not by
their *drôle de guerre*, then by their unworkable, party-domi-
nated republics.

If the stability fashioned by de Gaulle was applauded, the
other side of the coin—the claim, endlessly repeated, that since
1940 one man alone had been invested with the authority to
speak for France—was losing strength. The collateral claim
that for the first time in a half-century France was not beset
by war or other drama became a reminder that, twenty-three
years after the Liberation and six years after the Algerian
settlement, the state should modernize its institutions. If not,
the plebiscitary prince in the Élysée Palace risked becoming as
irrelevant to national needs as the archaic university and merit-
ocratic system upon which the state was based.

It has been commonplace, since Tocqueville, to remark that
authority and activity are excessively concentrated in the capital
by a centralized, bureaucratic state, constructed under the *ancien
régime*, and completed by Napoleon on the ruins of the Revolution. This centralization means also that relatively limited problems of public order in central Paris may threaten the govern-

ment of all France, as in 1830 and 1848. It also helps explain
that permanent feature of French political life, the divorce between the state and citizen (sometimes dressed up as alienation),
and a style of authority brilliantly described by Michel Crozier,*
which encourages autocracy at the top and anarchy at the bottom
at one and the same time.

The effects of the traditional French style of authority and centralization have been more apparent since 1958 with the decline
of Parliament and the political parties, and the monarchical government of General de Gaulle. The collapse of any effective opposition and the special role of the Élysée have turned most
ministers of the Republic into something like the secretaries of
state of the old monarchy, half way between courtiers and quasi-
permanent under-secretaries. Increasingly recruited from the
upper ranks of the civil service, ministers (with a few notable
exceptions) became insulated from public opinion and the daily
problems of reconciling opposing political priorities, and grew
excessively concerned with administrative convenience, fixing
favoured interest groups, and avoiding initiatives and responsibilities which might compromise them with the Élysée. Mediocre
ministers often satisfied themselves with the complacent manipulation of public opinion, echoing the self-satisfaction of the
General at his press conferences.[5]

The crisis began without warning—students in Paris demon-
strating for reforms of the archaic, pitifully overcrowded, in-
differently administered university structure. Like students in
all the high-consumption Western countries, the protesting
French youth (mostly middle class) were also moved by a
sense of alienation from their society. Police brutality in putting down the demonstrations aroused a wave of public sympathy for the students. With the situation worsening, the regime
went on the defensive and the trade unions edged onto the
scene. The working class, of which a relatively small part is

---

* See his *The Bureaucratic Phenomenon* (Chicago: University of Chicago
Press, 1954).—J.N.

represented by the unions, harbored little sympathy for the students' complaints but moved now to demand redress of its own quite legitimate grievances. Strikes were called all over the country. The union leaders were violently antagonistic to the Maoist and Trotskyist elements spearheading the student rebellion, and sought to give direction to the contagion of protest, which in roughly two weeks swept across the country. By then the black flag of anarchy signaled the students' control of major university buildings, with the red flag hoisted above the headquarters of France's major industries. Established authority, both public and private, was in full retreat.

For nearly a month de Gaulle was aloof from the crisis. Blunder followed blunder, especially while Pompidou was away in Central Asia. De Gaulle himself refused to cancel a state visit to Rumania at this time; while he was there Russia put several divisions against the Czech border, raising a real possibility of invasion.

Throughout this same week, while the crisis deepened until the country was virtually paralyzed, the French saw and heard de Gaulle on television warning the Rumanians against the two "hegemonies" (while carefully assigning the Soviet Union a special position in Europe) and comparing Rumania's historic efforts to remain independent of "Slavs, Magyars, and Ottomans" with France "containing the German and Anglo-Saxon pressure, struggling to remain faithful to our heritage—Celt, Gallic, and Roman." [6] It was quite unreal—all this at a moment when the established order was crumbling in most French cities.*

---

* One measure of the gravity of the affair, which had still to reach its worst point, was that de Gaulle's activities in Rumania did not "lead" the principal television news programs. Almost certainly, this was the first time that a trip of the chief of state was not given star billing.

Ironically, de Gaulle's opposition to the Vietnam war earned him no credit with the militant student groups. Vietnam, as David Goldey writes, "pressed especially on French sensibility since France had fought her own '*sale guerre*' there from 1946 to 1954. It seemed to show that if the most

De Gaulle returned from Rumania Saturday evening, May 18; for days he did nothing and said nothing, while the tension, anarchic impulse, and general sense of excitement or foreboding (depending on one's point of view) sharpened with each passing day. Possibly the author of *The Edge of the Sword* was recalling this passage: "Sobriety of speech supplies a useful contrast to theatricality of manner. Nothing more enhances authority than silence. . . . To speak is to dilute one's thoughts, to give vent to one's ardor, in short, to dissipate one's strength, whereas what action demands is concentration. Silence is a necessary preliminary to the ordering of one's thoughts." [7] Finally, on May 24, de Gaulle appeared on television with a brief message that the country had waited six days to hear. It missed both the moment and the issue.

Extremists aside, much of the population had wanted the beginning of a dialogue with the paternalistic regime that had ruled them for ten years. Instead de Gaulle offered a blank check on a take-it-or-leave-it basis. He proposed in general terms to reform certain aspects of the state and (on tenuous Constitutional grounds) announced that a referendum would allow the country to approve the program his government would submit. Failing such approval, he would, of course, take leave of his presidential functions. France, then, was faced with the stark choice of rejecting this cavalier gambit and thus depriving itself of president, government, and parliament in the midst of a national crisis, or of endorsing a regime whose interest in adapting and modernizing French life was judged by

---

powerful nation in the world could be beaten by a small but determined people, revolution elsewhere, anywhere, was possible. 'Vietnam is the Stalingrad of Imperialism' was a favourite thought of the Maoists. Vietnam provided the Trotskyite and Chinese factions with a common platform, an argument against the official Communists, and a reservoir of sympathy and support which they otherwise would not have had, or risked forfeiting by their arid and endless doctrinal battles." (*Parliamentary Affairs*, XXI, 4, p. 314.)

many to be largely declaratory, a regime that had in the preceding month allowed what began as student demonstrations to become generalized chaos.

De Gaulle clearly had misread the situation. Giscard d'Estaing, a youthful aspirant to the Élysée and reluctant Gaullist ally, explained it by comparing Marianne with Eliza Doolittle: just as Eliza wanted something more from Professor Higgins than a claim to bourgeois values, so Marianne wanted from de Gaulle something beyond stability and a quixotic pursuit of grandeur. Both ladies sought respect, even a gleam of affection.[8]

Premier Pompidou strongly opposed the referendum, urging instead a dissolution of parliament and new legislative elections. He was swiftly borne out. Within 48 hours it became clear that the referendum could not take place: French printers threatened to refuse to print the ballots, and Belgian printers declared solidarity with the French.

De Gaulle's position steadily worsened, as the last climactic week of May began. "De Gaulle is alone," read the headline over an article by a widely read and well-informed columnist and few doubted it. The regime was on the edge of collapse, with de Gaulle appearing either not to understand, or to be cut off from, the frenzy of events. At the time it seemed as if any moderately well-organized opposition could sweep him from power. In fact, the disarray of the Gaullists was more than matched by that of the leftist opposition, bent on snatching defeat from the jaws of victory.

A brilliant two-day piece of theater returned the initiative to de Gaulle. A resounding statement given on May 30, as triumphant as any in his epic career, transformed the situation instantly. France was again governed. The referendum would be indefinitely postponed, Pompidou's plea for immediate elections upheld. That part of public opinion that normally expresses itself at the Place de l'Étoile instead of the Place de la Bastille had finally been mobilized.

A curiosity of the crisis was the tacit alliance of the regime and the French Communist party, both committed to maintaining order. The Communists were no less hostile than the government to the Maoist and Trotskyist splinter groups on the far left. Although it earned them nothing in the new elections, they acted as a stabilizing force. Their aim, of course, was not revolution but respectability, more precisely, an end to isolation and acceptance as a party capable of forming alliances and even sharing power.

Moscow and Washington were also in tacit agreement, each hoping de Gaulle would survive, both fearing the consequences if he did not. The Americans' clear preference for de Gaulle showed that in their eyes the quarrels with France, however bitter, were essentially family fights. And for the Russians, Gaullist foreign policy, although not without its troublesome side, offered immediate advantages that could not be expected from any loosely strung coalition of his adversaries. Domestically, his actions tended to polarize French politics, conceivably to the lasting benefit of the orthodox French Communists. (The ultraleft-wing militants were no less distasteful to Moscow than to the PCF.)

As it turned out the Gaullists waged the June election campaign on the issue of defeating totalitarian Communism. This was no less successful for being unjust; having acted as a force for stability, the PCF was cast in the opposite role and crushed; the Gaullists were returned with a massive absolute majority. A reasonable guess is that the voters voted first for stability; second for Pompidou, whose skill and steadiness throughout the crisis was the government's only visible asset; and third for de Gaulle himself.

Broad conclusions were swiftly drawn by journalists and diplomats in the wake of the crisis. De Gaulle's foreign policy was judged to be doomed. Ditto his monetary policy. He would cut a less formidable figure in the Common Market because France might require special assistance from the Community, as Italy had a few years ago. And so forth. May had been a trauma for France, and some overreaction was only natural. But it was true that the cost was certain to be heavy. The franc, for example, much weaker than it had seemed even before the crisis, was (and remains) enfeebled; de Gaulle's aversion to dollar balances and his penchant for gold were unlikely to cause further serious disturbance to the world-payments system.

His ability to speak for Western Europe as a whole further declined. The famous fourth generation of French strategic weapons was headed for the discard or, at least, a drastic curtailment and slow-down. And a somewhat more conciliatory attitude toward the United States appeared just as the crisis was reaching its peak, when Ambassador Sargent Shriver arrived at the Élysée to present his credentials and de Gaulle described differences between the two countries as "events of the moment," while stressing the strong link between the two, "whatever should be."

His China policy, moreover, became a mockery. During his trip to Rumania de Gaulle had told the Chinese Ambassador in Bucharest to convey his best wishes to Chairman Mao. Two days later, de Gaulle was burned in effigy in Canton. And when he spoke of the French riots being inspired and supported *"de longue main,"* most people thought of China (the only state whose propaganda supported the student rioters), even though certain members of the entourage put the blame elsewhere, i.e., on the United States (CIA) and Israel.

Still, de Gaulle remained in power, sustained and fortified by the election returns and determined to repair the ravages of weeks of national paralysis. His policies were not to be changed. Any doubt as to who would be in charge was swiftly erased by his abrupt dismissal of Pompidou early in July, relegating the Prime Minister to the swollen ranks of the Gaullist back benches. This remarkable gesture showed, among other things, a fine disdain for the sensibilities of the electorate, which had just massively endorsed the Pompidou government after a campaign in which he had been the dominant figure and popular favorite.

Pompidou had been right too often during the crisis; worse, perhaps, he was unimpressed by certain of de Gaulle's oldest and favorite notions—a defense policy for *tous azimuts* was only one example. Important differences between them were really centered on domestic issues. Also, in January, months before the crisis, Pompidou had scarcely referred to de Gaulle during a forty-five-minute interview on television. Finally, Pompidou was bidding for control of the Gaullist party apparatus.

For de Gaulle the second half of 1968, if less apocalyptic than the first half, was scarcely more agreeable. Gaullist foreign policy, linked as it was to *"détente, entente* and cooperation with the Soviet Union,"* was abruptly deflated by the Czechoslovakian invasion of August 21, by the hard reality of what was central and what was merely tactically useful to Moscow. Following talks with Pompidou's successor, Couve de Murville, de Gaulle had a brief, two-sentence statement put out, tending to blame everything on the "policy of blocs," the origins of which were traceable to Yalta:

> The armed intervention by the Soviet Union in Czechoslovakia shows that the Moscow government has not freed itself from the policy of blocs that was imposed on Europe by the effect of the Yalta agreements, which is incompatible with the right of peoples to self-determination and which could and can only lead to international tension.
>
> France, which did not take part in these agreements and which

does not adopt that policy, notes and deplores the fact that the events in Prague—besides constituting an attack on the rights and the destiny of a friendly nation—are of a kind to impede European *détente* such as France herself practices and in which she urges others to engage and which, alone, can ensure peace.

For the next several days the Yalta Conference was the subject of nearly as much official comment and attention on the government-managed television news programs as the invasion itself. By inference, then, the Americans and British were partly to blame for what was happening in Czechoslovakia. This bizarre interpretation of events, to put it charitably, aroused only modest resistance. André Fontaine, who, like Sulzberger, though for different reasons, is one of the journalistic continuities in the story of de Gaulle and the Anglo-Saxons, did clear the air a bit: "This division of the world, morally so revolting, is caused by the strategic balance and not, as the French Government seems to think, by the Yalta accords, which General de Gaulle should know, even if he wasn't a signatory, were never really applied. . . . The truth is that the [creation of American and Soviet power blocs was] the inevitable consequence of the loss of power of a Europe which could not regain the liberty destroyed by Hitler's ambitions without appealing to two powers, one of which was not completely and the other not at all European." [9] Raymond Aron was another dissenter. In an article entitled "Yalta, or the Myth of Original Sin," he flatly stated that "the Yalta accords admitted neither in letter nor in spirit the partition of the world or of Europe. They led to the partition of Europe perhaps, following a fatal chain of events, fatal to the extent that they were violated by the Soviet Union." [10] Lastly, although Washington reacted mildly to de Gaulle's references to the ghost of Yalta, Ambassador W. Averell Harriman, then leading the American delegation to the Paris talks on Vietnam, offered some pungent comments during a Radio Luxembourg interview. "There is one thing

which General de Gaulle says which is true: that he was not at
Yalta; and therefore his impressions have been gained not from
a knowledge of what went on, but a lack of knowledge."

The day before, September 9, de Gaulle had rehearsed the
Yalta argument during a press conference. Compared to
previous performances, it was subdued, revealing, perhaps for
the first time, a lasting change wrought by the events of May
and the shock of August 21. Everything de Gaulle said was in
the well-worn pattern, but the effect was considerably less resounding. His language had all of the old bite; the performance, as always, was elegant and flawless. What was missing
was the compelling quality, the sense that de Gaulle was im-
parting to great affairs the logic of his independent thought or
the force of fiercely held attitudes. In brief, de Gaulle's grip
seemed less secure, as if he had somehow gotten slightly adrift
of the main currents. The impression would remain.

For once, the greater part of his press conference was devoted to internal affairs, especially the events of May. The
harshest language was applied to the trade unions, which he accused of becoming political; the "great organs of press and radio," which he accused of emphasizing all that was violent,
scandalous, and destructive ("isn't that so, gentlemen of the
press?"); and various intellectual circles. For the French people
themselves, the judgment was also hard. They had gotten themselves "in distress"; the situation had "morbid" aspects; the
mass of the people had been "congealed."

The next month de Gaulle was in Turkey, his chips still resting on *détente* and "free hands" for all. Turkey and France, he
said, were resolved to "maintain their independence, to allow
no one to use their soil, their skies, their borders or their
armies; to play their own role and impose their own weight
on all the events and the settlements that concern one and
the other. . . . To us French, it seems that the Turks intend, as we intend, to see the system of two hegemonies,

which currently divide Europe and spread themselves into the Orient, give way to *détente, entente,* and cooperation." The line was unchanged, but, predictably, it failed to change the thinking of the Turkish government, for which the Czechoslovak invasion had stifled the impulse toward more balanced relations between the blocs and reduced emphasis on the United States and NATO. Also, a growing Soviet naval presence in the Mediterranean meant that Turkey was now threatened from the south as well as the north. Rather wistfully, the Turkish President observed, "We, too, had believed that this *détente,* so much hoped for, had become a reality. What happened in Czechoslovakia unhappily showed us that optimism . . . is not yet applicable." [11] French press treatment of the trip was understated and routine, with an undertone of nostalgia for the splashier days running through some of the articles.

Large amounts of capital had fled France during and after the May crisis. By the late summer and early autumn the flow was increasing rather than leveling off. The government, trying to reanimate the French economy, had opted for a boldly expansionist program—very possibly the rational and correct policy—but the chances of finding a passage around the financial reefs were lessened by the expanding deficit in France's international account, and by the government itself. Too much credit was made available, in too many cases to the wrong people; in effect, the government found itself contributing to the flow of hot money. A major *gaffe* was committed early in September when the exchange controls adopted in May were removed at about the same time that a raise in inheritance taxes was proposed. It mattered little that the controls had not been working, because they were difficult to enforce. Lifting them at such a moment invited the inevitable: about $200,000,000 left France in the next two weeks, and confidence in the government fell off sharply.

By mid-November Western capitals were in the grip of their third financial crisis in a year; but this time the pressure was on the franc. In Paris banking circles, devaluation seemed inevitable; the only question seemed to be how much. Devaluation between eight and twelve per cent would be acceptable and would not necessarily force other currencies to follow suit. Indeed, a modest French devaluation, if accompanied by a revaluation of, say, five per cent of the robust West German mark, would probably allow the international monetary system to totter along intact. Anything above 12 or 14 per cent—to say nothing of a "savage" devaluation in the neighborhood of 25 per cent—could easily have had a chain reaction. Also, a "savage" devaluation was too risky. The political and social repercussions in France might have overwhelmed the regime. And then, while it might in the end force a major revision of the accident-prone monetary system—an attractive prospect for some Gaullist ministers, for whom the system was synonymous with "dollar bloc"—France would suffer the heaviest penalty; the other major lenders in the International Monetary Fund would almost surely refuse de Gaulle the credit he so badly needed. That was the way it seemed.

To Bonn for a major meeting came the finance ministers and managers of the "Group of Ten," the ten leading industrial countries of the International Monetary Fund. Some of them believed the ideal solution would amount to an agreement by the West Germans to revalue their currency and thus possibly spare de Gaulle the need to devalue. To nobody's surprise, the heaviest pressure in favor of this solution came from Washington, London, and Paris. Naturally, the French wanted to avoid devaluation; naturally, Washington and London wanted to help them, so as to avoid heavier pressure on sterling and the dollar, the overburdened reserve currencies.

The irony of this Big Three alliance, albeit temporary, was lost on no one, but Bonn was not persuaded. Adjusting the value of money is unpopular in West Germany—even if a sensible case for it can be made—since Germans tend to think that money is too important to be exposed to the whims and notions of governments; and the last German revaluation, in 1961, had been unpopular. So the Kiesinger government said no, and, in the days that followed, was as unbudging as de Gaulle himself. The moment was intensely dramatic and heavy with political import. The Germans had said no to their most important allies.

The attending world press swiftly drew the conclusion that "Bonn Puts *Nein* Back into Its Vocabulary," to cite one headline. "For five years, the great fear of West German 'internationalists' has been that President Charles de Gaulle of France would finally teach the Bonn government to say 'nein' and that once relearned, the word would never be forgotten." [12] It was not, of course, the first time that Bonn had said no, either to de Gaulle or the Americans. But never had Bonn said no to both at once, or so unambiguously, or on an issue so vital to France.

In turn de Gaulle mounted another piece of high-grade political theater, his standard method for turning adversity to advantage, or, at least, for confusing the situation and staving off adversity.

He had two choices, either a modest devaluation or no devaluation with a Draconian austerity program. As usual, everyone was kept in the dark about de Gaulle's intentions. By Wednesday, November 20, Europe's major foreign-exchange markets were closed. On Friday some well-informed journalists were reporting a French decision to devalue by less than 10 per cent. The *Financial Times* of London said: "All indications this evening were that General de Gaulle had reluctantly agreed to let the franc be devalued by less than 10 per cent in conformity with the wishes of France's major trading partners." The weekly news magazine *l'Express*, which appears on Monday, went to press on Friday evening with a lead story analyzing the decision to devalue. On Saturday *Le Monde*, which reaches most news-stands about 2:30 p.m., reported that the decision to devalue was to be taken formally that very afternoon, and that the figure would be "on the order of 9.785 per cent." The headline read: "The Government Defines the Broad Direction of the Economic Program To Accompany Devaluation." Two excellent sources —one a high official in the Bank of France, the other an aide of the Finance Minister—had passed the word that the decision had been taken to devalue. Obviously, they were acting under instruction from either the Élysée or the Prime Minister's office.

In fact, de Gaulle had already decided, possibly as early as the beginning of the week, *against* devaluation. The trap was sprung late on Saturday, when it was also announced that de Gaulle would explain his decision on Sunday evening in a broadcast to the nation.

Perhaps de Gaulle would not have devalued the franc under any circumstances in November 1968. Whatever the technicians said, the pressure for the move was not overwhelming—not, at least, if Washington, Bonn, and the others supplied enough backing for the franc. And to devalue on the first anniversary of the British devaluation would have been especially embarrassing, even repugnant, for de Gaulle. In any case, besides earning political credit at home, the decision not to devalue—with its surprise of the unexpected—offered the occasion for another of the big theatrical events in which de Gaulle placed so much confidence and which would swiftly recall the inspirational moment of May 30. Then, he was pitting himself against the forces of agitation and chaos. On Sunday evening, November 24, it was "odious speculation" against the franc that was to be resisted and that would not be allowed to dictate French policy.

The grateful approval of his allies, upon which he had now to rely, was another plus factor. De Gaulle received a warm cable from Lyndon Johnson pledging that the Americans would cooperate "in any way we can." A $2,000,000,000 line of credit that the Group of Ten had been prepared to offer de Gaulle, provided his devaluation stayed beneath 10 per cent, remained available. The foreign-exchange markets immediately reopened. In France exchange controls were restored, with threats of stiff penalties for violations. Another financial crisis was over. "Once again General de Gaulle has succeeded, not just in creating suspense, as on May 29, but in taking his adversaries and partisans by surprise and, with them, France and the world." [13]

It is tempting to say that the shocks of 1968 brought de Gaulle down from the peaks of legend to the drearier mundane lowlands where other political figures must normally operate. And in part, that is what happened. At home and abroad, Gaullist political fortunes sank to an unprecedented low. The effect on his style was, however, negligible. The old attitudes were unchanged. What was missing had, to some extent, never been there anyway. His claims for France, along with the claims for Gaullism, had some validity, but not enough.

His quarrel with the Americans over nuclear and strategic policy, for example, reflected a normal European desire for a larger role, a stronger voice in East-West matters, plus a real doubt about the American commitment to defend Europe with nuclear weapons. But his alternative—West European security guaranteed by France alone—was unthinkable beyond the Élysée Palace. An independent Europe—de Gaulle's European Europe—is an ideal for many people, but few besides the General would deny the United States a continuing and major involvement in the struggle to remove the obstacles to a settlement of European problems.

Or again, to take a neutral position between the Arab states and Israel, as de Gaulle did on the eve of the Six Day War, was sensible, even laudable; and specialists on the Middle East in the three Western powers silently applauded his stand. But then to come down on one side of the quarrel chiefly to harass one big power (the United States) to the apparent benefit of the other (the Soviet Union) was to lose at once the credit acquired by the neutral stand. Greater French influence in the Middle East in and of itself was desirable and could be useful. But when this became a function of de Gaulle's global vision it undermined policy and set limits on French influence.

France's refusal to give Britain and easy passage into Europe was widely approved. Britain, after all, had had several chances to enter Europe in the 1950s and, to put it mildly, had missed them all. But to veto Britain in an absolute sense was an extreme that France's allies could neither approve nor modify. In each of the six capitals, Paris included, there was concern that all Europe would suffer from de Gaulle's intransigence (and that the obstacle to British participation in a politically balanced European community might eventually be West Germany, stronger in most ways than France and progressively less burdened by the baggage of the past).

To chivvy Washington's financial and monetary practices made a certain amount of sense, given the sensitivity of Continentals to what seems an American penchant for sponging up their economic patrimony while running large balance-of-payments deficits. But the sensitivity was declining, and inadequate phrases like "technology gap" were falling from fashion as the "gap" came into better perspective—appearing more properly as a collection of disparities between America and Europe, the benefits of which flowed in both directions. Meanwhile, France, having first been obliged to stop swapping dollars for gold, now, *mirabile dictu*, let it be known that despite de Gaulle's commitment to gold, his government was opposed to raising its price. The Bank of France's gold reserves were very large, but the stock hoarded or held by Frenchmen in private desposits was larger still, and raising the price would set off colossal inflationary pressure. Thus was the monetary policy launched by de Gaulle in the early weeks of 1965 shelved. Not surprisingly, it had caught his old Minister of Finance, Giscard d'Estaing, off balance. France was now pushed back toward the more balanced monetary policy that Giscard himself had advocated until de Gaulle turned the issue into another weapon in the great quarrel with the Anglo-Saxons.

Quebec, Biafra, and other issues were put to the service of that same enterprise. In his last New Year's Eve broadcast to the nation, de Gaulle noted that "we French are not presently a physically gigantic nation . . . for example, we have to leave to others the admirable merit of . . . going around the moon. We have, nevertheless, a part to play in the world to the benefit of all peoples, and it is a part that is truly ours. This means that, without in any way renouncing our traditional friendships, we must remain sound and independent." Then he ticked off the "acute problems of the universe . . . which anyone can enumerate." Czechoslovakia was not on the list, but claims were made for "the free exercise of a national life of its own for the French people of Canada [and] the recognition of the right of self-determination for valiant Biafra."

Although the tone hadn't changed, Gaullist policy was in fact coming under review, as the world was to discover in just a few weeks. The drama of May, the invasion of Czechoslovakia, and the financial crisis had all helped to release pressures that had been building for a long time, not just in France but in Bonn, too. As 1969 began, it seemed clear that time and events were working against Gaullist policy. Instability at home and the threat of an unmanageable German problem, the eternal problems never far from the center of any French leader's thinking, had been reawakened.

De Gaulle could scarcely have looked for a more compliant—indeed, a more "Gaullist"—Chancellor than Kurt Kiesinger. Yet the rift that had opened between the Élysée and Chancellor

Erhard was never closed by Kiesinger, despite his determination to do so; reconciliation and friendship with France were a political constant to which no one could have shown more sensitivity than Kiesinger. But the price of harmony with de Gaulle was now too great for any German government, however warmly disposed. Aware that the May crisis and the Czech invasion had weakened his position, de Gaulle reacted by applying even greater pressure on West Germany. An extreme of sorts was reached in the late summer when he sent an emissary to tell a few prominent West German figures that Bonn bore some responsibility for the Soviet invasion of Czechoslovakia. West Germany's "opening to the East," encouraged by de Gaulle so as to reduce Bonn's dependence on Washington, had gone too far, he judged, in Czechoslovakia: a highly visible West German commercial presence in Prague, plus a large West German loan, had raised eyebrows. Perhaps Bonn had gone too far, but to suggest that lack of West German finesse or discretion had seriously influenced the Soviet decision is not credible. Yet de Gaulle, it is known, broached the matter in similar, if perhaps softer, terms when he saw Kiesinger in Bonn in late September during one of the semiannual meetings. (Kiesinger, at the time, was resisting strong pressure from within his own party to defy de Gaulle by promoting some activity within the European community, including greater contact with Britain.) The fragile, accident-prone Paris-Bonn relationship—from which each sought so much that the other could not, or would not, accept—was slipping into another sharp decline. Within de Gaulle's entourage anxiety was often and vividly articulated by Michel Debré, who had replaced Couve de Murville as Foreign Minister. Bonn's flat refusal to bolster the franc by revaluing the mark not only was an irritant, but it served notice on all France that the dutiful, guilt-ridden West German attitude was yielding to something more assertive and, thus, more disturbing.

The financial crisis had lowered Couve de Murville's stock in the Élysée, while Debré's access to de Gaulle increased, if temporarily. His renewed concern about Germany obviously reflected de Gaulle's. Not surprisingly, Debré had also begun to think about improving France's relations with Washington and London. Here, too, he may well have mirrored de Gaulle's own thinking. German balkiness tends to arouse in the minds of French statesmen thoughts not just of alliance with Russia but also of the Entente Cordiale. Debré had been attracted for years to the idea of Paris and London together ridding Europe of the integrationist temptation. Both publicly and privately, de Gaulle himself had kept such an iron in the fire (along with others). Always hostile to the Common Market, like de Gaulle, Debré now began to talk more seriously about a larger and looser European grouping in which Britain could participate.

But by the winter of 1968–1969 even this double-edged fallback position had more allure than feasibility. British efforts to do serious business with the West Germans were at last making headway, a development which, if sustained, might mean that de Gaulle would be outflanked on matters of surpassing sensitivity affecting defense and technology.

Mixing deeply in Continental affairs doubtless exhilarated Britain's leaders, but gave the Germans cause for worry. French anxiety became that much greater and the possibility of a major European political crisis more likely. The point should not be pushed too far, however. The joint British-German projects (involving other governments as well) were not yet out of the negotiating, or analysis, stages; they might come to nothing; nor had the mutual suspicion and even mistrust that for years had divided Bonn and London been effaced. But the logic of events, reinforced by the failure of other policies and absence of other alternatives, had at last pushed the two closer together.

To take a conspicuous example, Britain, West Germany, and Holland were—and are—moving slowly toward creating a joint venture for producing enriched uranium by the gas-centrifuge method, an enormously difficult process. The tripartite arrangement is explained by the mutually complementary breakthroughs they achieved, of which the Dutch was probably decisive. Like gaseous diffusion, the standard process for making U-235, the origins of the centrifuge process date to the last war. The diffusion process was adopted by the United States and later nuclear powers because the technical problems it posed, although formidable, were soluble, while the centrifuge technology seemed full of intractable difficulties. Yet the advantages of the latter process are compelling. A centrifuge installation uses only a fraction of the power needed by gaseous-diffusion plants, which are fantastically expensive to run; also, diffusion plants are huge and impossible to conceal, whereas the operating scale of a centrifuge installation is smaller and, perhaps more important, can be built up gradually, becoming in the end a kind of giant honeycomb of centrifuges.

Agreement of the three countries is still not assured, but the prospects are promising, if complicated. Something like twenty negotiating subgroups from the three countries are struggling with various aspects of the collaboration. If all goes smoothly, the consortium may have an installation completed as early as 1972. This would mean an alternate source of U-235, the industrial need for which will grow at a high rate in Europe in the next decade. It will also tend to hold down American prices for U-235. Politically, the centrifuge technology means that the spread of thermonuclear weapons, which are normally triggered by U-235 atomic bombs, may be more difficult to discourage. The effect of the British-Dutch-West German collaboration on the nuclear nonproliferation treaty is at the moment unclear. Indeed, the implications of the centrifuge breakthrough are so sweeping as to defy swift comprehension.

What may be safely said is that the formation of a three-country centrifuge club in Western Europe had a disturbing effect on de Gaulle and his government. The French have

invested staggering sums in their gaseous-diffusion plant at
Pierrelatte. But Pierrelatte's capacity is meager and barely
sufficient to satisfy French military requirements for enriched
uranium. In December 1967 the French pressed their Community partners to divide with them the cost of building a larger
diffusion plant in France which one day could supply low enriched U-235 to European industry. They were turned down;
their partners were unwilling to run the risk that dissent from
Gaullist political attitudes would jeopardize their access to the
plant, just as de Gaulle had been unwilling to depend on Washington as his source. Now, another and possibly cheaper source
loomed on the horizon. Even more ominous was the idea of
Britain and West Germany collaborating in an area as sensitive
as the production of enriched uranium.

Another joint project of great sensitivity is the so-called
Multi-Role Combat Aircraft (MRCA), a project involving a
$4,000,000,000 investment for the fabrication of perhaps a
thousand planes. Here again a European consortium may be
organized without France. The partners would be Britain, West
Germany, and Italy. Because it is unlikely that any one country
can afford to build a supersonic, multi-role swing-wing airplane on its own, collaborative arrangements are required. A
few years ago it appeared that France and Britain would build
a swing-wing all-purpose fighter plane together, but France
canceled the agreement.

With French participation the MRCA project would take less
time and would cost less. France has a long lead in swing-wing
technology and has built and tested a remarkably smooth and
bug-free prototype. Moreover, France can design and develop
high-quality combat aircraft as well as any of the world's man-
ufacturers, and probably more efficiently. But while technicians
(and many political figures) in both Great Britain and Germany would prefer to work with France than with each other,
the MRCA is supposed to promote Britain's presence on

the Continent and to give the aviation industries of Britain and Germany the major share of what is likely in the 1970s to be Europe's largest and most advanced aviation project. Most "political airplanes"—those that are jointly produced —either never fly or, if they do, are uneconomical. The Franco-British supersonic transport "Concorde" could make this point dramatically; the MRCA may be no exception either; in the end it might conceivably be France, working with either Germany or Britain, which makes the airplane. (British and West German requirements for the MRCA are so different that current plans envisage a two-place British version and a single-place German version.) France and Germany could probably agree on a substantially similar version. Still, in the spring of 1969, the systems-analysis phase of the MRCA was reasonably well advanced, a working agreement had been signed, and France faced exclusion from still another European joint venture in an advanced sector of high sensitivity.

For de Gaulle, defense and defense-related technology was a most sacred realm. To rest indifferent while Britain "Europeanized" in this area was out of the question. As 1969 began de Gaulle maneuvered for tactical advantage and fresh leverage. But the margins for maneuver were narrow. The West Germans were saying no not only on large matters but on small ones as well. (For example, the bid by a partly state-owned French oil company to purchase West German oil interests was vetoed in Bonn. That stung.) And the Soviet link was returning no important dividends; France had made numerous concessions, political and otherwise, and had obtained little if anything of substance in return. A joint project for launching a French satellite (the Roseau) with a Soviet rocket in Russia was canceled by Paris because of heavy budgetary pressure. Moscow had agreed to buy France's color-television process and tube—but other West European countries have opted for the West German system, which, while somewhat inferior to the French, is simpler and cheaper. To date, other options for the extraordinarily expensive and elaborate French system have been taken only by the East Europeans (notably Hungary and East Germany), plus Egypt and Lebanon. Again, France is isolated from the real market—Western Europe—and is having great difficulties in developing a tube that can be sold at competitive prices. Moreover, the West Germans are far from pleased at seeing France and East Germany making this sort of trade arrangement.

In short, the policy of "free hands," far from allowing de Gaulle to arbitrate great problems, was tending to isolate him —not only from the Anglo-Saxons but from Western Europe as well. He had failed either to unify Europe around France or to dominate Germany. His military forces, both nuclear and non-nuclear, were falling behind the stated goals, with further reductions and slowdowns ahead.

The early weeks of the new year were tumultuous, foreshadowing the European political crisis or political rearrangement that could not be far off. De Gaulle was seeking a way out from his confinement. With a new President in the White House, he tried to restore the appearances of Franco-American amity. And he was contemplating an initiative with the British.

Unfortunately, the notion that Europe should organize itself around France and Britain has been shown to have the defects of its obvious virtues. Alas, the symmetry is almost too perfect. The pain of giving up the old empires, together with the efforts to continue to be leading powers in the world, has unfairly taxed the resources of both nations. Just to deploy and maintain modern nuclear weapons might in the end be too costly for either to do alone. Quite a large segment of the British policy-making apparatus would favor not replacing nuclear weapons as they became obsolete, a sentiment that finds an echo of sorts in Paris, where numerous officials and civil servants believe that France's nuclear-weapons program is creating "European," as distinct from French, strategic options. Believing, too, that France cannot indefinitely sustain the economic burden of creating and maintaining a balanced nuclear-weapons capability, they see joint Franco- British efforts as a possible way of moderating the problem.

Politics and habit have divided France and Britain on familiar lines. Still, Debré's idea of a loosely organized confederate Europe based on a warmed-up Entente Cordiale has tempted key members on both sides of the House of Commons (indeed it was with precisely such a structure that Britain sought to sidetrack the Common Market in the late 1950s).

For some months in late 1968 a paper urging just such an approach, bearing Debré's blessing and rounding off the argument he had been putting to de Gaulle, had been going the rounds of the Quai d'Orsay. During the same period the new British Ambassador, Sir Christopher Soames, had been trying to arrange a talk with de Gaulle; a tête-à-tête luncheon was set for February 4.

Some days later the trouble began, oddly enough in the Western European Union, a consultative organization of interest mainly because its membership links the Common Market Six and Britain. France has taken a suspicious view of the WEU, alert to possible efforts to use it as a kind of "back door" for Britain to enter Europe. These suspicions were well grounded: first the Belgians, then the Italians, proposed using the WEU as a forum for policy discussions on matters not specifically covered by the Rome Treaty. The Foreign Office moved with dispatch to exploit this opening. At almost the same moment that de Gaulle and Soames were lunching together, Whitehall was preparing to arrange a WEU meeting on the Middle East. As the item found its way onto the WEU agenda, Paris suddenly woke up, instructed the French delegate to boycott the meeting, and declared that henceforth no such meetings could be held without the unanimous approval of all governments. The other Five rejected this position, attended the meeting, and, after some wavering in Bonn, have since attended others with Britain. The opening had been made; Britain was meeting with France's Continental partners on matters of broad political importance.

Soames' luncheon seemed to present yet another opening, and again the British moved with haste—as it turned out, too much haste. The gist of de Gaulle's remarks at lunch, according to Soames' version, was that France would consider scrapping the Common Market and replacing it with a large free-trade area in which Britain, Ireland, Scandinavia, and so on, could participate. European political cooperation would be left to an inner council of the four largest countries, Britain, France, West Germany, and Italy. He stressed the importance of an independent Europe, noting that among West European countries only France had achieved the necessary degree of freedom from the United States. And, he said, an independent Europe would have no further need of NATO, although it was not clear whether de Gaulle proposed a clear break by all the European members with NATO. He did propose that as a first step Britain and France should have talks on political, defense, and economic matters; Britain, he said, should propose the talks, an initiative to which France would respond favorably.

In a state of some excitement Soames returned to his embassy and with his staff worked long and hard on a report to Whitehall of the luncheon conversation. The following day he and a staff member showed their account of the talk to Bernard Tricot, de Gaulle's Chief of Staff. Tricot agreed to show it to de Gaulle but suggested that Soames obtain verification from Debré, who was then visiting Spain. Soames saw Debré on February 8 and was told that de Gaulle had read the account and found nothing inconsistent with his remarks. (Debré himself had not had time to read it and was relying on a memo from Tricot.) Moreover, a senior member of Debré's staff congratulated Soames on the "excellence" of his version and volunteered that "someone at the Matignon" (the Prime Minister's headquarters) had also expressed his admiration for it. Clearly, Soames' detailed account of the conversation had been read by a number of senior figures; for whatever reasons, the affair was considered important by the regime.

Prime Minister Wilson was scheduled to see Chancellor Kiesinger in Bonn on February 11–12, just a few days later. Two deceptively persuasive reasons tempted the British to tell the West Germans exactly what de Gaulle had said to Soames. To reveal the proposals could mean banking credit in Bonn, specifically at de Gaulle's expense. Second, the British sensed a trap: in suggesting that the initiative for Franco-British talks should come from London de Gaulle might have hoped that Wilson would accept, thus allowing him to tell the Five that Britain, far from being a serious candidate for the EEC, still clung to the hope of changing it into something much looser and different.

To tell or not to tell? The Foreign Office, by no means opposed to revealing the proposals, strongly urged Wilson to observe the proprieties by giving the French advance warning of his intentions. Alas, this Wilson was unable to do, because he did not decide to tell Kiesinger until the second day of the visit. Soames was instructed to inform the French Foreign Ministry immediately, but of course it was too late. The other interested capitals were also informed at the same time or a few hours later.

Meanwhile, the WEU crisis had dominated the front pages of European newspapers for some days. France had announced a full boycott of the institution and even suggested that the other members, by continuing to hold meetings with the British on political matters, ran the risk of provoking a break-up of the Common Market.

Then, on February 21, leaked versions of the luncheon conversation began to turn up in the French press, which inspired the British to release a summary of the "agreed version." Relations between Paris and London plunged to another low, with one French official accusing Britain of "diplomatic terrorism." The official French position was that what Soames and his colleagues had taken to be French proposals amounted only to an exploratory conversation on de Gaulle's part. None of it, they said, was really new. And they denied that Debré or any other official source had authenticated Soames' version of the conversation, which, they said, was not precisely accurate on certain points. Actually, France's clarified version scarcely differed from the British; but that was of little consequence.

The importance of the affair lay in what it told about the state of European politics in early 1969. De Gaulle was taking, or seemed to be taking, an important step *toward* the British, only to have the ground cut out from under him. After years of trying to turn the other EEC members, West Germany especially, against the British (and Americans), he had abruptly suggested something that might have turned Britain against them. The British could not ignore the possibility of entrapment. De Gaulle did few things for one reason alone, always had several irons in the fire. If the British had taken the bait, he might have seriously pursued a bilateral course leading to the dissolution of the Common Market in its current form, or he might simply have used the affair against them. Nobody will ever know, although the best guess is that he was in earnest.

De Gaulle was probably the net loser from the episode; without a word of warning to his partners he was opening a dialogue with Britain apparently aimed at breaking up or transforming the European Community. Still, the British earned little credit. It may be that Wilson had acted swiftly in order to disarm those elements in both the Labour and Conservative parties which are drawn to what de Gaulle was offering. (For those who recall Wilson's open hostility to the Common Market in Macmillan's day, this aggressive Europeanism was among the most pointed of the numerous ironies running through the episode.) But he overlooked an important point. Logic and fashion had conspired to focus attention on *après-Gaullism*, and a kind of tacit agreement had emerged that de Gaulle should not be provoked for the remainder of his days in power. His mandate ran to 1972, but events could inspire an earlier departure. In any case, since he was unlikely to agree to important initiatives that satisfied the others, the idea was to wait for a less inflexible and more realistic French leader —a Pompidou perhaps—and meanwhile hope that de Gaulle would not feel pushed to take some destructive action. Wilson missed the point.

Even to avoid entrapment he was not immediately obliged to tell the West Germans about the Soames luncheon but, instead, could have informed the French that proposals such as de Gaulle had made could not be discussed bilaterally but only in concert with the other Common Market countries; the British could then have proposed general discussions on European political organization with the Six, and informed France that a report of the luncheon conversation would be made available to the other members, together with Britain's reaction. Or the British could have let events—press leaks and so on—push them to release the "agreed version," being left at such a point with no alternative.

So swiftly was the Soames affair defused, by tacit agreement on all sides, that only days later it seemed like a tempest in a teapot. More likely it was one sign, the WEU troubles another, of a political crisis that might eventually lead to the break-up of the Common Market in its current form. The crisis has persisted, if less visibly at some moments than at others, pitting France against Great Britain, with West Germany in the middle.

On some issues Bonn must choose between Paris and London, on others between Paris and supporting the continuation of the Common Market. Rightly or wrongly, the West Germans feared that if de Gaulle lost on a major issue, he really would destroy the Common Market, whatever the cost, and perhaps in a way that would make *them* appear at least equally responsible.

The issue might be something as apparently banal as financing the EEC's agricultural policy. France is the EEC's granary and produces large food surpluses. Current arrangements provided that the other members share in the cost of subsidizing French agricultural exports and modernizing French agriculture. A great deal of money was involved in this scheme, and nobody, least of all the West Germans, who were obliged to pay the largest share, larger even than France's own, was happy with it. This was the issue which had paralyzed the EEC for six months in 1965; it had to be renegotiated again before the end of 1969.

The United States could not rest indifferent to the collapse of the European movement. Nor could Washington be content to see the Common Market replaced by a large free-trade bloc, innocent of political content or potential and in conflict with American trading interests. The United States encouraged the Common Market, quite willing to risk the effects of a competitive trading bloc in return for the political advantages of the enterprise.

Richard Nixon's administration said early on that it would not try to influence the direction of the European movement, a primarily family affair. Perhaps this attitude will survive the divisions and hard realities of European politics. But inevitably Washington will be drawn in; the American involvement in

Europe's problems is central; for the problems themselves are central to American interests, whether political, economic, or financial.

One object of President Nixon's visit to Western Europe early in 1969 was to gain the Europeans' assent to his negotiations with Moscow. He obtained it, which meant that the dialogue to which de Gaulle had always objected could go forward with a kind of clearance, or tolerance, on the European side which may or may not endure—depending on the talks themselves. What may be said is that never since the war have the European nations had so little to contribute to the East-West discussions on arms control and other pivotal issues. And the drop in influence was most marked in Paris; until the end of 1961, when de Gaulle withheld approval of the Berlin talks, Paris, as well as London, had always been closely consulted by Washington, and had participated directly in most East-West negotiations.

Indeed, the West's Big Three had once dealt with Moscow as political equals, even though the military strength lay with the Americans. Britain was still consulted on a fair number of issues, thanks to the vestigial remnants of the "special relationship." But Washington and Paris were far apart. To have free hands really meant that France had only marginal influence with either of the great powers. Unable to forget or to forgive his absence from Yalta, de Gaulle was once again isolated from the main event.

He could have been President of a United States of Europe; it bears repeating. Or he could have maneuvered eventual acceptance of the tridirectorate he had begun by proposing. Or he might even have had his French-led coalition of states organized on something approaching his own terms. But through the years de Gaulle ignored the substance of power in order to keep faith with its shadow. He did much for France, having twice restored a sense of honor and self-respect, and once perhaps having averted a civil war.* As theater it was superb, but what is called Gaullism was a misfortune for Europe, not least for France, which for a time had such need of him. The glory to be found in a global vocation, a paternalistic hold on one's errant people, a concern for the future limited to consecrating one's own monumental example—these were the considerations that animated de Gaulle's rule.

"To persuade the states along the Rhine, the Alps, and the Pyrenees to form a political, economic and strategic bloc . . ." This celebrated passage from his memoirs expressed de Gaulle's passion. The Europe he left behind is unlikely to resemble the integrated structure against which he thundered and fought—certainly not for a long time—but still less will it be the French-led coalition for which he struggled. De Gaulle once compared the effort to build Europe with the time, patience, and dedication required to construct a cathedral. It was not a bad metaphor. The realist in de Gaulle saw as clearly as anyone that Europe's organization would emerge only slowly, painfully, and in stages. But the romantic in him made claims for France for which the realist could entertain no real hope.

What is certain is that no European structure is possible without a strong and creative French presence. And, although inconceivable in de Gaulle's day, France's European policy should in time become more moderate and orthodox. Pompidou has never harbored "European" sympathies, but he is a problem-solver, burdened by neither ideological baggage nor experience with foreign affairs. And he must take some account of the non-Gaullist elements who supported him and provide part of his political base.

---

* It also bears repeating that before returning to power he used none of his considerable influence to help deflect the forces carrying France toward the abyss.

Equally, sweeping changes in French policy and in Europe's development cannot be expected. Negotiations on another British application to the EEC may go forward, but full British participation will be a matter of years, not months. De Gaulle's departure did not mean that France would return to NATO. It did mean that French cooperation within the Alliance machinery would be greater, the French position less ambiguous and less subject to the Gaullist tendency to dart between East and West.

This was starting to happen even before he left. Pressure from the French armed forces, a squeeze on the military budget, and the absence of acceptable alternatives were all pushing the regime toward closer rapport with NATO. Curiously, just two days after de Gaulle's reversal on April 27 the same defense review that printed the famous *"tous azimuts"* article by General Ailleret reproduced an address delivered to an institute of defense studies by Ailleret's successor as Chief of Staff, General Michel Fourquet.[14] Interred in measured language was the Ailleret concept, as well as a great deal of what passed for strategic doctrine in the Gaullist years. Fourquet (no less a Gaullist than his predecessor) spoke of "graduated actions" which would precede recourse to "nuclear deterrence," and asked how France could go so far if "our NATO allies did not themselves seem decided to raise the stakes." He spoke of French forces "engaged on the northern and eastern frontiers in close coordination with our allies against an enemy coming from the East." This passage restored the distinction between the Soviet Union and the United States that Ailleret (and de Gaulle) had removed.

The cost of advanced weapons systems grows constantly. The ability of European countries to deploy modern military forces is likely to decline unless there emerges some combination of more "cost-effective" procurement procedures and a new political dynamic within the Western Alliance. The point is taken by many people within France's defense community, and in Britain clearly reflects the attitude of numerous leaders of both major parties as well as the Whitehall bureaucracy. Official circles in London, some of them anyway, now think of Britain as virtually a part of Western Europe. The notion of a "European caucus," or a separate European personality, within NATO is being pushed by Britain. Nobody knows exactly what it means, if anything, but at least it shows a perception that efficient use of the resources available in Western Europe for defense can only be found in some form of reasonably close cooperation. In the end Europe's defense and ability to adapt may require a strong central institution that would manage defense spending within the framework of a general policy agreed to by all the governments. That will not happen soon; it may not happen at all. The process of disunity may continue to outpace the unifying process, in which case the Europeans will remain fully dependent on the United States and unable to influence American policies affecting their own security. Discussions between the United States and the Soviet Union on limiting strategic arms—known as SALT (Strategic Arms Limitation Talks)—may prove to be one of the most protracted yet significant negotiations of the era. Equally, they may greatly strain the cohesion of the Western Alliance. Although the United States is sensitive to the unease of the Europeans, who are absent from the talks, and is prepared to consult closely with them, it will be difficult to quiet their anxiety about possible deals being made above their heads.

The will to unite may have faded, but the practical arguments for close European organization are reinforced by the absence of acceptable alternatives and by the spur of SALT. How to reach the American negotiating position if not by creating some means whereby the European can speak with fewer voices? One much-discussed possibility is Franco-British military cooperation at both nuclear and non-nuclear levels, a step the British could contemplate only if France's opposition to their participation in Europe's political development were removed and if French and British nuclear forces were closely coordinated with America's, as Britain's are now. Relying on Anglo-American agreements Washington could and probably would veto any arrangements that fell short of such coordination.

Ironically, London and Paris may eventually seek arrangements similar to those which Kennedy and Macmillan offered de Gaulle in December 1962. It will be recalled that in return for France's assigning units to NATO and working out joint targeting arrangements, the Kennedy Administration was prepared to give France nuclear assistance, provided Congress agreed. A nuclear tridirectorate might have emerged, though not in precisely the form laid down by de Gaulle in 1958. After 1963 the political climate ruled out reconsideration of the idea. Even now, the traditional resistance of Congress, fortified by concern for the progress of SALT, may exclude trilateral nuclear arrangements. Washington's priorities are not yet clear.

Opposition to a European caucus, to say nothing of a West European defense institution, may come most strongly from West Germany. Instead of welcoming such ideas, the Germans —at least so far—have regarded them as measures which, far from promoting their security, on the contrary give the Americans a convenient excuse to hasten the day when they can withdraw large numbers of their forces based in Europe.

L'Europe à la carte is a modish phrase describing how Europe may develop—not within the Common Market or any existing structure, but through various steps in various directions over an indefinite period of time; the MRCA, the gas-centrifuge project, a Franco-German agreement to build a short-haul "air bus" are examples of such steps. In fact, the *à la carte* impulse is unlikely to create closer organization or unity, for the process lacks coherence. The MRCA, for example, is an alluring project, whether for London, Bonn, or Paris. But clearly, the three could not all have a major role in developing the aircraft. Fixing the division of labor between just two—Britain and West Germany (while assigning a lesser share to Italy)—has proved very difficult. Briefly, it is not possible to fit every major European country into every large joint project. No one country can undertake them independently, but the other extreme—a share for everyone—is an equally irrational use of limited resources.

Some of the joint projects have a modest political content, others virtually none (except, of course, if they fail, in which case the political effects are negative). They are attempts to manage large requirements on a correspondingly large scale, but they do little to promote the kind of equilibrium in which each participating country is assured that its continuing interests are protected and its advanced industries given maximum opportunity to mature. Shifting and expedient arrangements do not achieve this equilibrium. What might achieve it is the sort of institution that animated the early success of the Common Market—a commission authorized to make decisions on behalf of member countries and responsible for making certain that if the interests of Country A are favored over Country B's in one case, the circumstances will be reversed in another.

Before de Gaulle resigned it seemed that the movement toward some form of European unity would be obliged to hit bottom before reviving—if ever it did revive. De Gaulle froze the European movement, but now the situation is at least fluid. A thaw is beginning. Still, the stronger tendency to deal bilaterally and *à la carte* on matters of concern within Western Europe remains dominant. The identity of interest between London, Paris, and Bonn is clearer than in the past, and the asymmetry of their attitudes has declined. But the nationalistic impulse, reawakened by Gaullism as much as anything else, con-

tinues to beat strongly. Neither of those old adversaries—de
Gaulle or Monnet—will in the end be entirely borne out. And it
is too early to predict which will come nearest to carrying off
the prophetic honors, such as they may be.

Europe, then, is caught in the backwash of earlier achievements and in a political struggle at some moments muted, at
others uproarious. Britain and France, while still competing for
Continental support, are tempted by the possibility of bilateral
military cooperation, although each currently assigns a higher
priority to arrangements with the United States.

Franco-American relations are carried on at several levels,
of which the political is clearly the most consequential. But the
performance of de Gaulle and various American Presidents
in translating mutually hard political attitudes into the practical world of finance and commerce was uneven, to say the
least. The virtual collapse of political relations between the
two countries was not matched at these other levels; and it
should not have been. France and America, after all, are part
of a system that has grown up since the war for working out
the political, military, commercial, and financial arrangements
of its members. However imperfect, the system does represent
their best interests. Like any system, it has certain tolerances.
These were strained but not overcome by the endless skirmishing between de Gaulle and his antagonists in Washington and
London.

From the beginning the great if seldom declared issue was
whether America and Britain should assist or discourage
France's nuclear-weapons program. The White House most
often accepted the State Department's judgment that nothing
should be done which would reduce the cost to France in resources and time required to develop a nuclear capability.
Quite apart from the West German problem, Washington had

little interest in advancing the date when France would be able and perhaps willing to sell even the non-nuclear parts of advanced-weapons systems to other countries.

For one reason or another this "hard-line" policy was not applied as rigorously as some had hoped. Production licenses have been issued for guidance, tracking radar, and numerous systems of high sensitivity. An American study cites a reliable French publication as saying, "The Americans, whether voluntarily or not, furnished precious assistance to the French technicians [in] the difficult and delicate field" of inertial guidance.[15] French commercial missions and various data-collection programs have accomplished a great deal. The sale of KC-135 jet tankers gave de Gaulle's "first-generation" nuclear weapons such operational plausibility as they have. Another example was the sale to France of high-performance computers (Control Data *6600*) in July 1966, just when the Johnson Administration was trying to decide how to react to de Gaulle's withdrawal from NATO. (This was a reversal, and represented a typical case of bureaucratic skirmishing along the Potomac. France's first request for the computers was turned down. Somebody then suggested to the French government that it disavow any intention to use the computers in weapons-connected research. This was done, and the first decision reversed.)

Some say that Washington has fallen between two stools. Notwithstanding official policy, the French advanced-weapons program has drawn heavily on American experience and aid, whether direct or indirect. The hard line, it is argued, has not been applied with sufficient rigor. And in making occasional exceptions, as in the case of the high-performance computers, the United States has not gained the political benefits that might have accompanied a more lenient policy. By denying technical assistance to France, others say, Washington has merely encouraged the growth of a broader and more independent technological base in France and thus set in motion a process that works against America's long-run interests.

Probably none of these assessments is realistic. It was never likely, for example, that France would become significantly dependent on American technology. A former Pentagon official with long experience in the sale of American hardware says the French were never really interested in buying complete weapons systems, or subsystems, but rather in obtaining components, materials, and data. (They have, he says, the best and largest data-collection system he has seen.) Nor was a policy of full denial ever really possible. Aside from the United States' balance-of-payments difficulties and the pressure to sell abroad, France and the United States were allies with a long history of close commercial and technological links. Full denial, ruthlessly applied, would have added to the tensions between the two countries and further strained the tolerances of the Western system. Occasional relaxation of American policy, while it had no effect on de Gaulle, did provide some comfort to his Continental neighbors, for whom the Franco-American dispute often created embarrassment and difficulty. They tended to look to France to put the European case before Washington. But they had to continue to depend on the latter; a choice between the two was intolerable.

Most often it was de Gaulle who forced the choice. Never did he consider himself an ally of the United States except in the most limited and pragmatic sense. If the source of disagreement did not exist, then the pretext for disagreement was called up. To shift French destiny into its true current, he felt obliged—this bears repeating, too—to liberate France from the Anglo-Saxons.

Whatever the mistakes of the American and British leaders of the period—and these were numerous—there never was a possibility of doing serious business with de Gaulle on reasonable terms. Still, in both Washington and London, numerous thoughtful men devoted much of their time, often the better part of it, to trying to find the key to a productive relationship, or *any* relationship, with de Gaulle. Internal differences grew within both the American and British governments. The issue of de Gaulle, and of who or what should speak for Continental Europe, poisoned relations between equally gifted civil servants and officials who dealt with the problem. Unfair and misleading labels, such as "theologians" and "hard-nosed school," were applied on the American side by one group of bureaucrats to another. For those who were assigned such dreary labels, the heat has gone out of the issue, but a residue of bitterness— even misunderstanding—remains.

Yet on every side it should be recognized that because one official figure was closer to being right and another wrong it does not mean that the first was necessarily wiser or more useful to his government and the second less so. Those who deal with complicated events often become their victims, due to pressures of time, political dynamics, and the weight of multiple responsibilities. And a retrospective study of the relative validity of the judgments of any one decisionmaker would show the dips and rises of a fever chart.

The same review applied to the taxing problem of dealing with General de Gaulle would seem to show that the heavy investment in effort and time made by so many sensible and well-intentioned Americans and Britons—Presidents and Prime Ministers among them—was wasted. It was a tragic waste; de Gaulle was a tragic figure. The theater he created, the scenes he played, drew in the others and, in greater or lesser degree, touched them all.

Reference Notes
Index

Reference Notes

Chapter 1: On the Eve of Power

1. Charles de Gaulle, *The Edge of the Sword*. London: Faber & Faber, 1961, p. 61. Originally published in France in 1932 under the title *Le Fil de l'Épée*.
2. François Mauriac in l'Express, September 3, 1959.
3. General André Beaufre, *L'Expedition de Suez*. Paris: Grasset, 1967, p. 34.
4. J.-R. Tournoux, *Secrets d'État*. Paris: Plon, 1960, p. 154. See also Jacques Fauvet, *La IVe République*. Paris: Fayard, 1959, p. 323. Fauvet notes that on the French side only four people managed the Suez affair; all the other Ministers, kept in ignorance, later lodged a complaint with the President of the Republic.
5. Tournoux, *op. cit.*, p. 176.
6. *Ibid.*, p. 177.
7. Hugh Thomas, *Suez*. New York: Harper & Row, 1967, p. 154.
8. Bertrand Goldschmidt, *Les Rivalités Atomiques 1939–1966*. Paris: Fayard, 1967, pp. 226–27. At least, this is what French officials believed at the time. The fact is, their British colleagues almost certainly would not have transferred such data to France, but they doubtless found it convenient to put the responsibility for the decision on Washington. I discussed this and the other charges made by Goldschmidt, a distinguished French scientist and a director of the French Atomic Energy Authority (CEA), with three qualified Britons, all of whom held positions of high responsibility at this time in British atomic-energy programs and related British

activities. Two of them denied that Britain has ever seriously contemplated giving assistance of this nature to France. The third
implied that Goldschmidt was technically correct.

9. Laurence Scheineman, *Atomic Energy Policy in France under the
   Fourth Republic.* Princeton University Press, 1965, p. 186.
10. *Ibid.,* p. 180.
11. Alfred Grosser, *La IVe République et sa politique éxterieure.*
    Paris: Armand Colin, 1961, p. 58.
12. Tournoux, *op. cit.,* p. 154. Also, Fauvet identifies the four "arti-
    sans" of Suez as Mollet and Bourgès-Maunoury and their respec-
    tive *directeurs de cabinets,* Émile Noel and Abel Thomas. Thomas,
    he says, had special responsibility for the "liaison" with Israel.
13. Robert Osgood, *NATO, The Entangling Alliance.* University of
    Chicago Press, 1962, p. 220.
14. Fauvet, *op. cit.,* p. 340.
15. Michel Debré in *Carrefour,* April 23, 1958.

Chapter 2: The General

1. Quoted in Milton Viorst, *Hostile Allies.* New York: Macmillan,
   1965, p. 67.
2. Robert Sherwood, *Roosevelt and Hopkins.* New York: Harper,
   1948, pp. 775, 781–82.
3. *Ibid.,* p. 858.
4. Charles de Gaulle, *War Memoirs I—The Call to Honor.* New York:
   Viking, 1955, Simon and Schuster, 1959, p. 104.
5. Charles de Gaulle, *Vers l'Armée de Métier.* Paris: Berger-Levrault,
   1934.
6. Charles de Gaulle, *The Edge of the Sword.* London: Faber &
   Faber, 1961, pp. 20–21.
7. Jean Lacouture in *Le Monde Diplomatique,* January 1968.
8. Charles Maurras, *Kiel et Tanger.* Paris, 1912, p. 139. I am indebted
   to Pierre Hassner, the political scientist, who first directed me to
   this work of Maurras. See Hassner's "From Napoleon III to de
   Gaulle," in *Interplay* magazine, February 1968.
9. J.-R. Tournoux, *La Tragédie du Général.* Paris: Plon-Paris Match,
   1967, p. 92. See also Lacouture, *op. cit.*
10. Charles de Gaulle, *War Memoirs III—Salvation.* New York: Simon
    and Schuster, 1959, p. 330.
11. De Gaulle, *War Memoirs I,* p. 4.
12. De Gaulle, *The Edge of the Sword,* pp. 13–14.

13. Paul-Marie de la Gorce, *De Gaulle Entre Deux Mondes.* Paris: Fayard, 1964, p. 61.
14. De Gaulle, *The Edge of the Sword,* pp. 39–40.
15. *Ibid.,* pp. 53–55, 58, 61–62.
16. De la Gorce, *op. cit.,* p. 120.
17. De Gaulle, *War Memoirs III,* p. 205.
18. *Ibid.,* p. 53.
19. *Ibid.,* p. 61.
20. *Ibid.,* p. 77.
21. *Ibid.,* p. 51.
22. *Ibid.,* p. 57.
23. Address by de Gaulle at the National Press Club. Washington, D.C., April 24, 1960.
24. De Gaulle, *War Memoirs III,* p. 60.
25. Maurras, *op. cit.,* p. 140.
26. Cited in an article by André Fontaine in *Le Monde,* January 30, 1963, concerning a conversation between de Gaulle and American Ambassador Charles Bohlen. This aspect of the conversation, it would appear, was leaked to *Le Monde.*
27. Memorandum dated September 17, 1958, delivered to the Governments of the United Kingdom and the United States on September 25.

Chapter 3: Seeding the Quarrel

1. John Newhouse, *Collision in Brussels, The Common Market Crisis of 30 June 1965.* New York: W. W. Norton, 1967, p. 20.
2. *Le Monde,* July 7, 1958.
3. George W. Ball, *The Discipline of Power.* Boston: Atlantic–Little Brown, 1968, pp. 128–29.
4. *Ibid.,* p. 129.
5. *Combat,* July 4, 1958.
6. *London Daily Mirror,* April 2, 1958.
7. Franz-Josef Strauss, "An Alliance of Continents," in *International Affairs,* April, 1965, p. 200.
8. Speech at Compiègne, March 7, 1948.*
9. Speech to the Rassemblement du Peuple Français (RPF), April 17, 1948.*

* Notes 8–12 and 19–21 are citations of statements by de Gaulle collected by Edmond Jouve in his doctoral thesis, *Le Général de Gaulle et la Construction de l'Europe* (3 vols.), Paris, 1966.

10. Interview with United Press, July 10, 1950.*
11. Press conference, August 17, 1950.*
12. Speech at Vélodrome d'hiver, February 11, 1950.*
13. Stanley Hoffmann, "Les Conflits Internationaux," in *Revue Française de Science Politique*, April 1964, p. 319.
14. Press conference, May 31, 1960.
15. Press conference, November 10, 1959.
16. Address at the École Militaire, November 3, 1959. It concluded by quoting, without acknowledgment, the final rousing paragraph of *The Edge of the Sword*.
17. General Charles Ailleret, "Défense 'dirigée' ou défense 'tous azimuts,'" in *Revue de Défense Nationale*, December 1967, pp. 192–93.
18. *Le Monde*, March 2, 1967.
19. RPF speech at Lille, February 12, 1949.*
20. Press conference, March 29, 1949.*
21. Press conference, November 14, 1949.*
22. Alfred Grosser, *French Foreign Policy under de Gaulle*. Boston: Little Brown, 1967, p. 66.
23. David Schoenbrun, *The Three Lives of Charles de Gaulle*. New York: Atheneum, 1965, p. 284.
24. *Le Monde*, September 16, 1958.
25. *Le Monde*, September 16, 1958.
26. J.-R. Tournoux, *La Tragédie du General*. Paris: Plon-Paris Match, 1967, p. 321.
27. B. J. Cutler in New York *Herald Tribune* (Paris Edition), June 29, 1959.
28. *Ibid.*
29. *Paris-Presse l'Intransigeant*, December 17, 1958.
30. Guy de Carmoy, *Les Politiques Étrangères de la France 1944–1966*. Paris: La Table Ronde, 1967, p. 331.
31. Ball, *op. cit.*, p. 129.

Chapter 4: Allies at Cross Purposes

1. James L. Richardson, *Germany and the Atlantic Alliance*. Cambridge, Mass.: Harvard University Press, 1966, p. 267.
2. *Ibid.*, p. 267.
3. Don Cook, *Floodtide in Europe*. New York: G. P. Putnam's Sons, 1965, p. 240.

4. *The Times* (London), March 4, 1959, cited in Richardson, *op. cit.*, p. 268.
5. Dwight D. Eisenhower, *Waging Peace.* Garden City, N. Y.: Doubleday, 1965, p. 412.
6. *The New York Times*, September 29, 1959, cited in Richardson, *op. cit.*, p. 277.
7. *The New York Times*, August 23, 1959.
8. Text in *ibid.*, February 5, 1960.
9. Text in *ibid.*, February 19, 1960.
10. J.-R. Tournoux, *La Tragédie du Général.* Paris: Plon-Paris Match, 1967, p. 498.
11. See Robert Kleiman, *Atlantic Crisis.* New York: W. W. Norton, 1964, p. 63.
12. *Paris-Presse l'Intransigeant*, April 23, 1960.
13. *Le Monde*, April 24–25, 1960.
14. New York *Herald Tribune* (Paris Edition), April 27, 1960.
15. *Le Monde*, April 27, 1960.
16. *The Times* (London), April 26, 1960.
17. *Agence Économique et Finance*, April 25, 1960.
18. *Le Monde*, April 26, 1960.
19. Hans Speier, *Divided Berlin, The Anatomy of Soviet Political Blackmail.* New York: Frederick A. Praeger, 1961, p. 95.
20. *Ibid.*, p. 97.
21. *Ibid.*, p. 103.
22. *The New York Times*, December 16, 1959.
23. *The Washington Post*, April 15, 1960, and *The New York Times*, July 23, 1960. Cited in Robert Osgood, *NATO, The Entangling Alliance.* University of Chicago Press, 1962, p. 232.
24. *The New York Times*, May 15 and June 10, 1960, cited in Osgood, *op. cit.*
25. David Schoenbrun, *The Three Lives of Charles de Gaulle.* New York: Atheneum, 1965, p. 296.
26. Letter from the Under Secretary of State to Senator J. W. Fulbright, dated August 11, 1966, in *Hearings before the U. S. Senate, 89th Congress, Second Session* (summer 1966), pp. 507–508.
27. Schoenbrun, *op. cit.*, p. 321.
28. Guy de Carmoy, *Les Politiques Étrangères de la France, 1944–1966.* Paris: La Table Ronde, 1967, pp. 342–43.

Chapter 5: The Education of John F. Kennedy

1. Roger Hilsman, *To Move a Nation*. Garden City, N.Y.: Doubleday, 1967, p. 131.
2. C. L. Sulzberger, *The New York Times*, April 30, 1961.
3. *Ibid.*
4. *Le Monde*, April 29, 1961.
5. New York *Herald Tribune* (Paris Edition), March 20, 1961.
6. C. L. Sulzberger, *The New York Times*, April 7, 1961.
7. *Ibid.*, April 9, 1961.
8. Hilsman, *op. cit.*, p. 243.
9. Alain Peyrefitte in *La Vie Française*, April 7, 1961.
10. *Le Monde*, April 4, 1961.
11. *Ibid.*, May 31, 1961.
12. C. L. Sulzberger, *The New York Times*, June 2, 1961.
13. *Ibid.*, March 26, 1962.
14. James Reston, *The New York Times*, June 1, 1961.
15. Robert Kleiman, *Atlantic Crisis*. New York: W. W. Norton, 1964, p. 43.

Chapter 6: Nuclear Aid to France—the Great Temptation

1. Arthur M. Schlesinger, Jr., *A Thousand Days*. Boston: Houghton Mifflin, 1965, p. 358.
2. *The New York Times*, April 18, 1962.
3. Albert Wohlstetter, "Nuclear Sharing: NATO and the N + 1 Country," in *Foreign Affairs*, April 1961.
4. William W. Kauffman, *The McNamara Strategy*. New York: Harper & Row, 1964, p. 114.
5. *John F. Kennedy Papers II*, #184, p. 387.
6. *John F. Kennedy Papers II*, #157, p. 344.
7. Schlesinger, *op. cit.*, p. 208.
8. Theodore C. Sorensen, *Kennedy*. New York: Harper & Row, 1965, p. 559.
9. Robert F. Kennedy, *Thirteen Days: A Memoir of the Cuban Missile Crisis* (New York: W. W. Norton, 1969), p. 67. Copyright © 1969 by W. W. Norton & Company, Inc. Copyright © 1968 by Mc-Call Corporation.
10. Sorensen, *op .cit.*, p. 558.
11. *Ibid.*, p. 571.

Chapter 7: The Psychodrama of Skybolt and Rambouillet

1. "Problems and Trends in Atlantic Partnership," a *Staff Study of the Committee on Foreign Relations, U. S. Senate,* September 14, 1962, p. 37.
2. Henry Brandon, "Skybolt," in *The Sunday Times* (London), December 8, 1963.
3. *Ibid.*
4. Ward Just, "The Scrapping of Skybolt," in *The Reporter,* April 11, 1963.
5. Brandon, *op. cit.*
6. *Ibid.*
7. Theodore C. Sorensen, *Kennedy.* New York: Harper & Row, 1965, p. 564.
8. Brandon, *op. cit.*
9. Hugh Thomas, *Suez.* New York: Harper & Row, 1967, pp. 51, 95.
10. Cited by Just, *op. cit.*
11. Cited by Brandon, *op. cit.*
12. Cited in *ibid.*
13. *Le Monde,* December 15, 1962.
14. *Ibid.,* February 7, 1963.
15. Cited in an article in *The Guardian* (Manchester), December 17, 1963.

Chapter 8: The Anglo-Saxons Routed

1. Theodore C. Sorensen, *Kennedy.* New York: Harper & Row, 1965, p. 568.
2. Brandon, *op. cit.*
3. *The Times* (London), December 19, 1962.
4. Arthur M. Schlesinger, Jr., *A Thousand Days.* Boston: Houghton Mifflin, 1965, p. 864.
5. Sorensen, *op. cit.,* p. 570.
6. *Ibid.,* pp. 558–59.
7. Cited in a *Staff Report of the Committee on Foreign Relations, U.S. Senate,* June 17, 1963, p. 21.
8. Robert Kleiman, *Atlantic Crisis.* New York: W. W. Norton, 1964, p. 59.
9. *The New York Times,* January 2, 1963. Although this was a "not for attribution" news conference, British correspondents quoted the President's words, forcing the White House to issue a partial

transcript. The incident created a stir in Western Europe as well as at the White House, where it caused considerable annoyance.

10. *Le Monde*, January 3, 1963.
11. Sorensen, *op. cit.*, p. 60.
12. Kleiman, *op. cit.*, pp. 570–71.
13. Cited in an article in *The New York Times*, January 3, 1963.
14. New York *Herald Tribune* (Paris Edition), January 12, 1963.
15. Sorensen, *op. cit.*, p. 644.
16. *Le Monde*, January 10, 1963.
17. Cited in an article in the New York *Herald Tribune* (Paris Edition), January 15, 1963.
18. *The New York Times*, January 26, 1963.
19. *Les Échos*, January 24, 1963.
20. André Passeron, *De Gaulle Parle, 1962–1966*. Paris: Fayard, 1966, pp. 340–41.
21. Sorensen, *op. cit.*, p. 579.
22. *The New Republic*, December 14, 1963.
23. Schlesinger, *op. cit.*, p. 914.

Chapter 9: Contact with Moscow

1. André Fontaine, *Histoire de la Guerre Froide. II: De la guerre de Corée à la crise des alliances, 1950–1967*. Paris: Fayard, 1967, p. 463.
2. *The New York Times*, January 7, 1964.
3. New York *Herald Tribune* (Paris Edition), January 21, 1964.
4. *The New York Times*, January 16, 1964.
5. Charles Maurras, *Kiel et Tanger*. Paris, 1912, p. 140.
6. Jacques Fauvet, *La IVe République*. Paris: Fayard, 1959, p. 106.
7. C. L. Sulzberger, *The New York Times*, February 3, 1964.
8. AP interview, April 21, 1964.
9. *The New York Times*, June 5, 1964.
10. New York *Herald Tribune* (Paris Edition), September 12, 1964.
11. *Ibid.*, April 17, 1964.
12. James Reston, *The New York Times*, May 5, 1964.
13. *Le Journal de Genève*, July 8, 1964.
14. *Le Monde*, July 26–27, 1964.
15. *L'Année Politique, 1964*, foreign-policy section (October), pp. 297–98.
16. *Le Monde*, October 22, 1964.

17. Monthly Bulletin of European Documentation, European Parliament, November-December 1964, p. 9.
18. *L'Express*, January 25–31, 1965, p. 16.

Chapter 10: De Gaulle between the Blocs

1. C. L. Sulzberger, *The New York Times*, December 28, 1964.
2. Charles de Gaulle, *The Edge of the Sword*. London: Faber & Faber, 1961, p. 58.
3. *Le Monde*, March 12, 1966.
4. *Ibid.*, April 1, 1966.
5. André Fontaine, in *Le Monde*, July 12, 1967.
6. Marc Ullman, "De Gaulle's Secret Diplomacy," in *Interplay*, August-September 1967, pp. 38–41.
7. *Ibid.*
8. Cited in *ibid.*
9. Cited in *L'Express*, August 21–27, 1967.
10. *Le Monde*, September 12, 1967.
11. *France-Soir*, September 13, 1967.
12. Stefan Kisielewski, in *Interplay*, November 1967, pp. 40–41.

Chapter 11: Decline and Departure

1. Paul Fabra in *Le Monde*, November 22, 1967.
2. *Newsweek*, December 4, 1967.
3. General Charles Ailleret, "Défense 'dirigée' ou défense 'tous azimuts,'" in *Revue de Défense Nationale*, December 1967, pp. 1923–1932.
4. Pierre Messmer, "L'Atome: Cause et Moyen d'une Politique Militaire Autonome," in *Revue de Défense Nationale*, March 1968, p. 398.
5. David Goldey, *Parliamentary Affairs*, XXI, 4 (Autumn 1968), pp. 308–309.
6. Speech at University of Bucharest, May 18, 1968.
7. Charles de Gaulle, *The Edge of the Sword*. London: Faber & Faber, 1961, p. 56.
8. *Journal Officiel*, May 22, 1968.
9. André Fontaine, in *Le Monde*, August 24, 1968.
10. Raymond Aron, in *Le Figaro*, August 28, 1968.
11. Cited in an article in *Le Monde*, October 27–28, 1968.
12. New York *Herald Tribune* (Paris Edition), November 25, 1968.

Reprint of an article from *The Washington Post* of the previous day.

13. Jacques Fauvet, editor in chief, in *Le Monde*, November 26, 1968.
14. General Michel Fourquet, 'Emploi des Différents Systèmes de Forces dans le Cadre de la Stratégie de Dissuasion," in *Revue de Défense Nationale*, May 1969, pp. 757–67.
15. Citation from *Air et Cosmos*, September 30, 1963, p. 18, in "The Diffusion of Combat Aircraft, Missiles, and Their Supporting Technologies," a report by the Browne & Shaw Research Corporation prepared for the Office of the Assistant Secretary of Defense for International Security Affairs, October 1966.

Index